RELIGION
AND DOUBT

Second Edition

RELIGION
AND DOUBT

Toward a Faith
of Your Own

RICHARD E. CREEL

Ithaca College

PRENTICE HALL, Englewood Cliffs, New Jersey 07632

Library of Congress Cataloging-in-Publication Data

CREEL, RICHARD E., (DATE)
    Religion and doubt : toward a faith of your own / Richard E.
Creel. — 2nd ed.
        p. cm.
    Includes bibliographical references and index.
    ISBN 0-13-772286-9
    1. Religion.   I. Title
BL48.C725   1991
200—dc20   90-40650
                                                       CIP

Acquisitions editor: Ted Bolen
Editorial assistant: Helen Brennan
Editorial/production supervision
    and interior design: Rob DeGeorge
Cover design: Bruce Kenselaar
Prepress buyer: Herb Klein
Manufacturing buyer: Dave Dickey

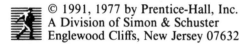 © 1991, 1977 by Prentice-Hall, Inc.
A Division of Simon & Schuster
Englewood Cliffs, New Jersey 07632

Printed in the United States of America

10 9 8 7 6 5 4 3 2 1

ISBN 0-13-772286-9

PRENTICE-HALL INTERNATIONAL (UK) LIMITED, *London*
PRENTICE-HALL OF AUSTRALIA PTY. LIMITED, *Sydney*
PRENTICE-HALL CANADA INC., *Toronto*
PRENTICE-HALL HISPANOAMERICANA, S.A., *Mexico*
PRENTICE-HALL OF INDIA PRIVATE LIMITED, *New Delhi*
PRENTICE-HALL OF JAPAN, INC., *Tokyo*
SIMON & SCHUSTER ASIA PTE. LTD., *Singapore*
EDITORA PRENTICE-HALL DO BRASIL, LTDA., *Rio de Janeiro*

To Diane—truly my other half

To my parents, Richard and Grace—for a lifetime
    of love and encouragement
    and

To my brothers, Dan and Randy—fellow seekers and finders

Contents

3   INTERPRETATIONS OF RELIGION   33

4   ROOTS OF RELIGION IN HUMAN EXISTENCE   56

5   TRAITS OF A HEALTHY RELIGIOUS FAITH   71

x   *Contents*

Foreword

When I was asked if I would prepare a foreword for Richard Creel's book, my reaction was one of surprise, delight, and hard-nosed realism: What an unknown author does not need is another unknown author to introduce his book.

But then, quite by accident, I discovered that what I had thought was spelled "forward" is spelled "foreword"! This put the matter in an entirely different light; in effect, I was being given the opportunity of getting in the *first word*. This is a point of chivalry, an advantage seldom granted by philosopher or theologian to a layperson. So, on behalf of my fellow readers, I make the following comments.

The First Word—is a complaint, not about Richard Creel, but about philosophers and theologians in general. They dig and dabble in the ultimate truths and in the precious mysteries of life; indeed, they discover and package these truths in such precise, concrete structures of logic and language that they become almost forever sealed from the throngs of would-be seekers. Hence, what philosophers and theologians need is a translator. That is the complaint.

Suddenly along comes Richard Creel, loping over the hills by Lake Cayuga's waters. He actually sits down with his readers and chats! Without fuss or pretense, he tackles topics that ordinarily leave us tongue-tied. He slips us questions and some of the answers, till, presently, lo, we discover we are acquiring for ourselves some of the tools of philosophical and theological thought. Indeed, we find that to grow in personal faith is something more than to study religion.

The Second Word—is that I had a better title for this book! It should have been called *Dandelions of Faith.*

"But," says the author, who is trying to think like his publisher (very important!), "no one will understand from *that* title what my book is about. People do not naturally equate dandelions with religion, let alone doubt."

"A pity," says she.

"Explain the metaphor," says he.

"Dandelions . . . You mean dandelions??? Well, it's like this. There is a thing about dandelions. We uproot them, we poison them, we try to get them out of our manicured lawns . . . but they persist, are absolutely indestructible, will appear even in the cracks of a concrete superhighway. And that is the way also with this thing called faith, this thing called religion, and this thing called doubt. Dandelions are simply descriptive of our human and religious predicament."

"Predicament??!"

"Ah, *hah* . . . don't you see?

1. No matter how hard institutional religions attempt to codify and structure our faith, we persist in heretical intuitions and doubts, and
2. no matter how hard secular society would infest us with doubt and relativity, there is something deep within us which hungers for truths and patterns, for forms of eternal meaning."

"And so . . . ?"

"And so what seems inevitable is that our faith, our doubts, and, to a certain extent, our religions are like the dandelions, which refuse to be exterminated, and which have a beauty and a freedom all their own.

"Moreover, our personal faith and our understanding of religious phenomena is usually a hodge-podge of experience and perception; it is not a well-groomed, manicured lawn. I suppose, systematically and theologically speaking, we are a Lovable Mess.

"Hence, I propose that, if our very own personal faith is alive and kicking, we are not like a lawn but a meadow, albeit possibly or properly fenced with tradition, logic, or dogma. And within this meadow there is a constant flowering of new thoughts and intuitions which give color and pattern. And after the blossom, the seed which floats on tails of fluff from one meadow to the next—crazy, unsystematic . . . quite defying

> the logic and training and
> instincts of a theologian
> or a Vatican Council."

"I think I'm gettin lost in your meadow-phor!"

"Lost?? You can't be. You are the one who has gathered the dandelions. You have lined up the meadows of mind and spirit, and, theologically speaking, helped us to fence them in.

"What is more, Professor Creel—all metaphors aside—you have done it rather well . . . and we
Thank You."

HARRIET CRAMTON
Ithaca, New York

Preface

Readers familiar with the first edition of *Religion and Doubt* will not find many startling changes in this second edition, but I hope they will find a more mature volume. I have had a decade to develop as a person, scholar, and writer and believe I have made some progress, which I have tried to express in this revision of *Religion and Doubt*. Regarding form, I have tried to make the structure and development of the paragraphs and chapters clearer and to focus my points more sharply and explain them more fully. I have also tried to be less abrasive to those who do not share my enthusiasms and convictions.

Regarding substance, I have done several things. First, I have added a section on secularism in order to acknowledge a viable alternative to the religious point of view—an alternative which I did not acknowledge in the first edition when, in good Tillichian fashion, I was seeing everything as religious. My discussion of secularism makes this edition more adequate in terms of the worldviews it covers, and it enables me to make the nature of religion clearer by virtue of contrast. Second, I have included a more extended, discriminating discussion of communism, and I think I argue much more persuasively than I did in the first edition that communism can be considered a religion; however, I also, thanks to discussions with my colleague Stephen Schwartz, point out that there are nonreligious forms of communism—an important point which I did not understand a decade ago. Third, I present a fuller discussion of similarities and differences between philosophy and religion. Fourth, I discuss explicitly the difference between religion understood institutionally and religion understood devotionally. The institutional understanding is so common because it is easy to talk about and comprehend, but it is profoundly inadequate because it is in fact *devotion* which is at the heart of religion and which has given rise and vitality to religious institutions. Fifth, my most satisfying accomplishment in this edition is to have distilled my earlier thoughts about religion into the concepts of agathism and agatheism, according to which the right way and the religious way to be human is to live in wholehearted pursuit of and devotion to absolute goodness. In the first edition of *Religion and Doubt*, Chapter 7 was even to me a puzzlingly short chapter with no subsections. Now I realize it was waiting for this new material concerning agathism. Finally, the notes in this edition do much more work than they did in the first edition, so I hope that students as well as teachers will refer to them.

A new category for the bibliography in this edition is that of "Women and Religion." That topic is not yet discussed in *Religion and Doubt*, but it has recently become one of the most exciting and fruitful topics in religious studies and will continue to be so. It is an intriguing, illuminating gateway into history of religion, sociology of religion, psychology of religion, comparative religion, scriptural studies, mysticism, and so on. Hence, I want to alert my readers to it, and I deeply appreciate the fact that my colleague Dr. Alice McDowell, an expert on women and religion, has compiled for this book a well-balanced list of anthologies and essays on women and religion by major feminist voices. Her list should get anyone off to an excellent start.

From readers' reactions to the first edition of *Religion and Doubt*, it is clear that Harriet Cramton's original foreword and illustrations are too exquisite to change, so I gratefully pass them on again.

In addition to the many people whom I thanked in the preface to the first edition, I would like to thank the following people for discussions that have resulted in some of the most important corrections and improvements in this second edition: my friend Stephen Schwartz of Ithaca College, and my friend James Keller and his students at Wofford College.

Richard Creel

1

Introduction

There have been eras when it was easy to believe wholeheartedly in a particular worldview. Medieval Europeans were largely convinced by the Christian worldview. Many twentieth-century people believe in a scientific-atheistic worldview. Characteristic of such eras is the feeling of obviousness which attaches to the belief in question. To many medieval Europeans the Christian view of the world seemed obviously true; to many contemporary people the scientific-atheistic view seems obviously true. Yet in every era of faith there have been doubters—not malicious or cynical people, but people who, for diverse reasons, have not been firmly convinced by the prevailing worldview in their society, or, for members of minority groups, by the worldview within which they have been reared.

Perhaps you are such a person. Chances are that you are, for our own era of faith seems to be crumbling. On the one hand, science hasn't given us what we expected of it (some now think of it as a Frankenstein monster which is causing more harm than good), and theories being proposed by subatomic physicists and scientific cosmologists are becoming as strange and counterintuitive as some of the more troublesome doctrines of religion.

On the other hand, because of extensive and increasing international communication and travel, we can hardly fail to feel challenged by the fact that there are numerous ways of understanding the world other than in our own way—ways among which we must choose because they are incompatible with, and sometimes even attack, one another.

A natural response to the challenge of these other points of view is to attempt to study all of them in order to expose the false ones and choose the true one. But there are so many of them and they are so deep and complex that such an endeavor quickly becomes perplexing and exhausting, impelling us to drop the whole enterprise, declaring it hopeless. Still, a desperate decision to become agnostic, to say, "I don't know the truth and there is no way to find out, so I'm going to quit trying!" is a resolve that is rarely kept. Most of us cannot escape from the nagging desire to have some sense of what we are, why we are here, where we have come from, and where we are going. Consequently, after resolving to forswear these kinds of questions, without even realizing what is happening we become involved in a discussion or a book or a thought or a situation that leads us right back to those central questions of religion: What is death? What is the nature of the reality within which I live and move and have my being? Who am I? How ought I to live my life? What is worthy of my wholehearted devotion? Hence, our challenge is not to decide *whether* to take these questions seriously; rather, it is to discover *how* to take them seriously in the most beneficial way.

Helping you with that *how* is what this book is all about. Along the way I will present to you the views of many writers in religion, philosophy, and psychology, but my ultimate intention is not to teach you what they say; rather, it is to *provoke* you into reflection by means of what they say and to *involve* you in the process of thinking their ideas through and making up your own mind about them. My sincerest wish is that you will find yourself caught in the flow of these ideas and pulled along by your own deep interest until you have reached the end of this book—an end which, if I am successful, will prove to be a launching pad rather than a stopping place. Through this process I hope you will acquire a more profound understanding of the nature of religion and some assistance in understanding and furthering your own spiritual growth.

THE SECULAR AND THE RELIGIOUS

Prior to the nineteenth century most people, including high officials and governing bodies of nations, understood in a religious way who they were and what their responsibilities were. During the nineteenth century, searing blasts were aimed at the religious point of view by Karl Marx, Friedrich Nietzsche, and Arthur Schopenhauer, so that the twentieth century is the first century in which large numbers of individuals, including high officials and governing bodies, have lived their lives and understood their responsibilities from a secular point of view. This book is primarily about the religious point of view, but the one point of view can be understood adequately only in contrast to the other, so I want to convey something of the contrast before proceeding to other topics.

This is especially important because people to whom the one point of view is profoundly natural often seem as though they are tone-deaf to the other point of view. They don't disagree with it so much as they just don't feel its attraction at all and cannot understand how anyone could be attracted to it except for neurotic reasons. I once took a group of Introduction to Religion students to visit a Pentecostal worship service. The members of the church, as they always did, broke out into spontaneous songs; prayers; and confessions of weakness, guilt, gratitude, or joy, as they felt "moved by the Spirit" and they spontaneously hugged one another and cried and rejoiced together. To be in the midst of such a thing can be a very emotional experience for people who, like most of my students, have never been exposed to it before. After the service, as we were walking to our cars, one of my students said, "You know, that was a beautiful experience. I want to go back and learn more from those people."

Soon thereafter I took my other group of Intro students to The Love Inn. The worship service went very much as it did before, but this time as we were returning to our cars one of my students said to me, "Those people are sick!" I couldn't help but chuckle and sigh at the extreme difference between the two reactions. It seemed clear to me that each student would have a very difficult time seeing and feeling the merits of the other point of view. I would like to say a few things here to try to bridge that gap.

The secular mentality, or worldview, is one that senses nothing of transcendent reality or value in life. This is not necessarily a pessimistic or morally indifferent view, but to this way of thinking there is nothing beyond nature, and death is the end of the individual. Moreover, nature is not thought of as sacred. Nature is what science tells us it is, and science tells us that nature is a mindless swirl of physical particles interacting unintentionally with one another. From within the secular framework, then, life is experienced, understood, and lived on the plane of "everydayness." The mottoes of the secularist are "Seeing is believing" and "What you see is what you get."

To be sure, the secularist would agree that drugs or meditation may be used to enhance our ordinary experiences or to give us experiences which are not had in ordinary life, but the secularist would add that those experiences should not be interpreted as revealing anything transcendent or religious about life or reality. Wonderful as those experiences might be, they are simply the result of unusual electrochemical states brought about in the brain by drugs or meditation.

Here, then, are five contrasts between the two points of view:

SECULAR POINT OF VIEW	RELIGIOUS POINT OF VIEW
1. The secular point of view is sometimes called the *profane* point of view; it holds that there is nothing more to reality than the physical world.	1. The religious point of view is sometimes called the *sacred* point of view; it holds that there are beings or aspects of reality that transcend the merely physical.
2. The secular point of view is "this worldly"; it holds that this world is our only world, and this life is our only life. Consequently, we should focus on the good things and problems of this life.	2. The religious point of view holds that we have spiritual needs that the merely physical aspects of the good things of this world cannot satisfy. Moreover, the most important problems are those that concern our relationship to eternal values such as truth and beauty, and eternal beings such as God or Brahma.
3. According to the secular point of view, life and history have no inherent meaning. The only meaning that a life has is that which the individual gives to it.	3. According to the religious point of view, life and history have an inherent meaning given to them by a transcendent being or good; that meaning is there to be found by us.
4. Secularism is relativistic about values: There are no absolute values or rights or wrongs. There are just individuals and societies with different likes and dislikes.	4. The religious point of view is absolutistic: There are some absolute values. These absolute goods and bads, rights and wrongs, are not created by us; they are discovered by us.
5. According to secularism, religion arose from human creativity responding to natural situations, needs, and emotions. Some negative sources of religion are fear, superstition, wishful thinking, and efforts to control people by means of religious fear and guilt. Some positive causes of religion are our need for social unity and identity, moral formation, and rites of passage to honor critical events in human life, such as birth, puberty, assumption of the responsibilities of adulthood, marriage, and death. But we can celebrate or honor these events without getting caught up in beliefs about a being or realm or values that transcend this life.	5. According to the religious mentality, religion is the human response to a transcendent realm or value or being that has revealed itself to humankind or been discovered by humankind. Religion is a response of adoration, gratitude, and devotion to something or someone that transcends the purely physical aspects of reality.

RELIGION AND PHILOSOPHY

Religion and philosophy are associated closely in the thinking of many people. Numerous colleges have a Department of Philosophy and Religion. Some people think of philosophy and religion as being basically the same thing. They are intimately related, especially by what they are interested in, for example, the nature of reality and the content and authority of morality. However, there are profound differences as well.

Philosophy is the *pursuit by means of reason* of the truth about reality, value, and knowledge. When philosophizing, one wants to see what can be understood about these important topics solely by use of one's reason and experiences. Nothing is to be accepted merely on the authority of another person.

Religion, by contrast, involves *self-conscious commitment to a holy or sacred reality* which seems to penetrate and perhaps fill this world but also transcend it in some important way. Reason and ordinary experience need not have played an important role in the occurrence of one's awareness of the sacred. This awareness may have been brought about by divine revelation or meditation, or by being in the presence of an extraordinary person, animal, or object (more on this in Chapter 2 under History of Religions). The commitment brought about by a sense of the sacred usually results in (and sometimes arises from) *rituals, stories,* and *symbols* which relate the individual to a community of fellow believers, to the world at large, and to the transcendent reality that gives life richness, meaning, and purpose. There is in Western philosophy little parallel to these concrete ways in which religious conviction expresses itself in the lives of ordinary as well as extraordinary people.

Another difference between religion and philosophy can be seen in how each relates to metaphysical claims, that is, claims about the nature of reality. Religion *declares* a proposition and calls for *commitment* to it. Consider, for example, the Jewish Shema: "Hear O Israel, the Lord our God, the Lord is One" (Deut. 6:4). Philosophy, by contrast, *questions* the meaning of such a proposition and calls for *justification* of it. A philosopher would ask, "What is meant by 'God' in the Shema? What is meant by 'one'? One what? One in what way? What reasons are there for thinking that God is one? What is meant by 'Lord'? What reasons are there for thinking that the Lord is God? What reasons are there for thinking that such a God exists other than as an idea?"

Another way to understand the differences between philosophy and religion is to note how different the study of the history of philosophy is from the study of the history of religion. The study of the history of philosophy is usually a study of the conclusions at which philosophical geniuses have arrived, of the distinctions and arguments whereby they arrived at those conclusions, and of the reasons why they did or did not agree with their predecessors and contemporaries. The history of religion pays attention to its own geniuses, such as Buddha, Moses, Jesus, and Mohammed, but there is usually little attention paid to *why* they believed what they believed about history and reality, and there is always much attention paid to how their lives and teachings became a part of the lives of ordinary people and manifested themselves in stories, rituals, symbols, special clothing, dances, creeds, moral codes, forms of social organization, artifacts, buildings, and music which have endured and evolved over centuries and sometimes millenia. There is no comparably rich institutional side to philosophy.

WHY STUDY RELIGION?

There are many reasons for studying religion, but three seem especially important. First, if to be well educated means to be well acquainted with the fundamental aspects of human existence, then it is impossible to become well educated without acquiring a mature understanding of religion. Why? Because religion is one of the most ancient, universal, enduring, and influential components of human existence.

Regarding its antiquity, as far back as we can trace human culture, we find evidence of religious beliefs and practices. The evidence, such as modes of burial and paintings on cave walls, is clear with regard to Cro-Magnon and Neanderthal humans, and is present possibly even earlier.[1] Though such evidence is subject to a wide range of interpretations, it does seem to indicate clearly that humans as many as 100,000 years ago were seeking more than survival and comfort and were sensitive to more than the pragmatic aspects of their experience. There seems to have been a mystic sense of kinship with nature and animals. There seem to have been rituals whereby values were preserved and the community related to a larger reality. There were paintings and statues rich in symbolic significance. There was belief in spirit powers and quite likely in survival of the dead. There appear to have been sacramental acts (perhaps involving the consumption of human brains and the special arrangement of human skulls!) by means of which an exalted sense of self was sought. Hence, ambiguous as the evidence may be, it does seem clear that quite early humans were not merely living in the world but were interpreting it, forging an understanding of it, and in turn being forged by that understanding as it found its expression in rituals, dances, sacraments, artwork, songs, and eventually creeds and codes.[2]

Religion is not, however, an ancient but isolated phenomenon. Today, as yesterday, no matter where we look on the face of the earth, we find that people there have a religion—not always in a biblical sense, to be sure, but always in some sense. In Africa there is Islam; in Europe, Australia, and the Americas there are Judaism and Christianity; in Asia and Japan there are Hinduism and Buddhism; and on each of these continents there are members of each of the other faiths named, as well as devotees of additional faiths which are smaller in number but often powerful in influence, for example, Sikhism, Shinto, Taoism, Confucianism, Unitarian-Universalism, and Baha'i.

Further, in spite of predictions that religion would be "outgrown" in this century—some have said that the idea of God died in the nineteenth century and that religion is scheduled to die in the twentieth—it is as vigorous as ever, almost like the mythical many-headed Hydra which sprouted two heads for each one cut off! Thus, there is no empirical reason to think that religion is on its way out of the human scene. Indeed, one of the things which has frustrated Soviet Communists is the fact that religion in the Soviet Union has not disappeared on schedule. Karl Marx, the founder of modern communism, predicted that once capitalism was replaced by socialism, religion would wither like a plant plucked from its native soil. However, the Soviet Communist party has not merely waited for religion to wither. It has repeatedly and aggressively sought to discourage and extirpate religion from Soviet society. Yet after decades of official opposition, various religions remain widespread and robust in the Soviet Union.

In brief, religion in the world today seems as irrepressible, as deeply natural to human existence as are philosophy, art, and science. Particular religions may come and go, even as particular styles of art, schools of philosophy, and theories of science do, but—as I shall argue in Chapters 3 and 4—religion itself will thrive as long as there are humans.

A second important reason for studying religion is to better understand and communicate with our contemporaries. The world is increasingly crowded because of population growth, and the population is increasingly mixed together by ease of travel and mass communication. Hence, the need to communicate in nonoffensive ways with people of persuasions other than one's own is increasingly urgent. Among the most important things to know about a people in order to communicate effectively with them and to develop mutual respect and appreciation are certainly their religious beliefs and practices. Why? First, because the religion of a people embodies and celebrates many of the things that are most precious to them. Second, the religious beliefs and values of a people condition the very way they see the world and respond to it. These beliefs and values, writes W. C. Smith,

matter not only in the sense that their adherent cherishes them, regarding them as supremely precious. More subtly and elementally, he thinks by means of them, feels in terms of them, and acts by them, and for them, and through them—even when he is thinking, feeling, and acting in the matters that we regard as political and economic.[3]

Later Smith adds that unless people "can learn to understand and to be loyal to each other across religious frontiers, unless we can build a world in which people profoundly of different faiths can live together and work together, then the prospects for our planet's future are not bright."[4] In order to understand another person, then, it is valuable, perhaps imperative, to understand his or her religion. Prudence requires it, and so does human solidarity.

The third reason for studying religion is a personal reason. Religion is directly and intensely concerned with issues that haunt all of us: meaning and meaninglessness, right and wrong, love and hate, community and loneliness, war and peace, life and death, illusion and reality. Hence, it is natural that we study religion not only out of intellectual curiosity and social responsibility, but also out of personal passion; not only as an interesting diversion and an act of social prudence, but also as an attempt to find or forge a viable understanding of ourselves and the reality of which we are a part. It is understandable, then, in the words of Huston Smith, that a living religion is not a "dull habit" but "an acute fever." "And whenever religion comes to life," he adds, "it displays a startling quality; it takes over. All else, while not silenced, becomes subdued and thrown without contest into a supporting role."[5]

FAITH AS A SEED WITHIN

To be sure, not everyone is obsessed by religion. Some are hostile to it, some are indifferent, some are simply curious. Still, I believe, religious concerns are like seeds that lie dormant in all of us. In some of us they germinate earlier and in some of us later. (And in some, perhaps, not at all?) Where *you* are right now in your religious growth I do not know—you may not be sure yourself. Is your primary attitude toward religion one of curiosity as to how people can get so excited about it? Or perhaps religion has developed into a curse and a plague, afflicting you with unanswered questions and unsatisfied yearnings? Or perhaps it is the greatest source of strength and happiness in your life? Wherever you are, it does seem true that much as we awaken socially and sexually, we also awaken religiously. And when we do, our religious concern "takes over." It becomes our ultimate concern because it is our concern about what is ultimate.

Why study religion, then? In order (1) to broaden and deepen our understanding of a fundamental aspect of human existence; (2) to better understand and communicate with our contemporaries; and (3) to respond personally to the ultimate issues that confront us each and all.

Reprinted by permission of UFS, Inc.

Notes

1. For an introduction to this fascinating aspect of human history, see the opening chapter, John B. Noss, "Religion in Prehistoric and Primitive Cultures," *Man's Religions*, 5th ed. (New York: Macmillan, 1974).

2. I say "eventually" creeds and codes because I suspect that a statement attributed to Arthur Darby Nock is more right than wrong: "Primitive religion is not believed. It is danced." Songs, dances, and rituals almost certainly preceded abstract creeds of belief and codes of behavior.

3. Wilfred Cantwell Smith, *The Faith of Other Men* (New York: Mentor Books, 1965), p. 96.

4. Ibid., p. 116.

5. Huston Smith, *The Religions of Man* (New York: Mentor Books, 1960), p. 10.

2

Approaches
to Religion

- How does phenomenology of religion differ from comparative religion?
- How does history of religions in the broader, more recent sense differ from history of religions in the narrower, more familiar sense?
- What kinds of information do social scientists, such as the anthropologist, the sociologist, and the psychologist, try to discover about religions?
- What kinds of questions about religion fall outside the realm of the social sciences?
- How does philosophy of religion differ from theology?
- What are some characteristics of the existentialist approach to religion?
- If a person is personally committed to and involved in a particular religion, can he or she evaluate that religion fairly and adequately?
- If a person is *not* personally committed to and involved in a particular religion, can he or she evaluate that religion fairly and adequately?

Once you've decided that it is important to study religion, you might think, "Well, okay, I'll dive right in!" But it's not that simple. Where do you dive in? What is it you are going to dive into? And what kind of a dive are you going to take? I'm sure you'll agree that in a book of this length not everything interesting and important about religion can be said. But enough can be included that you will be able to get your bearings on this mammoth field of study, so let's take a look at nine different ways of approaching it. Such an overview of contemporary approaches to religion will enable me to make more clear what we will and will not be doing in the remainder of this book, and it will help you know where to turn regarding those aspects of religion I do not treat.

I hope my descriptions will give you a working sense of the richness and diversity of the approaches that can be taken to religion, but please keep in mind at all times that I am painting with a very broad brush and am therefore leaving out a great deal of detail and nuance. Each of these approaches can be firmly distinguished from the others in broad terms, but among some of the approaches there is considerable overlap, and some of the differences are subtle. An examination of these subtle differences and areas of overlap belongs to a more technical book than this, so I shall not pursue these issues. All of these approaches can be connected in theory, however, and many of them are intimately related in practice. Indeed, each of these approaches, in my opinion, makes a distinct and valuable contribution to the division of labor necessary for a comprehensive understanding of religion. Further, each approach provides a distinct and fascinating point of view from which to look at religion. If you do not get a sense of the excitement, value, and mystique of each approach, the fault is mine, and I urge you to turn to some of the books listed in the bibliography. Finally, you should be aware that some knowledgeable persons will find my descriptions controversial. That's okay with me as long as my descriptions enable *you* to enter the controversy!

PHENOMENOLOGY OF RELIGION

Phenomenology of religion is a method for coping with a problem which besets us all. When dealing with familiar things and persons, we often discover in retrospect that we have attributed to them meanings that were not there. How many times a defensive reaction to what a friend or mate has said has proved unwarranted! How many times we have misjudged people's character on the basis of their appearance! If such things can happen so frequently with familiar objects and persons, how much more likely they are to happen when we are dealing with a foreign culture! You might be thinking, "Actually, we'd do better with a foreign culture because we would be more careful, realizing the difficulty of understanding its people and their culture correctly." There is something to that response, I agree, but it misses the more fundamental point that our most serious misinterpretations are not the result of not being careful; they happen because we fail to realize that we are systematically distorting what we are looking at by interpreting it automatically in terms of deeply ingrained preconceptions of our own—preconceptions that are as spontaneously a part of us as our posture, gait, and style of speech.

Phenomenology, founded by Edmund Husserl, a nineteenth-century German philosopher, is a rigorous method designed to help us escape from our preconceptions in order that we might get to "the things themselves," without distortion, or at least with a minimum of distortion from our habitual ways of understanding the world. By "bracketing out" our preconceptions—something one doesn't learn to do overnight—we allow things to present themselves to us *as they really are.* By applying this method of study to a particular religion, we come to understand that religion as it is *in its actuality for its adherents,* and not merely as it appears to an outsider. We come to see and feel the world of nature through the "eyes" of those people, and we come to appreciate the religious significance of the objects and actions that make up their social world. Surely it is this kind of knowledge that we want of a religion, and not, as W. C. Smith puts it, the kind of knowledge a fly must have of goldfish in a bowl. To be sure, our anthropomorphic fly might learn a good deal about goldfish by wandering around the outside of the bowl and staring in. But that is not enough. Our goal, as Smith puts it, is "not only to ascertain the institutions, beliefs, and practices of a tradition but to ascertain also, if one can, what these things mean to those who participate in them."[1]

In addition to this hermeneutical task (that is, the task of interpreting accurately and fully what religious phenomena—divine beings, scriptures, rituals, sacraments, and so on—mean to their devotees), phenomenologists also endeavor by means of their method to disclose the structures and essences of the specific religions they study and, ultimately, the general essence of religion itself. Because these structures and essences manifest themselves in and through the external features of a religion, they can be apprehended accurately and deeply only by a properly unbiased and sensitive approach—and that is what phenomenology is about. Understandably, then, the English title of one classic in phenomenology of religion is *Religion in Essence and Manifestation,* authored by G. van der Leeuw.[2]

COMPARATIVE STUDY OF RELIGIONS

Whereas phenomenology of religion may be new to you, *comparative religion* is almost certainly not. Most of us are reared in or around some religious tradition and encounter yet other religions rather early in life.

These other religions seize our attention by claiming to be superior to our own religion, or just by being different from it, and so we rather naturally and early find ourselves comparing religions. But whereas comparing religions has been going on for thousands of years, comparative religion, *as an academic field,* was established only in the nineteenth century.[3] Two of the major factors resulting in the establishment of departments of comparative religion were the following: First, there was a great increase in world travel during the nineteenth century. This increase was motivated largely by commercial interests and facilitated greatly by improved means of travel. Such travel took many Europeans and Americans into direct contact for the first time with religions of which they had only heard, and into contact with many more religions of whose existence they had been oblivious. Predictably, these travelers often brought back fascinating but incredible and conflicting stories about these religions. Hence, there was a need for someone to discover the facts. Second, Christian churches took vigorous advantage of these new opportunities to carry out their responsibility to take their message to the ends of the earth (Matt. 28:18). On the one hand, then, there were people who were simply fascinated with these other religions and found themselves telling about them and comparing them. On the other hand, there were missionaries who needed to know in advance something about the indigenous religion(s) of the people to whom they were going. Thus, the missionary enterprise of the nineteenth century created a practical need for the teaching of comparative religions, and it was primarily in response to that need that comparative religion became established in the seminaries and church-related educational institutions of Europe and America.

Motivated by the practical needs of missionaries and operating in a context of Christian commitment, it is understandable that most comparativists (scholars of comparative religion) performed an apologetic as well as an informative function. That is, as well as simply giving students some idea of the number and diversity of religions on earth, the comparativist also endeavored to evaluate these religions in order to show how they stood relative to one another in terms of their various levels of development. This approach to comparative religions was quite in the spirit of the times, considering the dominance then of the evolutionary theory of history. This theory held that history is a gradual and continual development from lower to higher forms of existence in religion as well as in biology, science, technology, art, and so on. Because part of the widely accepted evolutionary hypothesis was that history moves forward irreversibly and inexorably, comparativists also tried to determine from the past and present the direction in which religious growth was moving. It was assumed that that direction, when grasped clearly and correctly, should be taken as the direction in which we *ought* to move as well as the direction in which history *is* moving.

Today comparativists have largely dissociated themselves from the assumption that religious progress has moved forward throughout history in a relatively straightforward manner, and that by an examination of history we can assay the direction in which further religious development should and will take place. This is not to say that comparativists now believe that religions cannot be compared normatively. It means that such comparisons are no longer defended by means of highly abstract, speculative interpretations of history. Rather, it is now widely held that such comparative judgments must be based on an intimate grasp of the details of religions and on a profound grasp of the nature of religion, a grasp that proves its authenticity by being acceptable to religious scholars from diverse religious traditions. In the absence of widely accepted criteria for what is better religiously, comparativists have tended in recent decades to restrict such judgments to developments *within a single tradition*—so that a certain practice in Hinduism, for example, might be judged as an *advance* upon an earlier, similar practice; conversely, yet another practice might be judged as a *corruption* of an earlier practice. Such judgments within a single tradition are less controversial than judgments between traditions, but inevitably, I believe, the standards that are clarified for use *within* a tradition will eventually be used to compare traditions to one another. Hence, conceptual progress in the more narrow enterprise will eventually contribute to evaluative discussions in the broader enterprise.

As comparativists today generally dissociate themselves from the once popular evolutionary approach, which assumed uncritically that later religions are better than earlier religions, they also dissociate themselves from the apologetic task, that is, the task of showing that their own religion is superior to all other religions. There are a number of reasons for this. The most general reason is that whereas an apologetic approach is appropriate in a seminary, which is by its nature devoted to the training of religious professionals in a specific religion, it is inappropriate in a strictly academic context. Hence, (1) as comparativists sought to establish departments of comparative religion in *public* and *nonreligious* institutions of higher education, (2) as persons *without* a religious affiliation became fascinated with the study and teaching of comparative religions, and (3) as comparativists *with* a religious affiliation became interested in practicing their discipline in a *nonapologetic* context, comparativists came to identify their tasks with such things as the following: (a) identifying those themes and elements which cut across and are common to all or most religions (for example, ritual, myth, sacrifice, symbolism); (b) showing the diversity of forms which such things as ritual, myth, sacrifice, and symbolism have taken in the world's religions; (c) comparing and contrasting—in an appreciative, nonjudgmental manner—specific religions on these and other common topics; and (d) serving as "brokers" between religious traditions—helping the peoples therein to achieve an accurate and deep understanding of one another and helping them find the terms and concepts by means of which they can explain themselves to one another and understand one another.

The preceding, in broad terms, is where much of comparative religion is today. There is, however, something new and important happening—something that has been made possible in part by the careful, respectful work of comparativists in recent decades. Specifically, many philosophers, theologians, and scholars of religion have come to have a deep respect for religions other than their own and have begun to see them as authentic paths to the divine. Some have come to regard world religions, including their own, as historical, cultural expressions of humankind's relation to the divine—expressions which must change as histories and cultures change. These new points of view have motivated some thinkers to look for ways in which their own religions can be enriched and even transformed by other religions; some of these people from different religions are in dialogue with one another trying to go beyond the theologies of their own religions to a universal theology which discloses and honors the truth and goodness in all of the great religions and, perhaps, will set the stage for the emergence of a new religion which will weave together the good and true and beautiful aspects of the great historical religions. Some of the books pertinent to these discussions have been entered into the bibliography under Comparative Religion and will be obvious by their titles.

HISTORY OF RELIGIONS

"History of religions" is no doubt a phrase with some immediate meaning for you, given your long acquaintance with the word "history." But today, people who use the phrase "history of religions" may mean much more than you think they do. So let's take a look at both the narrower, more familiar meaning and a broader, more recent meaning. In its narrower sense, history of religions is concerned with searching for the origin of each religion (and when this is impossible, pushing back as far as possible), with tracing its development, and with relating it to the social, political, and economic realities of its cultural context. (This may hardly seem like a narrow approach! But I think you'll agree later that it is narrower than the second approach at which we shall look.)

What is the motive for examining a religion in its historical context—especially if it claims to be a revelation of God rather than a creation of man? The motive is the assumption that even a revelation from God would occur within a specific historical context and be addressed to it. It would be cast in the language of a specific people, coined in their metaphors, and aimed at their lives *as they are lived* at the time of the revelation. In this spirit, Mircea Eliade, distinguished professor of the history of religions, responds to the question, What can "history" mean to the student of religion? "For the student of religion," he writes,

> "history" means primarily that all religious phenomena are conditioned. A *pure* religious phenomenon does not exist. A religious phenomenon is always also a social, an economic, a psychological phenomenon, and, of course, a historical one, because it takes place in historical time and it is conditioned by everything which had happened before.[4]

To say that religious phenomena are conditioned by other cultural factors is not to say that they can be explained away in terms of those factors or reduced to them. A religious phenomenon is as distinctive as an economic or artistic phenomenon and will never be adequately understood until it is understood as a religious phenomenon. Eliade addresses this point too:

> To try to grasp the essence of [a religious] phenomenon by means of physiology, psychology, sociology, economics, linguistics, art or any other study is false; it misses the one unique and irreducible element in it—the element of the sacred. Obviously there are no *purely* religious phenomena; no phenomenon can be solely and exclusively religious. Because religion is human it must for that very reason be something social, something linguistic, something economic. . . . But it would be hopeless to try and explain religion in terms of any one of those basic functions. . . . It would be as futile as thinking you could explain *Madame Bovary* [or any other great novel] by a list of social, economic and political facts. . . .[5]

To expand on this point a bit, the economy of a nation is sometimes influenced by political events; but that doesn't mean that economics is nothing more than an extension of politics. Similarly, religion is sometimes influenced by economic events, but that does not mean that religion is nothing more than a byproduct of economic processes. We need to keep these and similar distinctions sharp, because they amount to a pragmatic way of distinguishing human reality into meaningful, manageable parts of the whole. The interrelationships between these various aspects of human existence—such as politics, philosophy, art, religion, economics, technology, and morality—need to be studied in order that we might understand better their impacts on one another. Nothing seems to be gained and something does seem to be lost whenever we collapse the distinctions between any of these areas or presume to reduce one to another. To be sure, it is not easy to say with precision what religion is, but neither is it easy to say what politics or economics is. These concepts are not the precision instruments we would like them to be, but they do acknowledge the fundamental differences that our experience reveals to us, and we ignore such differences only at the cost of a profound misunderstanding of religion.

We might say, then, that whereas phenomenology of religion is concerned primarily with the methods whereby the meanings, structures, and essences of religious data are apprehended authentically, and whereas the comparativist is devoted to discovering and investigating (concretely as well as abstractly) those themes and elements which are universally characteristic of religions, the primary concern of the historian of religions—in the narrow sense—is to gather, organize, and make a meaningful whole of the concrete data of the entire history of a religion or of some segment thereof. For a good example of the history of religions in this sense, see *The History of Israel* by Martin Noth.

The broader meaning of the history of religions has developed in the last several decades and is set forth nicely by Joseph Kitagawa in an article entitled "The History of Religions in America." After pointing out that the phrase "the history of religions" means different things to different people—some thinking of it as "a tour guide" to world religions; others thinking of it as "a historical discipline, analogous to church history" but dealing with many religions; and still others thinking of it as a philosophical search for the universal form of religion that lies beneath all the historical manifestations—Kitagawa writes:

> This apparent ambiguity of the nature of the discipline of the history of religions is reflected in the diversity of names by which it has come to be known, such as comparative religion, phenomenology of religion, science of religions, and history of religions. All these terms, with minor differences, refer to a general body of knowledge known originally as *Allgemeine Religionswissenschaft*. In the English-speaking world the imposing title of "general science of religions" [which is a literal translation of the German phrase in italics] has not been used widely, partly because it is too long and awkward, and partly because the English word "science" tends to be misleading. Thus, the world-wide organization of scholars in this field has recently adopted an official English title, "The International Association for the Study of the History of Religions." It is readily apparent that the term "history of religions" has come to be regarded as a synonym for the "general science of religions," and as such the nature of the discipline must be discussed in the total context of *Religionswissenschaft*.[6]

A number of different phrases in addition to "the general science of religions" have been used by Kitagawa and Eliade to clarify in English the meaning of *Allgemeine Religionswissenschaft*: "the science of religions," "the total science of religions," and "the religio-scientific study of religions." But Kitagawa is correct that any English translation of *Religionswissenschaft* which uses the word "science" stirs up images of physicists, chemists, biologists, and laboratories, whereas in German the term *Wissenschaft* refers not only to the natural sciences and the social sciences, but to *any* field that applies disciplined and rigorous methods of analysis to its subject matter. Hence, in the *Wissenschaft* sense of "science," the disciplines of history and linguistics are sciences, and there can also be a science of religion. But this notion of science is foreign to so many Americans and Britons that it would puzzle and mislead more than it would help. Hence, "the world-wide organization of scholars," to which Kitagawa refers, chose not to use the word "science" in the name by which it now identifies itself.

Clearly, those scholars intended that the history of religions should be a more comprehensive study of religions than a history of religions in the narrow sense would be, so let's look at some of the characteristics of the history of religions in its broader, more recent sense.[7] First, the history of religions takes with utmost seriousness the reality and uniqueness of the *experience* of the sacred. Recall, for example, Eliade's statement that it would be folly to try to appreciate *Madame Bovary* entirely in terms of social, economic, and political factors. Similarly, one has not understood a religious phenomenon until one has understood it as a *hierophany*—that is, as a manifestation of the sacred. What is the sacred? Eliade prefers not to make a direct statement in reply to this question, because any attempt to describe the sacred will only diminish or distort our understanding of it. Hence, the best thing to say is simply that it is the opposite of the secular. Much can be said to make that distinction clear, but what is most effective is not to try to describe the sacred and the profane but to tell stories and give illustrations that bring about in the listener a sense of the difference between the two. Eliade's *The Sacred and the Profane* is devoted to illustrating this difference, and you might take a look also at the first chapter and conclusion of his *Patterns in Comparative Religion*. But the important point here is that whereas the social scientist can legitimately ignore the category of the sacred when analyzing religious behavior, the historian of religions cannot, for like the phenomenologist and the comparativist, he or she is trying to understand specific religious phenomena as they are understood by the people for whom they are a revelation of the sacred.

The first point, then, is that the historian of religions finds the unity of religious studies in the experiences and embodiments of the sacred found among a people. That is the center from which and to which all such studies of religion move. It is the integrating factor in all that he or she does as a historian of religions. The second point is that for the historian, the passageway to an accurate and profound understanding of a people's religion is through the unique historical facts which constitute their lives. General impressions based on superficial experience are inadequate. Why? Because "every hierophany we look at is also an historical fact. Every manifestation of the sacred takes place in some historical situation."[8] Further, the sacred never manifests itself directly. Rather, it always expresses itself through something other than itself—the wind, the sky, a story, a voice, a stone, a book, a symbol, just about anything! And one's interpretation of these things is inevitably influenced by one's historical context. Further, one should keep in mind that historians of religion have long since given up the idea that "primitive" peoples worshiped these vehicles of the sacred. "It is not the tree, the spring, or the stone that is venerated," Eliade writes, *"but the sacred which is manifested through these cosmic objects."*[9] The proof of this point is that an object can return to the realm of the profane as well as enter the realm of the sacred. Hence, it is not the object that is worshiped, but the sacred that is manifested through it.

A number of the preceding points are captured nicely in the following passage by Eliade on the Konde people of Tanganyika, Africa:

> The Konde of Tanganyika believe in a Supreme Being, Kyala or Lesa, who, like all the Supreme Beings of the Africans, is endowed with all the majesty of a heavenly, creating, omnipotent and law-giving God. But Lesa does not only show himself by means of epiphanies of the sky: "Anything great of its kind, such as a great ox or even a great he-goat, or any other impressive object, is called Kyala, by which it may be meant that God takes up his abode temporarily in these things. When a great storm lashes the lake into fury, God is walking on the face of the waters: when the roar of the waterfall is louder than usual, it is the voice of God. The earthquake is caused by his mighty footstep, and the lightning is *lesa,* God coming down in anger. God sometimes comes also in the body of a lion or a snake, and it is in that form that he walks about among men, to behold their doings."[10]

Clearly, we begin to understand the Konde only when we understand what the roar of the waterfall and the stare of the serpent mean to them. Hence, the historian of religion eschews the popular practice of making easy generalizations about other peoples. Instead, he or she "seeks the basically religious by moving through individual historical religious experiences rather than by ignoring or moving around the peculiar or particular experiences."[11] Such a procedure is slower and more painstaking, but it will almost certainly decrease misunderstandings, misrepresentations, and mis-appreciations and lead to a much richer, more accurate sense of the nature and significance of the sacred in the lives of a people.

To gain such an understanding of the sacred in other people's lives requires something more than historical methods in the traditional sense. What more is required is, for the most part, precisely what we've talked about already—namely, phenomenology and comparative studies. That combination together with a historical emphasis is largely what the history of religions school of thought is all about. Eliade, the main spokesman for this approach, emphasizes that "the history of religions is *not merely a historical discipline,* as, for example, archeology or numismatics. It is equally a *total hermeneutics,* being called to decipher and explicate every kind of encounter of man with the sacred, from prehistory to our day."[12] Clearly, what Eliade is calling for is a comprehensive study of religious meaning that treats the experience of the sacred as unique and central.

We have said so far of the history of religions, in its broader sense, that (1) it takes the sacred seriously, (2) it focuses on the sacred as it is manifested in historical data, and (3) it goes beyond the traditional methods of historians in its efforts to explicate the religion of a people. The final point is that (4) historians of religions believe that their field has valuable cultural contributions to make. Among these are (a) a deeper and more adequate understanding of the nature of humankind, (b) better communications among people from different religious backgrounds, and—especially important to our own era—(c) an opportunity for people who have lost (or never had) a sense of the sacred to regain (or gain) an appreciation of what that sense has meant to people in the past and what it might mean to them now. Attractive statements about these cultural values of the history of religions can be found in Eliade's essay "Crisis and Renewal," in his *The Quest: History and Meaning in Religion,* and in Wilfred Cantwell Smith's paper "Comparative Religion: Whither—and Why?" in *The History of Religions,* edited by Eliade and Kitagawa.

ANTHROPOLOGY OF RELIGION

This method of approach to religion involves a comprehensive study of religious phenomena in their cultural context. A good example is A. P. Elkin's *Australian Aborigines: How to Understand Them.* A widely used and comprehensive collection of selections from studies such as Elkin's is the *Reader in Comparative Religion: An Anthropological Approach,* edited by W. A. Lessa and E. Z. Vogt. The methods and data of the anthropologist of religion are very much like those of the historian, except that the historian is interested in a broad sweep of time and of cultures, whereas the anthropologist is usually interested in an extant religion as it is now, as an integral part of a culture with its own dynamic tension and unity. Hence, the anthropologist, in order to speak with authority, normally lives among the people whom he or she is studying. In this way it is possible to observe directly the place of dances, lore, body paint, artwork, holy places, and ceremonies in the lives of the people. Having focused primarily on primitive peoples who have ways of understanding the world and of living in it which are alien to our European traditions, anthropologists of religion have produced some of the most fascinating literature in modern academia. Consider, for example, Clifford Geertz's description of the ritualization of birth in Java:

> The baby is washed, and then the mother; and there are spells for both of these performances too. The umbilical cord and afterbirth are wrapped in white muslin, put into a jug, salted, and buried outside the house. . . . A little wicker fence is erected around the spot or a broken earthenware pot is inverted over it to keep dogs or other animals from digging it up, and a small candle is kept burning over it for thirty-five days in order to prevent evil spirits from disturbing it.

Geertz continues:

> The burying of the umbilical cord is a serious matter. One woman blamed the death of her child, in convulsion after forty days of life, on the fact that the midwife did not put enough salt in the umbilical cord when she buried it, and so it "came up" and the child died. The cord and afterbirth, coming as it does after the birth of the child, is considered to be his spirit younger brother, while the amniotic fluid which precedes him (it is thrown out up into the air) is considered to be his spirit older brother. For the first thirty-five days they remain near the child and protect him against illness, the first under the ground, the other in the sky.[18]

Regarding the relation of anthropology of religion to history and phenomenology, the present tendency is for the anthropologists to restrict themselves to painstaking description of a particular culture and to leave the construction of broad, integrating hypotheses to historians and phenomenologists. Clearly, however, the phenomenological *method* is invaluable to anthropologists endeavoring to step out of the framework of their own culture so as to see and feel the world as their subjects of study do, and so as to appreciate the religious significance of the subjects' behavior, music, and creations.

SOCIOLOGY OF RELIGION

Sociological studies of religion usually take one of two approaches to religion. One kind we will call the *empirical research approach* and the other we will call the *social construction of reality approach*. In some ways these approaches parallel the empirical approach and the phenomenological approach of the history of religions, but a comparison of the two is unnecessary here. The empirical research approach (ERA for short) can be broken down into *functional, structural, conflict,* and *significant variable* studies. Even these aren't exhaustive, but a look at each should give you a good idea of the objectives of ERA.

Some sociologists focus on the question, What functions do religious institutions *in fact* serve in society X, and what are the unique functions of religious institutions in all or most societies? The two parts of this question are equally important, for we have discovered in this century—perhaps as never before—that the functions a religious institution serves may not be functions that it alone can serve. Formal education, for example, was handled for centuries by religious institutions. Now they have been largely relieved of that responsibility. Similarly, for centuries churches were the centers of the social life of a community, but now most social life (even for church members) takes place outside of the church. Sociologists want to know why these changes have come about and what impact they are having on religious institutions. Moreover (and this has to do with the second part of the question), do religious institutions have any social functions of their own which by their very nature cannot be taken away from them? Or are they like the onion which when all its layers are peeled away is reduced to nothing because it has no core of its own? If they are not like the onion, then what are the inalienable functions of religious institutions and what role do they play in the functioning of society as a whole?

Structural studies, as distinguished from functional studies—though these two are never absolutely separable—focus not on the roles a religion plays in the society of which it is a part, but on the various ways the members of that religion structure their environment, their activities, and their relations to one another. In Christianity, for example, the spectrum of social organization ranges from the tight, hierarchical organization of the Roman Catholic Church (which contains several levels of authority culminating in the authority of the pope) to the complete local autonomy of Congregationalist churches, in which decisions are made by democratic processes (the minister having no more authority than any other member of the congregation). Regarding each of these forms of religious organization, the sociologist wants to know not only its structure but also the peculiar problems and the peculiar strengths generated by that structure.

Conflict studies can be sorted into three basic types: (1) conflict within a particular religion, (2) conflict between different religions, and (3) conflict between religious and nonreligious institutions such as the state. Such studies, it should be noted, have a dialectical angle. That is, it is assumed that change comes about by means of the interaction of institutions, and that religious institutions are not merely products of social processes but are causes of change in those processes. The influence of nonreligious institutions on religious institutions is not unidirectional. The influence is reciprocal, so sociologists examine the ways in which religious and nonreligious institutions modify one another.

Structuralist studies lead naturally into examinations of the conflicts generated by the way a religious group is organized. For example, when I was writing the first edition of *Religion and Doubt* I pointed out that the Protestant Episcopal Church in America did not ordain women to their priesthood, and I predicted that because of vigorous opposition within the church, that policy would be changed before *Religion and Doubt* went to press (fall of 1976)—and I was right! Now there is an increasing number of women in the Episcopal priesthood, and because of continuing pressure by both women and men, on September 24, 1988, in Boston, Massachusetts, the Rev. Barbara Harris was ordained as the first woman bishop in the worldwide Anglican Church, of which the Episcopal Church in America is a part. These ordinations of women to priesthood and bishopric have caused controversy in the Episcopal Church in America and threaten to cause divisions in the international Anglican communion.[14] It is "microlevel" studies of these kinds of *internal* religious conflicts—including their causes and consequences and the people involved—that sociologists are trained to conduct.

Conflict between different religions is a matter of everyday news and has long been under investigation by sociologists. Catholics and Protestants fight in Northern Ireland, as do Jews and Muslims in Palestine, and Hindus and Sikhs in India. But to what extent are these *really* religious battles? And to what extent are the names "Protestant" and "Catholic" merely convenient labels with which to differentiate groups who only happen to be Catholic and Protestant and are really fighting over economic or other matters? And to what extent, sociologists ask, are the religions involved and their leadership serving to mitigate or exacerbate the conflict?

Third, sociologists investigate relations between religion and the state. The history of conflicts between religion and state in the United States is particularly interesting because European conflict between church and state helped populate America; yet the U.S. has hardly provided unrestricted religious liberty for its citizens. In the nineteenth century the Mormons were persecuted for practicing polygamy (though it was approved by their own religious laws), and in this century Amish children in Wisconsin have been required by state law to go to a state-accredited school through the tenth grade—in spite of the fact that Amish adults insist that formal schooling beyond the eighth grade is irrelevant to the rustic style of life to which they are religiously committed. (The Amish eventually won their case in court.) In other countries, newspapers and magazines tell of Soviet oppression of its Jewish citizens and of African persecution of black Jehovah's Witnesses (who believe in strict political neutrality and who are, therefore, a thorn in the side of nationalistic leaders who want every citizen to support them). The attacks haven't all been from the side of the state, of course. Mahatma Gandhi, a Hindu religious leader, helped India fight for its political independence from Great Britain, and religious groups in the U.S. have fought in behalf of racial justice and women's rights.

Perhaps I should add as a counterbalance that sociologists are interested also in the ways in which state and religion bolster one another. Sometimes religion is co-opted by the state, and vice versa, because it behooves a state to be able to declare divine authority for its earthly policies and because it behooves a religion to have the earthly power to implement its God-given mandates. In addition to the cooperative relations between highly visible religious institutions (such as Methodism) and the state, sociologists are also interested in what has come to be known as "civil religion"—a kind of distillation of elements from the spirit of nationalism and the mainline religions. Apparently civil religion is often more important to the citizens of a nation than the mainline religions to which they belong! Andrew Greeley calls civil religion the "super religion" (that is, the religion above the more obvious religions), while Will Herberg, thinking of his own nation, calls civil religion "the religion of Americanism." For a brief introduction to this fascinating phenomenon, see Chapter 7, "The Civil Religion," in Greeley's *Denominational Society.*

Finally, what I have called "significant variable studies" are efforts by sociologists to discover the cause-effect relationships of which religious phenomena are a part. It is a rather well-known fact, for example, that the denomination to which a Protestant Christian belongs can be guessed with a good degree of accuracy if you know the individual's socioeconomic status. But socioeconomic status is only one variable that can be linked up with religious facts. John Photiadis and B. B. Maurer, in a research project titled "Religion in an Appalachian State," took four religious variables—(1) intensity of religious beliefs, (2) need to use religion as a buffer from the outside world, (3) preference for a religious way of life, and (4) degree of church participation—and conducted research in order to see how these items correlated with fluctuations in the following kinds of nonreligious variables: age, family size, socioeconomic status, perception of one's own health, social alienation, and type of job. The correlations found were sometimes what you would expect, but not always. As would be expected, there was a larger percentage of "strong believers" among those who considered themselves to be ill than among those who considered themselves to be healthy, but the degree of church participation tended to *decrease* as intensity of religious belief *increased.*[15] Sociologists are also interested in determining the extent to which religious institutions are creators and critics of society and the extent to which they are products of secular forces. For example, to what extent have religious institutions made significant contributions to the quest for racial justice in the United States, and to what extent have they been, in the words of Martin Luther King, Jr., "taillights instead of headlights"? Also, regarding prejudice, do religious people tend to be more or less prejudiced than nonreligious people? And how does prejudice vary among religious groups? Is it true, as some wit put it, that "11 A.M. on Sunday is the most segregated hour of the week"? Do more religious persons than secular persons contribute to benevolent causes and involve themselves in social movements for justice? Or is it the other way around? Or are the two groups indistinguishable with regard to these questions?

The striking results of one sociological investigation were reported by the *National Health Federation Bulletin* in October of 1971. It reads as follows:

Dr. George Comstock of Johns Hopkins University recently conducted exhaustive tests on 567 men. The results proved that men who attended church regularly stood twice the chance of avoiding fatal heart attacks, cancer, tuberculosis, chronic bronchitis, suicidal tendency and cirrhosis of the liver.

The report goes on to say:

> NHF does not involve itself in religion, but this test, which was investigated by us, is so conclusive that we are reporting it. Apparently the psychic or emotional response to a religious oriented life in church relieves stresses that otherwise have a deleterious physiological effect on our bodies. An original survey on which the study was based included 91,000 persons.

We need more studies of this kind, and of the other empirical kinds, in spite of the fact that they may be embarrassing to religious institutions as often as they are flattering. After all, if we don't have the facts, we can neither criticize nor praise religion justly.

You should now have a good grasp of the kinds of questions that are investigated by sociologists who take the empirical research approach, so let's take a brief look at the social construction of reality approach (SCR for short). Philip Hauser points out that sociology is a specialized social science distinguished from the other social sciences by a basic fact with which it starts and a basic assumption which underlies its investigations. "The basic fact is the relative helplessness of the human infant at birth who is always born into, and depends for his survival upon, a social group. The fundamental assumption is that the conduct of the person—his ways of thinking and ways of acting—and the nature of the social order—its structure, function, and values—are to be understood as a product of group life."[16] It is this "fundamental assumption" which provides the key to SCR. It is, to be sure, a "methodological assumption"—that is, a working hypothesis rather than something one must believe to be true. But the fact that it is a working hypothesis rather than a certitude in no way relieves the sociologist from his or her responsibility as a sociologist to see if all human behavior can be explained adequately according to this assumption.

The point of this assumption is quite radical, compared to our ordinary ways of thinking, for ordinarily we attribute a good deal of an individual's behavior to "free" choice, or we say, "That's just the way she is." But look at that fundamental methodological assumption again (hereafter, FMA). It says that not only an individual's ways of acting but also ways of thinking are generated from the interaction between that individual and his or her social context. This is a claim we accept easily when we limit it to common ways of behaving, such as shaking hands, and common ways of thinking, such as arithmetic and certain historical facts. But the point of FMA is much more radical than that. It is claiming that even what we do in our deepest moments of solitude is a product of the interaction between ourselves and our social environment (and remember, all we are at birth is an unconditioned organism—all the conditioning comes from our natural and social environments, not from ourselves). I must admit that I am sometimes startled at how profoundly a child embodies the gait, the posture, and the gestures of a parent. At times it is sufficiently eerie that I begin to realize the extent to which not only his gait, posture, and gestures, but also his values, moods, beliefs, and ways of perceiving and feeling the world have been instilled into/absorbed by him from his social environment, unwittingly.

The sociologist of religion who takes the SCR approach is profoundly interested in the socialization processes whereby a particular interpretation of reality—for example, the Christian interpretation—*becomes reality to the individual,* usually a child. As Berger and Luckmann put it in their *Social Construction of Reality,* "The child does not internalize the world of his significant others as one of many possible worlds. He internalizes it as *the* world, the only existent and only conceivable world, the world *tout court.*"[17] To the child the world *is* the way it is interpreted to him or her by significant others—that is, the adults who are most important to the child. That is his or her natural way of seeing the world. Hence, that particular interpretation of reality is reality to that child—and not only to him or to her but to all of us as children. To repeat, the SCR sociologist wants to understand better the social processes by means of which a particular interpretation of reality becomes reality to the child. The sociologist wants to understand the social genesis of religious attitudes, behaviors, and belief systems. He or she wants to know what means (for example, myths, rituals, symbols, behavior patterns) a religion uses to maintain its interpretation of reality in the everyday lives of its members. And how does it cope with the lure of other religions in a pluralistic society or with the doubts about religion that are engendered in a secularized society? How does it legitimate its own belief system and "illegitimate" that of others? What stratagems does it use to bring deviants back into line and to make other symbolic universes (interpretations of reality) appear unreal or unattractive? These kinds of questions and this approach are associated especially with the work of Peter Berger and Thomas Luckmann. See *The Social Construction of Reality* for the theoretical foundation of their individual works on sociology of religion, such as Berger's *Sacred Canopy* and Luckmann's *Invisible Religion.*

PSYCHOLOGY OF RELIGION

Psychologists of religion are especially interested in the effects that different religious beliefs and practices have on the integration and disintegration of personality. Do more theists or atheists experience mental breakdowns? Do more Protestants or Catholics commit suicide? More fundamentally, is the fullest development of personality possible apart from some kind of religious faith? One eminent psychiatrist, Carl Jung, reported in *Modern Man in Search of a Soul* that his extensive practice as a psychiatrist led him to the insight that all of his patients over thirty-five were ill because they had lost their religious understanding of the world, and they recovered their mental health only when they recovered that outlook. Such a claim by such an eminent psychiatrist cannot be overlooked. Yet neither can we overlook the contention of Sigmund Freud, founder of psychoanalysis and one of the most influential thinkers of our century, that religion is a form of neurotic immaturity (see his *Future of an Illusion*). Clearly, regardless of who is right about the impact of religion on personal development and maturation, this is a question that must be submitted to critical inquiry and not left to mere prejudice and opinion. Hence the need for the investigation of religion by psychologists.

Please keep in mind, however, that the psychologist of religion is not concerned to say "good" or "bad" about religious beliefs and practices. As a scientist, he or she is concerned only with clarifying the *consequences* to personality of being religious in a certain way or of being religious at all. Value judgments such as good and bad, right and wrong, ought and ought not do not fall within the province of the scientist as scientist. This is true for the sociologist, the anthropologist, and the historian, as well as for the psychologist. Neither do these persons in their capacities as social scientists normally ask about the truth or falsity of the religion they are investigating. Their limited but important objective is to *understand and describe*. This is a crucial task because until the facts about a religion are known, we can evaluate it neither fairly nor accurately. In conclusion, scientific studies of religion can be intrinsically interesting and are instrumentally important to intelligent decision making.

"But surely," you must be asking by now, "*some* discipline must engage primarily in the task of *evaluating* religions?" That task, I believe, belongs in a sense to each and every person, for it involves decisions that are much too personal for us to leave to others. Still, there is a discipline that facilitates the making of intelligent decisions about the truth of religious claims—namely, philosophy of religion.

PHILOSOPHY OF RELIGION

Whereas the social scientists use their methods of research to discover *what* people do and believe of a religious nature, philosophers of religion use philosophical methods of inquiry to try to ascertain the *truth or falsity* of people's religious beliefs and the *morality or immorality* of their codes of behavior. Philosophers of religion sometimes go further and ask more radical questions such as, Does the idea of an absolute right and wrong

28282828

make sense? (That is, if standards of right and wrong are based on human opinions, and if human opinions vary and change, can there be an absolute right and wrong?) And what does God have to do with what is morally right and wrong? (Isn't what is morally right independent of the will of God? What if God had commanded us to torture infants?) Moreover, does the idea of God even make sense? (We know what we mean when we talk about sticks and stones, animals and people, or even stars and planets, but what in the world can be meant by "God" if God is "an infinite, incorporeal spirit," as God is often said to be?) Also, is life after death even conceivable, much less possible? (Isn't it the case that when my body disintegrates, I lose my personal identity forever? How can it make sense to talk about me surviving the death of my body? How could a disembodied me be anything at all?)[18]

Clearly, philosophy of religion is a highly intellectual approach to religion. It wants to know whether a religious claim is meaningful (that is, makes sense), and if so, what kind of meaning it has, what its meaning is, whether it is true or false, and how its truth or falsity might be demonstrated. Such an approach to religion is as unavoidable as it is inadequate. It is inadequate because there is always far more to religious faith, as we shall see, than believing intellectually that certain propositions are true; yet, it is an unavoidable approach because none of us wants to believe that which is demonstrably false or wrong. We want to believe that which is true, or, if we can't establish what is true, we want to believe that which is most probably true, or, if we can't establish even that, we want at least to believe that which is possibly true! Hence, we inevitably become involved in questions of truth and falsity, probability and improbability, possibility and impossibility. And that is largely what philosophical inquiry is about.

THEOLOGY

Whereas philosophy of religion involves no initial assumptions about the truth or falsity of a particular religious doctrine or the morality or immorality of a particular religious code, theology *begins* with commitment to certain religious codes and doctrines and works forward from these. This is not to say that all theologians think they *know* that the claims of their religion are true. Some would go this far, but others would say only that they *believe* the evidence shows that their religion is the one which is most likely true. Still others would make the even weaker claim that they have a profound but nonrational *feeling* that their religion is true; and still others would say that they only *hope* that their religion is true. In Chapter 6 we shall look more closely at these four attitudes. For now it is important only to realize that when a theologian affirms a religious doctrine or code, he or she is not necessarily claiming to know that it is true. Hence, when reading a theologian, it is important to discover not only *what* is being affirmed but also the attitude of this affirmation. Still, the primary work of the theologian as theologian lies not in what he or she affirms, for he or she very likely shares religious affirmations with many people who are not theologians, at least in any professional sense; for example, a Catholic theologian shares the affirmation of the Apostles' Creed with millions of lay Catholics. Rather, the theologian's work as a theologian is primarily a matter of (1) *clarifying* in contemporary terms the meaning of that which is affirmed (such as the Buddhist idea of reincarnation), (2) *working out the theoretical implications* of these beliefs (by this process understanding becomes deeper and more detailed, and sometimes new doctrines are deduced, such as the Catholic doctrine of the Immaculate Conception), and (3) *working out the practical applications* of this faith to the contemporary social scene (Mahatma Gandhi rejected the ancient class of "untouchables" on the ground that it was contrary to the spirit of Hindu sacred literature). Clearly, the theologian works *within* a religious tradition and is a servant *of* it, whereas a philosopher, as philosopher, stands *outside* a religious tradition and directs questions *to* it. If I might brandish my infamous broad brush again, whereas the preacher (whose task is closely related to that of the theologian) *declares* a proposition and calls for *commitment* to it, the philosopher *analyzes* that same proposition and calls for *justification* of it. However, these two roles are not antithetical; they are the positive and negative poles between which the human spirit must oscillate in its search for that which is most worthy of commitment.

In view of the fact that I sometimes get from people the attitude that the philosopher is more honest than the theologian, since the philosopher hasn't "sold out" to some particular doctrine, I must add the following: There is nothing wrong with finding yourself committed to a belief and then trying to understand more fully its significance and implications. This is essentially what the theologian does, and I don't see how intellectual progress can be made except in this manner. Further, the philosopher *does* have his or her own presuppositions when investigating religious beliefs; it's just that they aren't about religious doctrines—more likely they are about logic, language, and the nature of knowledge.[19] Without such presuppositions, the philosopher would be able to do nothing since there would be no standards by which to make judgments; yet few, if any, philosophers these days claim that their presuppositions are demonstrably true. Hence, philosophers, too, are operating on the basis of presuppositions that are debatable. Yet neither the philosopher nor the theologian has "sold out." Both are simply proceeding according to the best that they know in their respective areas of inquiry.

Finally, it should be noted that *the same person can be both theologian and philosopher*. To be sure, in order to do theology a person must have a religious faith on which to reflect, but one can have such a faith without blinding oneself to the philosophical questions that can be put to that faith and to religious faith in general. Being aware of such questions, a person can choose to attempt to answer them, and by doing so is doing philosophy. The person must be careful, of course, not to let his or her faith interfere with the integrity and the intensity of the philosophical investigations. Finally, even as the professional theologian may raise philosophical questions about his or her faith, the professional philosopher is not prevented from having a religious faith by that vocation. As a person who must act on the basis of probability and hope or else perish, the philosopher need not, any more than any other person, allow the legitimate philosophical ideal of perfect and certain knowledge to impoverish his or her inner life and paralyze the ability to act. If we require 100 percent certainty before carrying on our daily lives, we will never move! And when we do move on probabilities, we don't move only 60 percent of ourselves because the probability of success is only 60 percent! We take 100 percent of ourselves into action—whether the odds are high or low, with us or against us. We cannot do otherwise. Whence some of the anguish of life.

EXISTENTIALISM

Finally, I call your attention to the existentialist approach to religion. This approach is not as completely cerebral as analytic philosophy of religion nor as impersonal as social science studies of religion. It is at one and the same time *emotional and intellectual, subjective and objective.* It is an approach in which you are deeply and personally concerned about yourself, about reality, and about your relation to it. A shift of perspective moves you from asking, What is man? to asking, Who am I? From asking, What is our duty as persons? to asking, What ought I to do in this situation? From asking, What is death? to asking, Why am I dying? Both types of questions are legitimate and important, but to ask the second kind of question is, it seems to me, an inevitable moment in the process of religious study, for at some point you will pass from the disinterested question, What do those people believe and do of a religious nature? to the personal and passionate question, What do their beliefs and practices have to do with my existence? A Catholic priest I once met was aware of this possible switch from being disinterested to being interested, so that when I took a group of students to visit his monastery for a weekend (we had also visited Jewish, Unitarian, and Hindu groups) the first thing he did was to impress upon the students that though they might be coming with a purely academic attitude, three days in such an atmosphere might precipitate some very genuine personal struggles. He did not want them to be caught unawares by such an event lest they think that it had been engineered. Such alterations in perception can be engineered of course, but they needn't be, for sometimes what we approach initially out of sheer curiosity we soon find ourselves very personally involved in. Perhaps I should issue a similar warning, for the remainder of this book is not a disinterested academic analysis of religion. Rather, it is an attempt to convey what religion has meant and can mean to human beings at its best. Hence, it is the existential approach we will be taking throughout the remainder of our time together, but with considerable doses of phenomenology of religion (regarding the essence of religion), philosophy of religion (regarding the essence of belief and faith), and psychology of religion (regarding religion and personal development). If you are interested in the other approaches mentioned, such as history of religions, anthropology of religion, sociology of religion, and comparative religion, they are included in separate sections of the bibliography at the end of this book. Parenthetically, it's a great bibliography, so I hope you'll do some browsing in it soon! In fact, it might be a good "change of pace" before beginning the next chapter.

Notes

1. Wilfred Cantwell Smith, *The Faith of Other Men* (New York: Mentor Books, 1965), p. 40.

2. Gerardus van der Leeuw, *Religion in Essence and Manifestation* (New York: Harper & Row, 1963).

3. See the brief "Chronological Survey" of the study of religions at the end of Mircea Eliade's *The Sacred and the Profane* (New York: Harcourt, Brace & World, 1959).

4. Mircea Eliade, *The Quest: History and Meaning in Religion* (Chicago: University of Chicago Press, 1969), p. 52.

5. Mircea Eliade, *Patterns in Comparative Religion* (New York: New American Library, 1958), p. xiii.

6. In Mircea Eliade and Joseph Kitagawa, eds., *The History of Religions* (Chicago: University of Chicago Press, 1959), p. 15.

7. Henceforth when I use the phrase "history of religions," I will be using it in its broader sense, unless noted otherwise.

8. Eliade, *Patterns in Comparative Religion*, p. 2.

9. Eliade, *The Quest*, p. 52.

10. Eliade, *Patterns in Comparative Religion*, p. 27.

11. Eliade and Kitagawa, *The History of Religions*, p. viii.

12. Eliade, *The Quest*, p. 58. Italics mine.

13. Quoted from *The Religion of Java* by Clifford Geertz, in Michael Pye, *Comparative Religion* (New York: Harper & Row, 1972), pp. 63–64.

14. See "Episcopalians' Semi-Schism: Upset over Women Clergy, Traditionalists Defy the Church," *Time* (June 19, 1989), p. 53.

15. See "Religion in an Appalachian State," by John Photiadis and B. B. Maurer, Appalachian Center, Research Report 6, West Virginia University, February 1974.

16. See "Sociology," by Philip M. Hauser, *Encyclopaedia Britannica* (1970), 20, 784.

17. Peter L. Berger and Thomas Luckmann, *The Social Construction of Reality* (Garden City, NY: Doubleday, 1966), p. 124.

18. D. Z. Phillips in *Death and Immortality* (New York: St. Martin's, 1970) argues the inconceivability and therefore the impossibility of survival of death. H. D. Lewis in *The Self and Immortality* (New York: Seabury Press, 1973) argues that survival of death is conceivable and is therefore possible.

19. See, for example, the kinds of philosophical tools that are developed in Wesley Salmon's *Logic,* 3rd ed., 1984, William Alston's *Philosophy of Language,* and Roderick Chisholm's *Theory of Knowledge,* 3rd ed., 1989, all published in Prentice Hall's Foundations of Philosophy Series. Get latest edition.

3

Interpretations of Religion

QUESTIONS TO THINK ABOUT

- What does it mean to be religiously concerned?
- What does it mean to have a religious faith?
- What shall we mean by the word "God"?
- What shall we mean by the word "deity"?
- What shall we mean by the word "Lord"?
- What is idolatry?
- What is Erich Fromm's definition of religion?
- What is pseudoreligion?
- What is cryptoreligion?
- What are the characteristics of authentic religion?
- What is meant by saying that reality is ambiguous?
- Why do I say the question is not *whether* to engage in the game of life but *how* to do so? Do you agree?
- Do you agree that there are assumptions about reality and value presently operative in your attitudes and actions?
- What are those assumptions?
- What do you think are the best reasons for being religious? for not being religious?

A METHODOLOGICAL PRELUDE

In this chapter and the chapters that follow, I will be setting forth an understanding of religion which I hope will prove provocative and valuable. But as I proceed, please keep in mind that I am not presuming to tell you what religion really is. The very idea of saying what something really is involves philosophical problems that could easily sidetrack us for many pages. Indeed, one can spend a lifetime on these problems, normally dealt with in philosophy in the subareas of *epistemology* (theory of knowledge) and *metaphysics* (theory of reality). I shall not be presuming, then, to tell you what religion is in some complete and final sense; yet neither do I believe that my understanding of religion is completely arbitrary. I think I am hitting the target—though perhaps not in the bull's-eye. I am trying to account for certain data in human experience and believe I am succeeding to some extent. So I hope you will take seriously what I have to say. However, I also hope that you will continuously ask yourself how well my ideas fit your own experience and thinking, for these may bring you to believe that my understanding of religion is inadequate and therefore needs to be supplemented, or is plain wrong and needs to be corrected. Hence, I invite your reactions. Fill the margins with comments and questions! It is only by acknowledging and clarifying our disagreements that we can discuss them honestly and fully, and it is only by rigorous dialogue that we shall make rapid progress toward a more adequate and convincing understanding of religion than either of us has now.

My method in setting forth that interpretation of religion which I find exciting and authentic will be to develop a set of terms by means of which we can better understand ourselves and others regarding religious matters. These terms will then serve as tools with which we can analyze religious phenomena and thereby understand better their structure and dynamics. My exposition of these terms, such as "God" and "faith," has been greatly influenced by the work of Professor Paul Tillich, but I have not attempted to restrict myself to Tillich's conclusions. Readers who are interested in Tillich's position are encouraged to read his outstanding little volume *Dynamics of Faith.*

RELIGIOUS CONCERN

Earlier we spoke of a person "awakening religiously," of a seed of religious concern germinating. But what does it mean to awaken religiously, to be religiously concerned? It means that a person is gripped by the question, What is *ultimately, eternally,* real and valuable? There are many versions of this question, but they all have to do with *the individual's existence in relation to reality.* These are never impersonal questions. They are always impassioned. They have to do with *my* origins, *my* destiny, all considered in a cosmic context. What is the nature of the reality within which I live and breathe and have my being? What is the nature of my existence within that reality? What within that reality, if anything, is sacred—that is, gives absolute meaning, worth, unity, richness, and exaltation to human life, and therefore to my life?

Now, if "to be religious" in its simplest sense means "to be religiously concerned," then every normal person is potentially religious, as every normal person is capable of being besieged by the questions, What is ultimately real and valuable? How am *I* related to it? How *should* I relate to it? Indeed, I think that a person cannot become fully developed until he or she has confronted these questions and thereby begun the religious quest. Moreover, it is difficult, perhaps impossible, not to enter on this quest. As John Magee puts it,

> . . . whenever a human being (1) speaks of the ultimate meaning of his existence, (2) considers his absolute obligations, or (3) relates himself by commitment or devotion to what he thinks is ultimately real—whenever he does any of these things, he is acting religiously, whether he realizes it or not.[1]

The circumstances of our lives virtually force us to engage in the first and second activities. In Chapter 4 we will specify some of these circumstances and see how they help germinate the seeds of religious concern and inquiry. Keep in mind, however, that though the religious quest is a virtually unavoidable phase of human life, religiousness (Magee's third activity), is not. Secularity is always an alternative. Some people start there and stay there. Some do not start there but do conclude there. Others leave but return to stay.

RELIGIOUS FAITH: GOD, DEITY, AND THE LORD

Whereas to be religiously concerned is to be concerned about what is ultimate, *to have a religious faith* is to feel that you have found that which is ultimately real and valuable (or that it has revealed itself to you).[2] Note that both states, concern and faith, are characterized by duality: There is a Subject (you) who is passionately concerned and an Object of that concern. Prior to faith, the concern of the Subject is to *discover* that which is ultimately real and valuable. After faith has emerged, the concern of the Subject is to *sustain* a right relationship to the Object which has been experienced as sacred, as worthy of worship, as worthy of absolute commitment and devotion. Such faith may be dynamic, for the individual may seek an ever deeper understanding of the object of his faith, and, if experience proves the object to be deficient, he may seek an ever more adequate object of faith.

Tillich suggests that this object of religious commitment should be called "God"—no matter what it is. In other words, the word "God" should be applied to *whatever* fulfills the function of giving to an individual the conviction that it is that which is ultimately real and valuable. That thing does, in fact, function as God (as the absolute) in that person's life. Now this might seem an odd, even blasphemous, use of the term "God," but it is really quite biblical. Consider, for example, a story about the ancient Israelite prophet Elijah. Disturbed by the defection of many Israelites to the worship of the Canaanite deity Baal, Elijah decided it was time to have a showdown with the worshipers of Baal. Elijah successfully challenged the priests of Baal to meet him on top of Mount Carmel in order that the true God might be revealed. When all were gathered he declared, "If Baal is God, then we should worship Baal; but if the Lord is God, then we should worship the Lord." Clearly, Elijah did not beg the question as to who was the true God, Baal or the Lord. He simply raised the question in a pointed way, using the word "God" to refer to that which is worthy of our worship, of our absolute trust and commitment. He left the resolution of the question to the contest that ensued. The progress of the confrontation is fascinating, Elijah proving to be a sharp-tongued wit. If you haven't read the book or seen the movie, I invite you to put down this book and turn to I Kings 18 in the Bible—but hurry back.

Tillich is correct to insist on the importance of having functional interpretations of religious terms, since such interpretations enable us to see more clearly how religion cuts across and finds expression in all societies and all lives. Still, it is not enough to define just one term, "God," in this manner, for that term gains clarity only against other terms. Hence, let's define "God," "deity," and "Lord," and see how the definitions of any two of these words help make more clear the meaning of the third. We shall use the word "God" to stand for that which *is* worthy of our ultimate concern and commitment because it is ultimately real and valuable. The word "deity" we shall use to refer to that which a person *treats as though* it is worthy of absolute commitment (whether it really is or not). A person's deity is that which actually dominates that person's life, giving it unity, direction, and inspiration, whether the person realizes what it is or not. Karl Jaspers, a twentieth-century German psychiatrist and philosopher, put this point nicely when he stated, "That which you hold to, upon which you stake your existence, that is truly your God" (though we would now substitute "deity" where he has said "God"). Jaspers goes on to make another point which shall be assumed throughout this book: "Man cannot help taking something as an absolute, whether willingly and knowingly, whether accidentally and fitfully or resolutely and steadfastly. Man has a kind of home in the absolute. He cannot evade it. In that home he must live."[3] (We shall return shortly to the phenomenon of a person being unaware of that which dominates his life.) Owing to the nature of its usage in English translations of the Bible, we shall reserve our third term, "the Lord," for reference to the deity of Jews and Christians.[4]

Many things other than the Lord have been deities, of course. One alternative was captured in a felicitous expression by a student who said that some people are "very religious about money"! Consider, for example, the experience of my brother Daniel, who drove a man a couple of hundred miles because the fellow was down on his luck and needed a break. When they arrived at their destination the man, whom my brother knew, handed him some money. My brother refused it and said, "I drove you because I'm your friend." The fellow dropped the money on his lap and said, "That's the only friend you'll ever have." And what about the Great Depression of the thirties? People committed suicide because their wealth was wiped out. It was as though they were saying, "God is dead, so I may as well be too." Other prominent deities for which people have lived and died include sex, fame, power, pleasure, security, success, the nation, justice, love, peace, self, and humanity. I'm sure you can think of still others. As Radhakrishnan, a Hindu thinker, put it, "The age of faith is always with us; only the object of our faith changes."[5]

IDOLATRY

Inasmuch as there are many possible objects of religious faith, we must ask, Are all of these objects equally worthy of our commitment, or are some more worthy than others? Most important, is there anything that is worthy of our *absolute* commitment and devotion? Is there anything that is truly worthy of *worship?* Kai Nielsen focused the problem sharply when he stated, "The religious quest is a quest to find a Z such that Z is worthy of worship."[6] Some objects certainly seem more worthy of devotion than others; for example, self-fulfillment should be valued over self-indulgence and the welfare of humanity over the supremacy of one's nation. Is not your own conviction that some things are more worthy of commitment than others? Now since the objects to which we can commit ourselves are many in number, and since they are not equally worthy of our commitment, we are faced with the problems of (1) deciding among them and (2) avoiding *idolatry*. What is idolatry? In its extreme form, it consists of *giving unconditional devotion to something that is not worthy of such devotion*—such things as money or winning or one's nation. From another angle we might say that idolatry consists of giving more of yourself to something or someone than it or that person deserves. The greater the discrepancy between the intensity of your devotion and the worth of the object of your devotion, the greater the idolatry.

If Tillich is correct that everyone is religious in the sense of having an ultimate concern, then that includes you and me, and we each need to ask ourselves what our deity is and whether it is an object worthy of our absolute commitment *or* is it an idol—that is, something not able to deliver what we expect of it, something which will disillusion us, something the deficiencies of which we must not notice or must blind ourselves to in order that we can remain committed to it. Is our deity God or an idol? Which deity is God? And how do we avoid idolatry? Karl Jaspers, in his *Way to Wisdom,* makes the interesting suggestion that idolatry results from mistaking for God that which only *points* to God. Instead of responding to the pointer—for example, political power—by transcending to God, we fixate on the pointer by becoming obsessed with it, as though there were nothing more important or greater. But the pointer, whether it be power, fame, ecstasy, or something else, is no more the same as God than a finger that points at the moon is the moon. Most of us have been amused and frustrated by our attempts to point something out to a baby. All the baby cares to look at is the finger that keeps punctuating the air with its pointing! Perhaps in more difficult matters we adults are still susceptible to mistaking the finger for the moon, the pointer for the referent.[7]

FRANKLY SPEAKING   **by Phil Frank**

IN GOD WE TRUST

'DON'T DISTURB YOUR FATHER WHILE HE'S PRAYING!'

THE NATURE OF RELIGION: ERICH FROMM AND PETER SLATER

Now I would like to begin setting forth a second analysis of religion—not because it contradicts the earlier analysis, but because it is so similar. What *is* different is the background of the author, Erich Fromm. It seems significant to me that Tillich, a believer in the biblical God (see his difficult but valuable lectures *Biblical Religion and the Search for Ultimate Reality),*[8] and Fromm, who rejects the biblical God (see his *Psychoanalysis and Religion*),[9] arrive at such similar conclusions about religion. People starting from such different perspectives and arriving at such similar conclusions must be on to something! Fromm, a practicing psychoanalyst and author of such popular books as *The Art of Loving* and *Revolution of Hope,* does not believe that the Lord is God, but believes nonetheless that religion is humanly important. He states in *Psychoanalysis and Religion* that by the word "religion" he understands, "any system of thought and action shared by a group which gives to the individual a frame of orientation and an object of devotion."[10] He goes on to claim that a human being (in the biological sense) cannot become a person without a frame of orientation and an object of devotion. Why? Because to be human is merely a biological matter, but to become a person requires a certain level of development, awareness, sensitivity, and commitment. Without these things we fall short of personal fulfillment and may even perish, owing to our lack of any instinctual frame of orientation or object of commitment. We are confronted, then, with the *opportunity* and *necessity* of choice; the religions and philosophies of the world confront us precisely as different ways to be human.

Before going on, let's analyze two deficiencies of Fromm's otherwise fine definition. First, Fromm has focused on two of the central concerns of religion—namely, the nature of reality and what is of genuine worth—but he has neglected a third and equally important concern—namely, the concern for rebirth, for transformation, for an extraordinary source of strength, peace, guidance, and joy. In biblical terminology, Fromm has provided for the Father (the Genesis frame of orientation accepted by Jews and Christians holds that the Lord created the heavens and the earth and is the ruler of history), and for the Torah/Son (Jews are devoted to study of and obedience to the commandments of the Torah—that is, the first five books of the Bible—and Christians are devoted to a person, Jesus, whom they believe to be the only Son of God), but Fromm has not provided for the Holy Spirit, which is described by Jews and Christians alike as their source of strength, joy, and transformation. To be sure, the devotion of Jews to the commandments of the Torah is of a different nature than the devotion of Christians to Jesus, and their interpretations of the Holy Spirit also differ significantly. I do not mean to deny these differences, but only to point out the functional similarity between three central foci of the religious faith of Jews and Christians. Moreover, I think these three elements—frame of orientation (a matter of the mind), object of devotion (a matter of the will), and source of transformation (a matter of the heart)—are central to any fully developed religion.

There are, of course, religions that are (1) almost completely moralistic, emphasizing the object of devotion to the neglect of the frame of orientation and the source of transformation; and there are religions that are (2) almost completely Pentecostal or Dionysian, emphasizing the source of transformation to the neglect of the other two elements of a fully developed religion; and there are religions that are (3) primarily a matter of the intellect, focusing on a particular understanding of the world without much regard for the inner life or the life of action. When we put two of these elements together without the third, we get combinations that sound familiar: (a) an emphasis on reason and morality with a neglect of the spirit, (b) an emphasis on morality and spirit with a neglect of reason, or (c) an emphasis on reason and spirit, with a neglect of morality. But no two of these factors by themselves, it seems to me, can provide what the human spirit is seeking in religion. In our religion we want to acquire a way of understanding the world, a sense of what is truly valuable, and a source of spiritual sustenance. Anything less is not enough. Perhaps that is why we see an increasing interest in mysticism among liberal religious groups and an increasing involvement in social action by Pentecostal groups. The very nature of our existence makes us discontented with anything less than a fully developed religion.

The second debatable aspect of Fromm's definition of religion is his claim that religion is, and presumably must be, "shared by a group." This cuts across the sentiment of many persons I've talked to. The eminent philosopher and mathematician A. N. Whitehead is also of the opposite opinion. In *Religion in the Making* he writes:

> Religion is what the individual does with his own solitariness . . . and if you are never solitary, you are never religious. Collective enthusiasms, revivals, institutions, churches, rituals, bibles, codes of behavior, are the trappings of religion, its passing forms. They may be useful, or harmful; they may be authoritatively ordained, or merely temporary expedients. But the end of religion is beyond all this.[11]

What do you think? Does religion have to be shared by a group? If so, then there can be no such thing as a personal, private religion. Right? But then, how could a new religion ever get started? Perhaps Fromm's point is that a religion which is not shared by a group will not survive and flourish. It is certainly an accurate historical observation that religion has been almost entirely a group phenomenon, but whether it must be or ought to be is a different matter.

Another, more recent, description of religion, by Peter Slater, emphasizes four aspects of religion: the personal, the communal, the traditional, and the transcendent. Slater writes in Chapter 1 of *The Dynamics of Religion* that a religion is "a personal way of life informed by traditional elements of creed, code, and cult and directed toward the realization of some transcendent end." He adds, "A personal way of life is both individual and communal" and "the transcendent end is the ultimate concern of those who follow a [religious] way [of life]." Indeed, ". . . the transcendent end is what is of ultimate value to those who are on the way. It is this which defines their sense of priorities." This emphasis on the centrality of value in religion is one that I will take up in my own definition of religion, but first for contrast let's look at some misinterpretations of religion.

MISINTERPRETATIONS OF RELIGION

The terms we have now defined are helpful for understanding religious matters, but they do not constitute a definition of religion in its authentic, healthy form. So let's keep pushing forward toward such a definition by examining some common misconceptions of religion. Against this backdrop of misconceptions, the definition of authentic religion to be provided later should take on a clearer, richer meaning. The two misconceptions on which we will focus are described by John Magee in his comprehensive text *Religion and Modern Man.*

Pseudoreligion (Segmental Religion)

Magee reports in *Religion and Modern Man* that according to two studies of student attitudes, made during 1957 and 1960, religion was perceived by most students as simply one thing among many, as something they held in common with many other students, but which often came off poorly in competition with the other things bidding for their time and attention—for example, studies, social life, sports, earning money, family. Moreover, religion was valued for the contribution it made to these other aspects of life, "but there was no hint that religion might call these other interests into question by judging them according to some higher standard. In short, religion, as they conceived it, is a useful convention for respectable people."[12]

For these students, then, religion was simply one concern among others, competing for equal time with education, social life, business, and family. These students have a lot of adult company, of course—adults who have a "service station" attitude toward religion: religion is what you turn to when your spirits are low and you need a fill-up, or when your oil is dirty with guilt and you want it changed, or when you want to meet likeminded persons or potential business contacts. After all, why join the smallest, poorest church in town if you sell Cadillacs for a living? In any case, religion here is thought of as a *segment* of life, lying alongside other segments rather than transcending them. It is thought of as something to be used for ulterior ends, rather than as something that has a bearing on the whole of life and stands in judgment on all personal and social enterprises.

Authentic religion, by contrast, should be thought of as *holistic, wholehearted,* and *transcendent.* It involves the whole person in relation to the whole of life—indeed, in relation to the whole of existence. It stands *over* the individual in judgment, and it stands *by* the individual for strength and guidance and transformation. In the light of this distinction between pseudoreligion and authentic religion, when the question arises as to what a person's religion is, it cannot be answered by simply asking him or her or by looking to see to what religious tradition he or she belongs. The question must be put on two levels: (1) what does Betty *think* is her religion? (2) What is *really* her religion? If what she thinks is her religion is *not* really her religion (according to the preceding definition of authentic religion), then what she *thinks* is her religion is a *pseudoreligion,* not her real religion.

It might seem impertinent to ask whether a person's purported religion is his or her real religion. After all, who should know better what Betty's religion is than Betty herself? If we don't accept her word as to what her religion is, aren't we implying that she may be deceiving us? Not necessarily. What must be kept in mind is that Magee is working with a functional interpretation of religion. When we ask, What is her religion? we are not asking, To what religious organization does she belong? We are asking, What in life does she take most seriously? What gives her integrity, purpose, and energy? What central concerns does she organize her life around and subordinate all other considerations to? She may not be aware of what her religion is in this sense. If she is not, we might provide a valuable service by helping her come to see and distinguish it from her pseudoreligion.

One has a pseudoreligion, then, when what one thinks is one's religion is not. To be sure, it might seem strange to say of an individual that Christianity is his or her pseudoreligion whereas professional success is his or her *real* religion—because we do not ordinarily think of the pursuit of professional success as a religion. After the initial awkwardness, however, I think you will find the functional definition of religion more illuminating in helping you understand yourself and others than the traditional institutional definition, which restricts the meaning of religion to one of the specific religions, such as Judaism, Hinduism, and so on. Once we clarify those characteristics that lead us to classify these things as religions, we must be willing to apply the word to whatever possesses those characteristics, regardless of whether it has been traditionally classified as a religion. (Parenthetically, as fascinating as it is to put the question, What is that person's real religion? to family and friends, you might just want to start with yourself!)

Cryptoreligion (Unwitting Religion)

Whereas pseudoreligion consists of thinking that your religion is one thing when it is another, cryptoreligion consists in thinking that you are not religious when you are. Whereas in pseudoreligion your professed religion is not what gives your life integrity, zest, and direction, in cryptoreligion you do not realize the religiousness of your activities and commitments because of too narrow an interpretation of religion. Consider those people who believe that science is humanity's only means of achieving truth and happiness. Aren't those people taking a religious attitude toward science? Can't it be said meaningfully that science is their deity? This kind of attitude toward science is sometimes called "scientism" and is exemplified by persons such as Sigmund Freud and B. F. Skinner.[18] In a similar manner, many atheists who have been convinced by the Marxist interpretation of human history show a commitment to communism which is religious in nature. Marxism provides them with a frame of orientation (dialectical materialism), an object of devotion (the Communist society), and a source of strength and transformation (the Communist party). Perhaps it seems odd to call communism a religion, since it rejects belief in a supreme being and is notorious for attacking religion. Yet, if we restrict the word "religion" to traditions that include belief in a supreme person, then we cannot apply the term to Taoism or Confucianism or certain branches of Hinduism and Buddhism, because none involves belief in a supreme, personal being. If we *do* define "religion" broadly enough to include those traditions, which are usually thought of as religions, then we find that it will also include communism, scientism, and nationalism.

What do you say? Is it a mistake to apply the word "religious" to systems that deny the existence of a supreme, personal being? Or is it a mistake to refuse to apply the word to systems that perform all the basic functions of theistic religions but do not include belief in a supreme, personal being? Let me share with you some ideas and quotations in defense of my claim that communism is a religion for many of its followers. If I convince you, then you will see that religion and religiousness are found more widely and deeply in human life than you might think.

IS COMMUNISM A RELIGION?

The Marxist-Leninist frame of orientation, usually called "materialism," maintains that nature is all of reality, is composed of nothing but matter, has always existed and always will. Moreover, nature is eternally in the process of development; "development is a progressive movement, an ascent from lower stages to higher stages, from the simple to the complex. In other words, development is *progress.'*[14] Thus, Marxist-Leninists believe that nature, by virtue of its inherent, essential characteristics, is eternally, unstoppably developing from one level of goodness to a higher one. There are obstacles, deviations, and setbacks along the way, but "history demonstrates that in the long run progressive movement overcomes all these temporary deviations and obstacles, and makes headway."[15]

Marxist-Leninists believe, then, that there are inexorable laws at work in nature, which includes humankind and its history. "Dialectics" is their name for the science of the laws of the development of nature. But the Communists responsible for founding and propagating modern communism have not been scientific observers who merely discover and report how things are and where they are going; they have been *enthusiastic* about the direction in which dialectics shows history to be moving, and they have devoted themselves to speeding its inevitable movement to universal communism. In the words of the Soviet manual *Fundamentals of Marxism-Leninism:*

> The struggle of the working class and the Communists convincingly refutes the stupid idealist lie that materialists are indifferent to ideals. For this struggle is being waged for *the highest and noblest ideal of all,* communism, and it produces legions of intrepid fighters *supremely devoted* to that ideal. [my italics][16]

Communists have, then, an explicit worldview, an object of devotion, and a source of inspiration. Their worldview is dialectical and historical materialism. Their general object of devotion is nature and its next step of progress, and their particular object of devotion at this time is the establishment of worldwide communism. The vision of worldwide communism together with the comradeship of fellow Communists and the profound conviction that history is on their side produces "the greatest of all energies—the energy of the builders of communism."[17] Indeed, "The advance to the shining heights of Communist civilisation will always engender in people unusual power of will and intellect, creative impulses, courage, and life-giving energy."[18]

In addition to the preceding there are numerous other statements in which Communist leaders and authors use the language of religion to communicate their points and sentiments: "Materialism is imbued with *the utmost faith* in the human intellect. . . . " "Materialism is in its very essence an optimistic, life-asserting and radiant philosophy, entirely alien to pessimism and *Welt-schmerz.*" According to the 1961 Programme of the Communist Party of the Soviet Union, "Labour for the benefit of society is the *sacred duty* of everyone." "The mainspring of [Communist] morality is *devotion to the collective,* readiness and ability *sacredly* to observe the public interests." Nikita Khrushchev expressed his support for "the fraternal Cuban people in their *sacred struggle* for their just cause." Having exalted the example and teachings of Vladimir Lenin, Khrushchev rallied the 22nd Congress of the Communist Party of the Soviet Union by saying, "So let us, comrades, always *sacredly cherish* and ever more consistently put the behests of our immortal leader and teacher into effect." Khrushchev concluded his speech by saying, "So let us, comrades, *devote all our efforts, and our energies* to hastening the day when the sun of communism will shine over our land!" The Soviet Communist party's motto in 1961 was, "Everything for the sake of man, for the benefit of man," echoing Ludwig Feuerbach's pre-Marxian sentiment that "man's God is MAN!" The first command in the 1961 Soviet Communist moral code was "*devotion* to the Communist cause." The conclusion of the 1961 Soviet Communist Programme states, "The Party is confident that the Soviet people will accept the new Programme of the C.P.S.U. as their own vital cause, as *the greatest purpose of their life* and as a banner of nationwide struggle for the building of communism."[19]

What are we to make of the religious flavor of the preceding statements and terminology? I know of no reason to think that they were insincere efforts to manipulate the emotions of the audience by using religious language to confer upon communism a dignity and glory which the speakers did not think communism really had. Also, I know of no reason to think that those uses of traditionally religious terms and phrases were just superficial uses that could have been paraphrased easily into nonreligious terminology. Rather, I think that religious terminology was used because it best captured the profound reverence, devotion, and enthusiasm that Khrushchev and others felt toward working-class people, the Communist vision of society, and nature's slow but inexorable and irreversible actualization of that vision on earth. Moreover, the profound moral outrage felt and expressed by Marx, Engels, and Lenin toward the evil aspects of slavery, feudalism, and capitalism was an outrage the like of which had not been seen since, perhaps, the biblical prophets Amos and Hosea.

It seems best to me, then, to understand communism as a form of religion for many of its advocates and to distinguish it from religions like Judaism, Christianity, and Islam by distinguishing between naturalistic religion and supernaturalistic religion. A *supernaturalistic* religion involves belief in and devotion to someone or something that exists beyond the realm of nature. Examples here are Moses' devotion to Yahweh and Plato's devotion to the Idea of the Good. A *naturalistic* religion involves devotion to nature itself, whether the whole or a part of it or some prominent force within it, or devotion to some possibility within nature. Examples of the former include the pantheism of Benedict Spinoza, the reverence for nature that is expressed in Native American religions, and the sacredness of nature and its ecological systems that is being experienced and expressed by more and more ecologically minded people. Examples of religious devotion to the possibilities of nature are the Communist movement and the Unitarian-Universalist Association.

AUTHENTIC RELIGION

As a conclusion to the preceding reflections on pseudo- and cryptoreligion, let me express my conviction that authentic, mature religion is not *segmental,* as is pseudoreligion, pertaining to only a part of life; rather it is *holistic* and pertains to the whole of life. Moreover, it is not *unwitting,* as is cryptoreligion; it is *self-conscious* and *conscientious.* John Magee captures most of these points quite well when he says that a person's religion

> is what he really takes to heart as most reliably real and most convincingly valuable; it is the standard by which he judges everything else. Another way of saying this is that a man's faith is the ground upon which the rest of his life stands; it is an estimate of what is ultimately trustworthy and dependable.[20]

Two of my students captured these ideas nicely when one of them wrote that "to be religious . . . means a total giving of oneself to his belief" and the other wrote that religion is "a supreme interest that grows in and with you."

Now I want to work from the preceding ideas toward what seems to me a plausible, useful definition of religion in its genuine, developed form. First, however, I want to speak of the definition of religion that seems to come to most people's minds when they are asked what religion is or what someone's religion is. This most common way of understanding religion is the *institutional* way: a religion is a group of people bound together by common beliefs and practices that focus on what they consider to be supernatural truths and realities. To have a religion means to affirm the beliefs and engage in the practices of some such group. For example, an individual who is baptized in a Congregational worship service, professes Jesus as her personal lord and savior, and promises to support that particular church becomes a Congregational Christian. This is a primarily external definition of religion because it focuses on what people publicly profess and do regarding the supernatural.

The *devotional* way of defining religion starts from a different point and places its emphasis internally instead of externally. It begins with the individual rather than the group, with subjective experience rather than objective experience, with an understanding of what it means to be religious rather than an understanding of what a religion is. From this starting point the devotional understanding of religion goes on to deduce what a religion is and to discover what religions exist.

According to this approach, to understand religion one must begin with the realization that to be religious in the clearest, fullest way, in the way that has given rise to the great religions and religious revolutions, is to be *devoted* to something which one believes to be worthy of wholehearted devotion. Such devotion arises out of one's sense of something that is so good as to be worthy of unqualified commitment and which calls for such commitment. For example, if it is Jesus of Nazareth whom one feels and believes to be worthy of unqualified commitment, and if it is the Congregational way of expressing such commitment that one finds most attractive, then one is religious toward Jesus, and Congregational Christianity is one's religion. The same kind of interpretation can be applied to being a Sufi Muslim, a Hasidic Jew, and so on, with different results, of course.

Note, however, that the devotional understanding of religion leads to some surprising results: (1) a person can be religious without believing in the supernatural; (2) a person can be religious without belonging to a religious institution; (3) a person who *does* belong to a religious institution might be religiously authentic or inauthentic. Let's examine each of these points. First, religiousness and religion do not require belief in supernatural truths or realities. For example, if an individual believes that truth is the highest value for humans, and if it is the search for truth that gives that person's life unity, energy, and direction, and if that person believes that it is only through science that we discover the truth, then according to the devotional definition of religion, truth is that person's deity and science is that person's religion. Earlier I argued for a similar conclusion regarding contemporary communism.

The second, perhaps less surprising, implication of the devotional definition of religion is that one does not have to belong to a religious institution in order to be religious or have a religion. Nevertheless, we should not fail to appreciate the fact that most religions have developed from an earlier religion and that most religious people have accepted or adapted an already established religion. Yet although the devotional understanding of religion does not require that a religion be shared by a group, it best enables us to distinguish religious institutions from other institutions such as education, science, government, and medicine. It also allows us to distinguish different religions from one another by dint of their different objects of devotion and/or different ways of expressing that devotion.

A third implication of the devotional understanding of religion is that there is an important distinction between authentic and inauthentic members of a religion. The institutional definition of religion does not account satisfactorily for the person who claims to be a Muslim and who does what is publicly required of a Muslim, for example, refrains from drinking alcohol and makes a pilgrimage to Mecca, but who does those things for family or business reasons and without religious sincerity. By contrast, consider the Muslim whose life is radiant with devotion to God. According to the institutional definition of religion, the religion of both of these people is Islam, period. Each claims to be a Muslim and keeps the public requirements of Islam. But it seems clear that the first person is not a Muslim; only those who submit their lives to God with sincerity are Muslims; people who engage insincerely in the public practices of Islam only appear to be Muslims. The same thing seems to be true of the individual's relation to any religion.

To be sure, the institutional definition can distinguish between "good" and "marginal" members of a religion by means of public criteria, for example in the case of a Muslim praying five times a day, not eating pork, and fasting during the month of Ramadan. We do not want to lose that important distinction, but public criteria do not capture the difference between someone who is a Muslim, even though a very imperfect one, and someone who claims to be and appears to be a Muslim but is not due to a lack of religious sincerity.[21]

If the preceding analysis is correct, then the devotional definition of religion is more satisfactory than the institutional definition primarily because it recognizes that religion is first and foremost a matter of subjectivity and passion directed toward what the individual considers to be an absolute good giving meaning, unity, and direction to life. It is from such passion that religious movements and institutions have developed and by which they have been sustained, enriched, and transmitted. Also, by distinguishing between authentic and inauthentic religiousness, the devotional understanding of religion enables us to see that some of what seems religious is not (such as worship by someone who merely goes through the motions to avoid being harassed by his or her parents) and that some of what may not seem religious is (such as the dedication to the dialectic of history by many Communists).

This last point is controversial because it allows for religions which do not require belief in the supernatural. Given the devotional definition of religion, it certainly seems to follow that Marxist communism, Unitarian-Universalism, and some forms of Buddhism and Hinduism are religions in spite of their affirmation or permission of atheism. Anyone is religious who is devoted to something which seems worthy of and calls for such devotion because of its great good; and the way that person relates to that great good is his or her religion. Moreover,wholehearted devotion to such things as worldly success or baseball or winning certainly strikes me as sometimes tragic, sometimes humorous, sometimes both (for example, a quote from a famous coach: "Winning isn't the most important thing; it is the *only* thing!"); but the inadequacy of these values and the worldviews that go with them does not mean that they are not religions. There can be inadequate, misdirected religions, and the institutional, supernaturalistic definition of religion tends to prevent us from seeing that.[22]

It does seem to me that the two basic options for defining religion are belief in the supernatural, on the one hand, and devotion to the good, on the other hand. The word "religion" comes from a Latin word, *religare,* which means "to tie together" or "to bind together." The most fundamental and persistent endeavor of the great religions, I think, is to bind us to the good, not to the supernatural. Some of these religions believe that ultimate goodness lies beyond the realm of nature, others believe it lies within nature; so it is understandable that we have some religions that are supernaturalistic and others that are naturalistic.

The devotional definition also illuminates the difference between religious and nonreligious Jews, Hindus, and so on. The religion of a religious person provides him or her with a frame of orientation and object of devotion; for the nonreligious participant that same religion—or at least the public aspects of it—provides only a means of acquiring cultural identity and self-understanding.

We must not, however, think that every act or object of devotion is religious. Simply because we are told that someone works on his golf game religiously, or is religious about golf, or golf is his religion does not mean that we should think that golf literally has religious significance for him. Such a statement is usually a figure of speech and means that someone is focused on golf, or something else, with the kind of enthusiasm and perseverance associated with devoutly religious people. Such uses of metaphor can be wonderfully illuminating and humorous, and I do not mean to discourage them. But I also do not want to rule out the possibility that golf can literally constitute the religious center of someone's life. Golf may seem an unlikely and bizarre religious object, but that is due to a consideration of whether it would be a *worthy* deity, not whether it *could* be a deity.

In conclusion, the religious question is the question of whether there is anything which is worthy of and calls for our wholehearted devotion because of its great and objective goodness. *Religiousness* arises from a positive answer to that question and consists of wholehearted devotion to that which one believes to be supremely good. A *religion* is what the individual thinks is a fitting and fruitful way of relating to that great good. A *supernaturalistic* religion holds that that which is supremely good transcends the realm of nature. A *naturalistic* religion holds that that which is supremely good is either nature itself or some part or aspect or possibility of nature. One expression of this position can be found in George Bernard Shaw's *Black Girl in Search of God.* One of Shaw's characters, a crusty, socialist Irishman, agrees that the word "God" is meaningful and valuable but insists that it refers to nothing more than "an eternal but as yet unfulfilled purpose." That purpose, he added, cannot be fulfilled unless it is "made reasonably easy and hopeful by Socialism."

Secularity is a negative answer to the religious question. Jean-Paul Sartre seems to be an excellent example of a secular person. He was a self-declared atheist who said that his philosophizing was an effort to think out all the consequences of atheism. One of those consequences, he argued, is that nothing has inherent value, that is, value in and of itself. Nothing has any value except the value which the individual gives to it, and that lasts only as long as the individual gives it.[23]

TO BE OR NOT TO BE RELIGIOUS

Clearly we cannot be secular and religious at the same time. To be religious is to reject secularity's claim that there is nothing which is good in itself and worthy of our devotion. To be secular is to reject religion's claim that there is something inherently worthy of wholehearted commitment. Still, there is, I think, a sense in which religiousness precedes secularity. The search for an answer to the religious question is itself religious. That quest is a hopeful enterprise which we would not undertake if we did not care whether there might be a positive answer. Moreover, while the quest is underway it is directed toward absolute goodness even if one decides eventually that such goodness does not exist. Sartre seemed to agree that the religious quest is a hopeful one, for he said he found it "very distressing" to conclude that God does not exist.[24] After all, to conclude that absolute goodness does exist, whether as actuality or possibility, should fill one with joy upon discovery of such goodness and gratitude for the opportunity to live in relationship to it.

It seems to me, then, that it is important to be religious in at least one phase of our life, namely, that phase in which we are earnestly seeking something worthy of our wholehearted devotion. As we have seen, the religious quest is a path that forks in two very different directions, the religious direction and the secular direction. To become fully developed and fully functioning, we need to confront that fork, deliberate over it to the best of our ability, and make a self-conscious choice. However, this does not mean that we must make a "now and forever" choice. We should always remain open to the possibility that new information and experiences, or a deeper understanding of old information and experiences, will call for us to change paths. This will always be possible because the path not taken is always forking off from the path we are on, no matter where we are on it. Hence, we are always responsible for the direction in which we are going and are always able to change direction—difficult and traumatic though it may be sometimes (and easy and joyous at others).

Sometimes we think that making such a choice when the information is so ambiguous, that is, open to various conflicting interpretations, none of which is demonstrably true, is too overwhelming, so we decide to *not* make a decision. But not to make a decision *is* to make a decision! It is a decision to stay wherever we are. If we are religious at the time, it is a decision to remain religious. If we are secular at the time, it is a decision to remain secular. Moreover, it seems that we must be one or the other; there is no third alternative. Let me try an analogy. If you are asked to choose between red and blue for the color of your car, you might reject both, for there are other colors. However, if you are asked to choose between red and not-red for the color of your car, you cannot reject both; to reject one is to accept the other. That, I think, is how religiousness and secularity are related, namely, as contradictory properties.

Many of us have philosophical claustrophobia and do not like to be closed in by only two choices. Actually, though, we do not have only two choices. There are unlimited ways to be religious and to be secular. The forced choice is whether to be religious or secular. To some people, this might seem unfortunate and intimidating, but it can also be exhilarating. It means that we cannot "sit out" the game of life. We are always in it whether we like it or not, so the question is not *whether* to step onto the playing field; we are always already on it as long as we are conscious and rational. Let's try another analogy: You can choose for your body to be in this part of space or in that part of space, but you cannot choose for your body not to be in space at all. Similarly, the only pertinent question is *how* to engage in the "game" of life, not *whether* to engage in it (even attempting suicide is a way of engaging in life). Hence, even if we cannot *prove* or *know with certainty* what is right or wrong, true or false, we must nonetheless *act* as though something is true or false and good or bad. We have no choice. Reality forces us to play the game.

Will Herberg, a modern Jewish author, teaches that human life and action is impossible apart from some assumptions about the nature of reality and value. "All men," he writes in *Judaism and Modern Man,* "whether they know it or not, make such overall affirmations." He continues:

> For men, unlike animal creation, cannot live out their lives in the fixed patterns of nature; in their freedom, they must live to some purpose—and that purpose, however inarticulate, however primitively conceived, is in effect one's "philosophy" of life and history. A "philosophy of history" in this sense is thus no theoretical question; it is quite literally a question of existence.[25]

Without such assumptions operative in our lives, all we can do is subsist as organisms—and even that won't last very long if we do not make a positive assumption about the worth of being alive!

An interesting illustration of the importance of having a religion or a philosophy of life can be found in the life of the famous Russian novelist and religious thinker Leo Tolstoy, author of *War and Peace.* Tolstoy, like most of us, lived the early part of his life with an unexamined conviction that life has meaning. Eventually he wanted to know what that meaning was, so he directed his powerful faculty of reason to discover it, and he found . . . nothing! He was shocked and distressed, and never found by means of reason a meaning for life. But he did find such meaning by another route.

Tolstoy became convinced that the meaning of life lies in the nature of our basic relation to reality. We must then grasp that relation, but not with reason, because reason can grasp only relations between similar objects or concepts, such as bananas and bananas or balloons and balloons. It cannot comprehend the relations between dissimilar objects or concepts, such as bananas and balloons, which is where the problem lies. We are finite, but the reality to which we want to know our relation is infinite—never were two things more dissimilar than the finite and the infinite.

Having despaired of reason, Tolstoy observed that millions of people had found meaning for their lives. Therefore, he concluded, there must be a source of knowledge in addition to reason. "In this way," Tolstoy writes, "I was compelled to admit that, besides the reasoning knowledge, which I once thought the only true knowledge, there was in every living man another kind of knowledge, an unreasoning one—faith—which gives a possibility of living." He continues by admitting,

> All the unreasonableness of faith remained for me the same as ever, but I could not help acknowledging that faith alone gave man answers as to the questions of life, and consequently the possibility of living. Reasoning knowledge brought me to the conclusion that life was meaningless, and my life stood still, and I wished to put an end to myself.

His discovery of faith put an end to that wish, instead of to his life, and he wrote that "faith is the knowledge of the meaning of human life, in consequence of which man does not destroy himself, but lives. Faith is the force of life. If a man lives, he believes in something. If he did not believe that there was something to live for, he would not live."[26]

For reasons that will be discussed in Chapter 6, I think Tolstoy would have been more accurate if he had said that "faith is *a conviction* of the meaning of human life," rather than "faith is *the knowledge* of the meaning of human life." Also, perhaps he is mistaken that reason can never find the meaning of life, but his emphasis on the importance of *having* a conviction that one's life is meaningful seems correct.[27]

There are, however, many competing claims about the meaning of life. Which one should we affirm? Your first response to this question, I believe, should not be to turn outward and survey what other people have to say about reality and value (though such a survey is eventually very important). Your first step should be to turn inward, for *you already have your own fundamental beliefs about the nature of reality and value.* It may not be clear to you what those beliefs are, but if you didn't have them, you wouldn't have made it this far in life! As Herberg puts it, every person "has his faith, whether he recognizes it or not, whether he avows it or not; the beliefs which a man really holds, it is well to remember, are not necessarily those he affirms with his mouth but those that are operative in his life."[28] Saul Bellow, an American novelist, emphasized this point in his Nobel Prize for Literature speech: "With increasing frequency," he stated, "I dismiss as merely respectable [those] opinions I have long held—or thought I held—and try to discern what I have really lived by, and what others live by."[29]

As there can be a difference between what people think their religion is and what it really is (pseudoreligion versus real religion), so there can be a difference between what people think they believe and what they really believe (pseudobelief versus real belief). Hence, we need to make explicit the beliefs which are implicit in our attitudes and actions. It is only when these beliefs are made clear that we can *affirm* them, *modify* them, or *reject* them. Until they are made clear, each of us is to some extent a puppet, acting unwittingly according to their influence. Moreover, until these beliefs are made clear, we are not prepared to gain maximum benefit from a study of alternative beliefs, for we will not be able to compare them clearly to our present beliefs.

Unfortunately, many of us are frightened away from a clear awareness of our own convictions by philosophical and religious bullies. One of my students had been clearly intimidated by the prospect of articulating her beliefs, for she wrote about an article by John Wisdom, "I especially enjoyed Wisdom's article because he gave to people like me, who are so afraid to express what they think, an encouraging note that if we try to speak we might have something worthwhile to say." How oppressive to philosophical and religious expression our social environment can be! And I suspect that as our impulse to verbalize our beliefs to others withers, so does our impulse to verbalize them to ourselves. Thereby we increasingly become puppets of feelings and behaviors built into us by our environments rather than acting on convictions consciously held and freely affirmed. The problem of self-ignorance is further compounded by our tendency to flee from facing up to our deepest convictions because of a dim awareness of the changes in our lives which would consequently be required.

It is possible, of course, to avoid facing up to our deepest beliefs and their likely discrepancy with our behavior, but it is no longer possible for us to hold our beliefs with the innocent certainty of a child. It is only in "bad faith" that we can say (1) that we have no beliefs about what is real and important (we have already seen why it is reasonable to assume that we do have such beliefs); or (2) that it is unimportant to clarify these beliefs to ourselves (surely you want to act on beliefs you freely hold, not on those that have simply been bred into you by parents, peers, teachers, and the media); or (3) that it is unimportant to investigate these beliefs critically (surely you want to believe the best that you can discover). To be sure, you don't *have* to explicate and evaluate your beliefs. It is possible to escape from spiritual uneasiness and anguish, at least to some extent. But there is no way to do so yet become as fully developed as you can. Yes, passionate grappling with religious questions might make for extreme discomfort at times, but that's okay, for as Socrates put it, "The unexamined life is not worth living"; and as John Stuart Mill put it, "It is better to be a person dissatisfied than a pig satisfied; it is better to be Socrates dissatisfied than a fool satisfied." What do you think?

Notes

1. John B. Magee, *Religion and Modern Man* (New York: Harper & Row, 1967), p. 22.

2. One of the most fundamental divisions among people who take religion seriously is between those who believe that the only religion worthy of human commitment is one which has been *revealed by God* and those who believe that the only religion worthy of human commitment is one which has been *created by the human community* out of the depths of its own experience and reflection. The first position is represented by Karl Barth's *Dogmatics in Outline* and the second by John Dewey's *A Common Faith.* My intention in this book is not to favor either position, but to develop a general theory of religion in terms of which both positions can be appreciated.

3. Karl Jaspers, *Way to Wisdom* (New Haven, CT: Yale University, 1954), p. 80.

4. "Lord" is used also by some translators of Oriental religious literature to refer to Buddha and Krishna, but that is probably due to the fact that the term was already being used by translators of the Bible to refer to the deity of Jews and of Christians. As we have seen already, Elijah, a Jew, believed that *the Lord* is God. Moreover, one of the verses of scripture most frequently uttered by Jews is the *Shema,* Deuteronomy 6:4, "Hear O Israel, the Lord our God, the Lord is One." In the New Testament, which is accepted by Christians but not Jews, "doubting" Thomas, to whom the resurrected Jesus has just appeared for the first time, is overwhelmed by the appearance of Jesus in the flesh and says to him, "My Lord and my God!" (John 20). Also, Jesus is frequently called "Lord" in the letters of the foremost Christian missionary, Paul. See, for example, his letter to the Romans, Chap. 10.

5. Sarvepalli Radhakrishnan, *Recovery of Faith* (New York: Greenwood Press, 1955), p. 73.

6. Kai Nielsen, *Ethics Without God* (Buffalo: Prometheus Books, 1973), p. 17.

7. The attempt to answer these questions will lead us back into philosophy, and especially into epistemology, that is, the theory of knowledge. Why? Because we must try to discover by what method or by what characteristics we can ascertain that a deity is God rather than an idol. This dialectic back and forth between philosophy and religion is inevitable, for it is essentially the dialectic between thought and action, evaluation and commitment.

8. Paul Tillich, *Biblical Religion and the Search for Ultimate Reality* (Chicago: University of Chicago Press, 1955).

9. Erich Fromm, *Psychoanalysis and Religion* (New Haven: Yale University, 1967).

10. Ibid., p. 22.

11. Alfred North Whitehead, *Religion in the Making* (New York: World, 1973), pp. 16–17.

12. Magee, *Religion and Modern Man*, p. 5.

13. For an introduction to Freud's work, see his *General Introduction to Psychoanalysis* (New York: Washington Square Press, 1960). For an introduction to Skinner, see *Science and Human Behavior* (New York: The Free Press, 1953) or *Beyond Freedom and Dignity* (New York: Bantam Books, 1971).

14. *Fundamentals of Marxism-Leninism* (Moscow: Foreign Languages Publishing House, 1963), pp. 16, 31–32, 59–60. No author listed.

15. Ibid., p. 86.

16. Ibid., 26.

17. *The Road to Communism: Documents of the 22nd Congress of the Communist Party of the Soviet Union, October 17–31, 1961* (Moscow: Foreign Languages Publishing House. n.d.), p. 188.

18. *Fundamentals*, p. 717.

19. All of these quotations are from the two books cited in footnotes 14 and 17. The italics are mine. For other arguments in favor of religious as well as nonreligious Marxism, see Peter Slater's *The Dynamics of Religion* (New York: Harper & Row, 1978), pp. 8–9, and Germaine Grisez and Russell Shaw's *Beyond the New Morality* (South Bend, IN: University of Notre Dame, 1988), pp. 229–33.

20. Magee, *Religion and Modern Man*, p. 5.

21. Such a discrepancy between appearance and reality regarding one's religion may occur because an individual wants certain advantages, perhaps economic or political, of being a member of a certain religion and so does what is publicly required to be thought a member. More often, I suspect, this discrepancy occurs because a person's confidence in a particular religion dissipates but he or she continues, perhaps for family or aesthetic reasons, to participate in the institutional aspects of that religion.

22. In the late 1980s there has been a spate of baseball movies with subtle to overt religious themes. See *The Natural, Field of Dreams,* and especially *Bull Durham.*

23. See Sartre's *Existentialism and Human Emotions* (New York: Philosophical Library, 1957).

24. Ibid., p. 22.

25. Will Herberg, *Judaism and Modern Man* (New York: Atheneum, 1970), p. 198.

26. Leo Tolstoy, *My Confession,* Chap. 9, any edition, or *The Religious Writings of Leo Tolstoy: Lift Up Your Eyes* (New York: The Julian Press, 1960), p. 78–79.

27. More recently, Dr. Viktor Frankl, a survivor of the Nazi death camps, has emphasized the importance of having a meaning for one's life. He developed a form of psychotherapy, namely, logotherapy, which is based on this conviction. See his very popular book *Man's Search for Meaning.*

28. Herberg, *Judaism and Modern Man*, p. 37.

29. *Ithaca Journal,* (Monday, Dec. 13, 1976).

4

Roots of Religion
in Human Existence

• What bearing do the following aspects of human existence have on the germination of religious concern and faith?

Alienation
Despair
Death
Meaninglessness
Emptiness
Fear
Curiosity

Beauty
Community
Presence
Gratitude
Morality
Peace and Joy

Religion is not something foreign to human life, something artificial, something imposed on it. It is an intimately human affair rooted in and growing out of human experience. What we will do now is look at some of the specific aspects of human experience out of which religious concern, practice, and belief develop. Inasmuch as religion is an attempt to cope with the negative experiences of life and to cherish the positive experiences, the development of religious concerns, beliefs, and practices is as natural and inevitable as the development of medicine or science or art or agriculture. Moreover, even if one particular religion is a gift of divine revelation rather than of human creativity—as, for example, Islam claims to be—still that religion is best understood, I believe, as God's ministration to the human needs evoked by the experiences we are about to discuss.[1] Of necessity we must discuss one of these experiences first, another second, and so on, but the order in which we shall examine them in no way reflects the diversity of their order of occurrence and importance in people's lives. For some people, the catalyst of religious faith has been a negative experience—such as despair—whereas for others the catalyst has been a positive experience— such as the feeling of community. Hence, nothing of importance should be read into the order in which we proceed here.

Beliefs and Feelings

Let's take a moment here to think about whether one's *understanding* of reality has any necessary influence on one's *feelings* about oneself, others, and the future. That is, do beliefs have any necessary, predictable influence on feelings? Most people would answer yes, I believe. Yet there seems to be some disagreement. For example, can a naturalistic faith (no personal God; Nature is everything) be as optimistic and rewarding as a theistic faith? Kai Nielsen, a Canadian philosopher, argues that it can. He states in *Ethics Without God* that an atheist "with secular knowledge alone can find clear and permanent sources of happiness such that whoever will avail himself of these sources of happiness can, if he is fortunate, lead a happy and purposeful life."[2] Bertrand Russell, British philosopher, mathematician, and social critic, disagrees, though he also believes that modern science has discredited theism. Hence, he wrote in his 1903 essay "A Free Man's Worship":

> That man is the product of causes which had no prevision of the end they were achieving; that his origin, his growth, his hopes and fears, his loves and his beliefs, are but the outcome of accidental collocations of atoms; that no fire, no heroism, no intensity of thought and feeling, can preserve an individual life beyond the grave; that all the labors of the ages, all the devotion, all the inspiration, all the noonday brightness of human genius, are destined to extinction in the vast death of the solar system, and that the whole temple of man's achievement must inevitably be buried beneath the debris of a universe in ruins—all these things, if not quite beyond dispute, are yet [due to scientific

investigation, Russell was convinced] so nearly certain, that no philosophy which rejects them can hope to stand. Only within the scaffolding of these truths, only on the firm foundation of unyielding despair, can the soul's habitation henceforth be safely built.[3]

Ernst Nagel, distinguished philosopher of science, has made a more recent statement to the same effect, and therefore to some extent in disagreement with Nielsen's optimism. Nagel wrote:

Though slavish resignation to remediable ills is not characteristic of atheistic thought, responsible atheists have never pretended that human effort can invariably achieve the heart's every legitimate desire. A tragic view of life is thus an uneliminable ingredient in atheistic thought. This ingredient does not invite or generally produce lugubrious lamentation. But it does touch the atheist's view of man and his place in nature with an emotion that makes the philosophical atheist a kindred spirit to those who . . . have developed a serenely resigned attitude toward the inevitable tragedies of the human estate.[4]

I encourage you to consider this question of the relation between beliefs and feelings because the way a religion makes you feel about yourself, others, and the future is a very real and a very important aspect of it, and different religions make us feel differently. To be sure, we shouldn't choose a religion simply because it makes us feel good. Religions include beliefs, and the question of the truth or falsity of beliefs cannot be settled by how good or bad they make us feel. Yet because the truth or falsity of a religion is a very difficult thing to establish with finality, I believe you will find that in choosing a religion your feelings play a legitimately more important role than they do in other contexts, such as the scientific laboratory, where they may be totally irrelevant.

Alienation

The first experience we shall discuss is that of *alienation*—alienation from ourself, from others, and from existence itself. We are alienated from ourselves in the sense that we know we are not what we *ought* to be. According to our *own* best judgment, we have not done what we ought to have done. Hence, we feel guilty, and surely guilt is a form of self-alienation. Further, we know that we are not what we *want* to be. We would like to be more intelligent or better looking or funnier. Hence, we feel inferior. Indeed, sometimes we hate ourselves. Finally, sometimes we are not even sure who we are; we suffer from a lack of *identity* so that, paradoxically, we go in search of ourselves! Religion is an attempt to help us deal with these kinds of alienation, to help us cope with our guilt, self-hatred, and lack of identity; to help us find out who we are, to help us accept ourselves for what we are, and to help us become in fact what we are in essence.

As though self-alienation weren't enough to cope with, we are alienated also from others. To be sure, we *say* that "what the world needs now is love, sweet love," but when it comes down to the nitty-gritty of our daily lives, we find ourselves caught in crushing competition with one another and we find ourselves alienated from one another by envy and contempt. Further, when it comes to laying our money and time on the line for those who are desperately in need, we all too often find ourselves profoundly indifferent. Religion is an attempt to get at the roots of our alienation from one another and to bring about reconciliation, caring, and commitment.

Finally, we feel alienated from the power or powers responsible for our existence. Without having asked for it, we have been thrown into existence, surrounded with circumstances with which we must struggle, desperately at times, and over which we have little control. We are burdened with physical features that are frequently not to our liking, tormented with various forms of suffering, and plagued by passions that destroy our peace of mind and threaten what social adjustment we do manage to achieve. All of this and then we are crushed by death. Alienated? You better believe it!

But must it remain that way? Is *indifference* or *hostility* our only possible attitude toward the power or powers responsible for our existence? The great religions insist that there is another way, a positive way. Alfred North Whitehead, speaking from a Western theistic tradition, put it like this: When we begin our religious journey God is a *void* to us—a matter of indifference. As we progress we perceive God as *enemy*—for God judges our desires and our actions and leaves our deepest questions unanswered. But if we move forward intrepidly, we come to know God as *companion.* Indifference and hostility are transcended, even though questions and yearnings remain.[5]

Despair

Religious concern is also awakened by the experience of *despair.* Sometimes we despair of *finding* the good. We don't know what to do; we have been unable on our own to discover what to do; and we do not want to act arbitrarily. We want to do that which is good and right, but we have no conviction as to what it is. If we do not despair completely, we wait in hope that the nature of the good and the right will be revealed to us, will impress itself upon us. Yet should this occur, we become liable to another kind of despair—namely, the kind that results when we find ourselves *unable* to do that which in our own opinion is right. It might be that we do not feel strong enough to do what is required or, more seriously, it might be that we find ourselves perversely betraying our own sense of the right. Experiences such as these take on religious significance by causing us to look beyond ourselves and the everyday world for some source of strength or transformation in order that we can do what we believe we ought to do and be what we most deeply want to be.

Death

Another source of despair is *death.* You and I know that we will die and that there is nothing we can do to avoid death—no matter how undesirable or outrageous it might seem. Our reaction to impending death leads us to ask questions about ourselves and about the power or powers which have brought us into being. Clearly, my body will die—but am I identical with my body? Perhaps I can survive the disintegration of my body? At least one four-year-old, my youngest son Christopher, seemed to think so. I was undressing him for bed one evening and said to him as I removed his footwear, "Off with your shoe! Off with your sock!" Then, without malice or forethought, I tugged at his foot and said "Off with your foot!" Well, he thought that was great fun, so we had to do it with his other foot, his legs, hands, and arms! Then he made a request that I, constrained by more rigid modes of thought, would never have thought of. He said with a twinkle in his eye, "Now take off my body!" So I put my hands around his waist and pretended to lift off the remainder of his body and place it to one side. Then I asked, "Now where are you?" and he broke into great laughter, which I couldn't help joining. Having nothing left to remove, I put pajamas on what remained and it was "lights off." Despite the intuitions of four-year-olds there are, oddly enough, adults who doubt that the self can be separated from the body. Still, even if they are correct, perhaps the power or powers which have brought us into being in the first place can bring us into being again.[6] And even if that is not possible—that is, if the sun of consciousness shall never dawn for us again after death—is there, perhaps, a power which will sustain the good we have accomplished and which will favor the efforts of all those who struggle on behalf of justice, peace, and compassion? Clearly, one could use such questions as springboards into escapist fantasy, but just as surely one can accept the ambiguities of our situation and still hope that death is not the end, that cruelty doesn't ultimately have as firm a place in reality as kindness, and that indifference is not the final word which shall be pronounced over all things.

If we do become convinced that the worst is true, then a pall is cast over our lives. As a college student who committed suicide stated in a farewell note, "I'm going to die anyway." Why not now rather than later? Why run the gauntlet of life, since no matter how successful we are at avoiding pain and achieving pleasure, upon our death it will not matter how much pleasure we enjoyed, since after death there will be no remembrance by us of good times past? The problem becomes especially urgent when one becomes aware of the scientific prediction that eventually *all* life will be destroyed in a cosmic collapse. Hence, even our contributions to posterity will come to naught. Surely this prospect must have some kind of reflexive influence upon the way we feel about ourselves, other persons, and our contributions to them. A wry comment by retired heavyweight boxing champion Jack Sharkey, at age seventy, seems relevant to this point. Sharkey, living in retirement in a small New Hampshire town, replied to an interviewer, "I've got everything I need here. The doctor lives across the street, the druggist is on the corner, the funeral parlor is nearby, and the cemetery is right up the street." In the light of such a comment we can understand better why John Magee writes, "The sting of death, then, is the poisoning of hope, the extinguishing of all possibility of a full human existence here and now."[7] How do you feel about this? What do you think?

Meaninglessness

A further source of religious awakening, a source closely related to the fact of death, is the sense of *meaninglessness* that haunts us from time to time. As Magee puts it,

> Life without ultimate significance is not only flat and stale, it leads finally to the negation of life itself. People lose heart even in the midst of success and physical well-being when they are convinced that their existence is meaningless. A person with a fine car but no place to go can hardly be happy. Similarly, a human being with all the means of life [money, looks, talent, ambition, but who sees no point to his life as a whole] will find himself in ever deepening frustration.[8]

The great religions are attempts to meet this need for meaning, to provide a framework within which our lives are graced with significance, to provide a foundation to which we can anchor ourselves in an infinite and sometimes stormy ocean. Walt Whitman, nineteenth-century American poet, brings out by analogy the nature of our ceaseless and sometimes desperate search for meaning:

> A noiseless patient spider,
> I mark'd where on a little promontory it stood isolated,
> Mark'd how to explore the vacant vast surrounding,
> It launch'd forth filament, filament, filament out of itself,
> Ever unreeling them, ever tirelessly speeding them.
> And you O my soul where you stand,
> Surrounded, detached, in measureless oceans of space,
> Ceaselessly musing, venturing, throwing, seeking the spheres to connect them,
> Till the bridge you will need be form'd, till the ductile anchor hold,
> Till the gossamer thread you fling catch somewhere, O my soul.[9]

Emptiness

Whereas in the problem of meaninglessness the prominent need is for a satisfying *intellectual* understanding of reality, in the problem of *emptiness* the need is primarily *emotional.* It is the need to *feel* uplifted and filled. Such emptiness is marked by a kind of spiritual hunger, by a restless search for "food" that satisfies. St. Augustine (A.D. 354–430) captured this experience in words when he said in a prayer in his *Confessions,* "Thou hast made us for Thyself, and our hearts are restless till they find their rest in Thee." In the same spirit, members of a contemporary Pentecostal group have told me that God creates each of us with an infinite void within and that nothing but God can fill that void—no matter how desperately we try to fill it with other things. Whether these people are correct that only the Christian God can fill the void is a question we shall not pursue in this book. But the experience of emptiness they talk about and the fact that religion endeavors to fill that emptiness seem to be universal facts. As John Magee puts it, man needs "a deep sense of well-being, an experience of joy, happiness, even ecstasy, that will not crumble under the attrition of life."[10] I would like to summarize this by saying that we sometimes feel a need for a sense of buoyancy. It is a sense of being unsinkable, even in a storm. Only when we have this feeling within us shall we have the guts to live courageously in the face of adversity; only then shall we have the single-mindedness to ignore the petty annoyances of life and to resist its trivial distractions; only then shall we have the resilience to pick ourselves up and start afresh after failure or tragedy. Religion is devoted to the acquisition of this pervasive sense of buoyancy.

Fear

There are those who say that *fear* is the primary source of religion. Bertrand Russell, for example, says, "Fear is the basis of the whole thing—fear of the mysterious, fear of defeat, fear of death."[11] That seems simplistic to me. The emergence of religion is the result of many factors, negative and positive. Though we have focused on the negative thus far, shortly we shall take a look at positive sources of religion. Nonetheless, I agree that fear has been a real and understandable source of religious thought and practice. People fear that they will not be able to withstand the suffering imposed on them by life, so they turn to an extraordinary source of strength and endurance. They fear that the values they are struggling to advance in this life may be destroyed by evil or indifferent forces, so they hope that there are forces of good which will prevail and can be tapped even now. People fear that they may be held responsible after death for the way they live before death, so they try to discover the will of the gods and to act accordingly. All of these are reasonable responses to our human situation. We need not apologize for them. Further, it seems to me that of the three types of fear which Russell specifies as sources of religion, only one, fear of defeat, is accurate. Regarding fear of the mysterious, people do not fear the mysterious simply because it is mysterious. Entry into the mysterious can be exhilarating as well as frightening. It all depends on one's intuitions and preconceptions. The mysterious can be alluring as well as alarming. One fears the mysterious only when one has an intuition that "bad things are going to happen" as a result of it, or when one already has a worldview which holds that the denizens of the mysterious are our enemies. No doubt fear of the mysterious has given rise to some religious beliefs and practices, but so has love of the mysterious. Perhaps the most lovely expression of this fact is a statement by Albert Einstein, scientific genius and sensitive religious spirit. He wrote:

> The most beautiful thing that we can experience is the mysterious. It is the source of all true art and science. He to whom this emotion is a stranger, who can no longer pause to wonder and stand, wrapped in awe, is as good as dead; his mind and his eyes are closed. The insight into the mystery of life, coupled though it be with fear, has also given rise to religion. To know that what is impenetrable to us really exists, manifesting itself as the highest wisdom and the most radiant beauty which our dull faculties can comprehend only in their most primitive form—this knowledge, this feeling, is at the center of true religiousness.[12]

Regarding fear of death, I do not believe it is accurate to say that people fear death at all! Why? Because fear is fear of an experience—for example, being bitten by a snake. Now let's divide everyone into two groups and see if either group can rightly be said to fear death. The two groups are (1) those who believe there is no life after death, and (2) those who do believe there is life after death. Those who believe there is no life after death will not fear death, I submit. To them death is not an experience which we have; rather, it is the end of experience. Hence, it is nothing to be feared. It is, to most of us, something to be *abhorred,* which means literally, "to shrink from," but that is precisely because it is not an experience but, rather, the end of experience. After all, if you're having a good time and believe that death is the end of good times, bad times, and any times at all, then you'll "shrink from" death; indeed, you'll run from it and fight against it. But it's not correct to say that you'll fear it, for, we are assuming, you believe that death causes neither pain nor pleasure, but the total absence of consciousness.

Okay, so those who do not believe in life after death will not fear death, though they may abhor it. But what about those who do believe that there is life after death? Again it seems inaccurate to say that this second group fears death. Some people who believe in life after death welcome death, for they believe it is the portal to paradise! Other people are made anxious by "the gnawing tooth of time" because they fear not death but what they believe lies beyond it—for example, judgment and punishment by the gods or God. Hence, here too it seems to me that Russell's explanation of the origin of religion is simplistic. Love of life and love of death have had as much to do with the origin of religion as have fear of life and fear of death, and perhaps more so.

Curiosity

"All humans by nature desire to know." Those are the opening words of Aristotle's *Metaphysics.* They constitute one of the most widely accepted claims ever made by a philosopher. According to some people, it is this insatiable appetite for knowledge that best explains the emergence and duration of religion. Religion, it is said, arose and developed over thousands of years prior to the emergence of modern science. During that time humans were no less curious than they are now, but they lacked the scientific ideas by which we understand and explain the world. However, our predecessors were not completely without ideas by which to explain natural events. They understood why they themselves did things. They did things because of anger, love, jealousy, hunger, and other such feelings. Consequently, they explained events such as storms, rainbows, headaches, and good crops as the results of the actions of spirits or gods and goddesses who were similar to humans but superior to them and usually invisible. Because it was thought that those beings were emotionally like humans, it was also thought that they could be influenced favorably by prayers, sacrifices, dances, and so on.

That way of understanding and explaining the mysteries of nature was plausible prior to the emergence of modern science, say critics of supernatural religion, but it is no longer rational for educated people to think that way. The scientific way of understanding the world explains all events by laws of cause and effect, such as the laws of physics, chemistry, and biology. I cannot think of any contemporary, educated religious person who does not agree that most events in the world can be explained by means of scientific laws of cause and effect. Indeed, some religious people *are* highly respected scientists.

Why, then, is there a conflict between religion and science? I think there are two primary reasons. First, there is the issue of miracles. Some people, including some scientists, believe that some events in history cannot be explained by science but can be explained by reference to a supernatural being or beings. Examples of such events include the Red Sea parting for Moses, Jesus rising from the dead, and Mohammed (who was illiterate) dictating the *Qur'an.* Other people believe that modern science has permanently discredited belief in miracles. Second, some people believe that no questions are meaningful or worth bothering with except those that can be answered by science. Others disagree and cite questions they think are meaningful and important, but that cannot be answered by science, which is limited to physical concepts and methods. Examples of such questions are Is there a God? Did time have a beginning? Is space infinite? Is abortion immoral? Is there life after death? Does life have meaning? If one believes that such questions are meaningful and their answers important, and if one believes that miracles, that is, events that cannot be explained scientifically, appear to have taken place, then it is only natural to look beyond science for answers to those questions and explanations of those events. Whether it is rational to do that is a question we will not pursue here, though it is receiving much attention in contemporary philosophy of religion. For our purposes it is sufficient to note that the human desire to understand why the world exists, why it is like it is rather than some other way, whether there is more to reality than the physical world, and how to explain "unnatural" events reported by seemingly reliable witnesses has given rise to religious concepts, convictions, and practices, and probably will do so forever.

Beauty

Now let's look at some positive experiences that have given rise to religious beliefs and practices. Among the foremost of these experiences is that of *beauty*. Review, for example, the statement by Albert Einstein, already quoted in the section on fear, who found the world to be suffused by "the most radiant beauty"—a beauty which struck him as coming from an impenetrable, divine source. Einstein found such beauty no matter how deeply he probed the physical world by means of telescope and microscope. But scientific genius is not required for having this experience. It is common for people of ordinary intellect to experience nature as a whole, and various parts of it such as flowers and sunsets, as too beautiful to be the result of mindless, accidental processes. Many times natural beauty is experienced as a gift, and a gift always comes from a giver.

In addition to the beauty of nature, there is beauty which seems to transcend nature. Speaking of this second kind of beauty, the philosopher Plato urged that we should develop "the passion for a beauty which is spiritual, not physical" (*Laws* 841.c). Clearly, such a passion and such experiences are religious in nature and significance, as are those reported in the scriptures of the world. The Koran speaks of "The Beautiful Names of God," and there is a list of ninety-nine such names in the Hadith literature of Islam. In the Bible, Psalm 27:4 speaks of the beauty of God: "One thing have I asked of the Lord, that will I seek after; that I may dwell in the house of the Lord all the days of my life, to behold the beauty of the Lord, and to inquire in his temple;" Psalm 96:6 speaks of the beauty of the house of worship: "O sing to the Lord a new song. . . . Declare his glory among the nations. . . . Honor and majesty are before him; strength and beauty are in his sanctuary." The King James translation of I Chronicles 16:29 speaks of the beauty of the act and raiments of worship: "Give unto the Lord the glory due unto his name: bring an offering, and come before him: worship the Lord in the beauty of holiness."

Community

Another source of religion to which John Magee points is man's need for *communion*. Sociologists have long been aware of the profound extent to which people participate in religious groups for the sake of the sense of community it provides them. Religions provide people with an opportunity to come together in a noncompetitive, nonutilitarian context which affirms their worth and their oneness, which encourages them to become involved in spite of timidity. Indeed, Martin Buber, Jewish existentialist, teaches that the best way to serve God is to build community.[13] Religious community is more than social, though, because loneliness can be cosmic as well as social. If we cannot say "Thou" to the universe which surrounds us, we experience that profound emptiness we spoke of earlier. Why? Because we are made for communion—for that kinship with all being which we sense in the beauty of the universe, for companionship with everything that lives, for "communion with the total soul of things."[14] Clearly, it is religion which endeavors to lead us to this sense of cosmic community.

Presence

Whereas religious *concern* grows out of such needs as the above, religious *faith* grows out of the moments in which these needs are ministered to—moments when guilt is replaced by forgiveness, confusion by direction, weakness by strength, self-hatred by self-acceptance, despair by hope. Since we have just spoken of our desire for a sense of oneness with the powers that be, consider the positive experience of a divine *presence* reported by persons throughout human history and across the face of the globe. Such experiences have not always been preceded by an intense feeling of need, but they have always created the conviction that one was in the presence of a divine person. Simone Weil wrote of her first religious experience, "God had mercifully prevented me from reading the mystics, so that it would be clear to me that I had not fabricated an absolutely unexpected encounter."[15] Of that first experience, she continued:

> In a moment of intense physical suffering, when I was forcing myself to feel love, but without desiring to give a name to that love, I felt, without being in any way prepared for it (for I had never read the mystical writers) a presence more personal, more certain, more real than that of a human being, though inaccessible to the senses and the imagination.[16]

In Chapter 8 we shall return to the topic of religious experience and look at naturalistic as well as theistic interpretations of it. Meanwhile, it should be clear that religious faith and practice often emerge from such experiences as those of Simone Weil.

Gratitude

Another contributor to the germination of religion is the experience of *gratitude,* which we feel occasionally toward reality itself, rather than toward a specific person. Because we feel grateful for our existence and for life itself, we give our thanks "to whom it may concern." G. K. Chesterton, British novelist and biographer of such persons as St. Francis and St. Thomas Aquinas, reported on one of his own experiences in the following passage from *Orthodoxy:*

> The test of all happiness is gratitude; and I felt grateful, though I hardly knew to whom. Children are grateful when Santa Claus puts in their stocking gifts of toys or sweets. Could I not be grateful to Santa Claus when he put in my stockings the gift of two miraculous legs? We thank people for birthday presents of cigars and slippers. Can I thank no one for the birthday present of birth?[17]

Again it is understandable that such feelings of gratitude should become part of a religious faith and give rise to such rites as offering and prayer.

Morality

There are at least two ways in which moral experience can give rise to religious conviction. Consider first that if the moral rules we are expected to live by are based on nothing more than the *preference* of a ruler or the majority of a society or our parents, then nothing is absolutely right or wrong because rulers, majorities, and parents have changed and will change their minds about moral right and wrong. Consequently, there seems to be no reason for us to follow such rules whenever we are sure we can get away with it or are willing to take the consequences if we get caught. After all, if moral right and wrong are only a matter of someone's preference, then when the risks of disobedience are acceptable to me, why shouldn't I follow my own preferences—whether or not they are the same as those of the government or a majority of fellow citizens or my parents?

The preceding type of position is called *ethical relativism.* Ethical *absolutists* reject that position emphatically. They believe that some rules of action are always wrong and some are always right; for example, it is always wrong to torture anyone for entertainment; it is always right to resist impulses toward cruelty. According to *theocentric* absolutists, that is, absolutists who are devoted to God, neither the preceding moral rules nor any others can have absolute authority unless backed up by a perfect being who *knows* what is truly right and wrong. Absolute moral authority cannot rest in human beings because none of us has any special moral authority over the rest of us; none of us has a right to say how all of us should live; but God—who is perfect in knowledge and character and is our creator—does have such a right, according to theocentric absolutists. Hence, they reason, because there are some absolute moral rights and wrongs (such as the two mentioned above), there must be a divine being who knows they have that status and perhaps gave it to them.

There is a second way in which moral experience gives rise to religious conviction. Some people experience the voice of conscience as being the voice of a divine being revealing that some action would be morally wrong.[18] That way of experiencing the voice or feeling of conscience is so strong to those people that they can no more take seriously the suggestion that conscience is merely an echo of the influence of other people's morals in their lives than the critics who make such a suggestion can take seriously the possibility that other people don't have thoughts or feelings.

The preceding points are tied together nicely in the position of Emil Brunner, a twentieth-century Protestant theologian. In *Our Faith* he writes,

> Moral seriousness is respect to the voice of conscience. If there is no God, conscience is but a complex of residual habits and means nothing. If there is no God then it is absurd to trouble oneself about right—or wrong. It all comes to the same ultimate chaos. Scoundrel and saint are only phantoms of the imagination.

Later Brunner adds that "There has never been a man without a conscience. The law of God is as though it had been engraved in the human heart."[19]

Not all ethical absolutists agree with Brunner that only the existence of God could give authority to moral commands. See, for example, the ethical systems of Plato (realism), Immanuel Kant (deontology), and John Stuart Mill (utilitarianism). Here, however, I am not trying to engage you in a consideration of basic questions in ethics. I am simply recounting one of the major reasons why religion has emerged and endured in human life, namely, in order to account for the interruptions of conscience and the voice of revelation, and in order that moral obligations and prohibitions might have absolute authority over all people in all places at all times.

Peace and Joy

Finally, how could we close a discussion of religious belief and practice without mentioning the experiences of peace and joy? I do not mean the peace and joy that come from identifiable worldly sources, such as the peace of mind you experience when your cancer biopsy comes back negative or the joy you feel when your marriage proposal is accepted. I am referring to the peace and joy that seem to come from reality itself or from that which lies beyond the physical world but is responsible for its existence, nature, and destiny. Moses, Jesus, Mohammed, Buddha, and Hindu mystics all spoke of a joy and peace that surpass human understanding but are available to us through certain beliefs and forms of life. It is perhaps these experiences of gladness of heart and peace of soul welling up within us from the ground of all existence which are the most powerful sources of religiousness. It is difficult to see how religion could *not* grow out of such experiences.

These, then, are some of the needs and experiences out of which religious concern, faith, and practice emerge. The list is not complete, and I hope you'll take a moment to see what others you can think of. Certainly on a fuller list would be included the *comfort* religion has traditionally provided to those in grief, distress, or depression; the *values* religion provides us, with which to guide our lives and nurture our children; the *significance* accorded to work and creativity; and the ability to *hope* in situations that are hopeless from a worldly point of view. Perhaps the most intriguing source of religious faith mentioned to me, by my friend Mildred Carver, was *family loyalty*. At first I was simply puzzled, but the idea is growing on me with increasing persuasiveness. Certainly the language of the family has played a central role in the endeavors of nearly all religions to explain our proper relations to one another and to the absolute. Further, someone who has had a good family experience is probably in a much better position to appreciate the religious concepts of mutuality, compassion, forgiveness, trust, and so on. In brief, as long as human existence continues to be characterized by such needs and experiences as we have discussed, people will continue to awaken religiously and to cherish and transmit those religious practices, beliefs, and symbols which enable them to live more richly.[20]

Notes

1. Much of our discussion shall draw on Part Seven of John B. Magee, *Religion and Modern Man* (New York: Harper & Row, 1967).

2. Kai Nielsen, *Ethics Without God* (Buffalo: Prometheus Books, 1973), p. 58.

3. Bertrand Russell, *Why I Am Not a Christian* (New York: Simon & Schuster, 1957), p. 107.

4. J. E. Fairchild, ed., *Basic Beliefs: The Religious Philosophies of Mankind* (New York: Sheridan House, 1959), p. 186.

5. Alfred North Whitehead, *Religion in the Making* (New York: World, 1973), p. 16. My friend Harriet Cramton, who is fascinated by children and religion, taken together as well as individually, has sometimes objected that my points are true enough of adults but not of children. For example, she pointed out (and I agree) that a child who is reared in a home of love and faith will know God initially as companion, not enemy. Still, she allows, it is quite common in our society for people to be expelled from the spiritual world of their childhood into the doubts and negations of adolescence, wherein God is often perceived as void or enemy.

6. The first possibility, survival by the soul of death of the body, is commonly called "immortality," whereas the second possibility, re-creation of the bodily self subsequent to real annihilation at death, is called "resurrection." For an introduction to the differences between these two conceptions of life after death see Krister Stendahl, ed., *Immortality and Resurrection* (New York: Macmillan, 1965).

7. Magee, *Religion and Modern Man,* p. 476.

8. Ibid., p. 35.

9. Gay Wilson Allen and Charles T. Davis, eds., *Walt Whitman's Poems* (New York: Grove Press, 1959), p. 198.

10. Magee, *Religion and Modern Man,* p. 36.

11. Russell, *Why I Am Not a Christian,* p. 22.

12. Louis Untermeyer, *Makers of the Modern World* (New York: Simon & Schuster, 1955), pp. 540–541.

13. Martin Buber, *Paths in Utopia* (Boston: Beacon Press, 1958), p. xvi.

14. William James, *The Will to Believe and Other Essays in Popular Philosophy* (New York: Dover, 1956), p. 40. See also Magee, *Religion and Modern Man,* pp. 449–450, 485–492.

15. Simone Weil, *Waiting for God* (New York: Capricorn Books, 1951), p. 25.

16. Ibid., p. 24.

17. Gilbert K. Chesterton, *Orthodoxy* (Garden City, NY: Image Books, 1959), p. 55.

18. For an intriguing example of this read Plato's *Apology,* in which he gives an account of Socrates' experience with what most of us would call the voice of conscience. See also Exodus 20 in the Bible, where Moses is described as receiving the Ten Commandments not through the inner voice of conscience but through the outer voice of divine revelation. In the cases of both Socrates and Moses, moral commands are understood as having divine authority behind them.

19. Emil Brunner, *Our Faith* (New York: Scribners, n.d.), trans. John W. Rilling, pp. 5 and 47.

20. An interesting analysis of the impact of the family experience on the development of religious faith can be found in "The Development of Ritualization" by psychiatrist Erik H. Erikson, in Donald R. Cutler, ed., *The Religious Situation: 1968,* (Boston: Beacon Press, 1968), pp. 711–33.

5

Traits of a Healthy Religious Faith

QUESTIONS TO THINK ABOUT

- What would the ideal religion be like?
- What is emotional integrity and why is it a trait of a healthy religion?
- What is intellectual integrity and why is it an important trait of a healthy religion?
- What is the relation of doubt to a healthy religious faith?
- If science is true, is religion false?
- Are humanism and religion incompatible?
- Is religion "the opium of the masses"?
- How does a healthy religion deal with the problem of evil?
- In what sense is a healthy religion optimistic? What would be the opposite?
- Wherein lies the value of beliefs that "bake no bread"?
- Is there a good sense as well as a bad sense in which religion can be a crutch?
- In what sense is a healthy religion an exercise in creativity?

In Chapter 3 I argued that we must choose between the religious and the secular ways of understanding and living life. I think the religious way is the better of the two, but the purpose of this book is not to convince you to become or remain religious. It is to help you understand better what the religious way is and why so many people find it attractive. I would like to continue with that objective by sharing with you some ideas about what makes a religion healthy. In the process I will also identify characteristics of an unhealthy religion.

You might want to stop reading now and make up your own list of healthy and unhealthy traits of a religion. Check it against my list as you read this chapter. When you've finished reading, see if you can combine these lists to come up with a result that is better than either list by itself. Then see if you can think of additional traits that were not included in either of the original lists.

EMOTIONAL INTEGRITY

The first characteristic we shall look at is *emotional integrity.* A healthy religion is one that draws all our energies to one object, one goal, one deity. The life of the individual is *unified* by a single object of devotion; whereas it is *fragmented* by multiple incompatible objects. If your own life is divided within, if your mind and heart are the arena of severe conflicts, it is probably because you are attracted to incompatible objects of commitment. The conflict will not be resolved until one of the objects becomes appreciated as superior to the others or until yet another object appears and causes your interest in the competing objects to diminish, even as the sun causes the stars to vanish at dawn. An inner conflict, then, should lead us to the following considerations: (1) Are all of the alternatives really equally worthy of my commitment, even after the most rigorous analysis? and (2) is there some new alternative that might banish the conflict by diminishing my interest in the present alternatives or by rearranging their order of importance?

It is important to transcend such conflicts and achieve emotional unity because inner conflicts are among the chief causes of personal misery and social disruption. People afflicted with an inner conflict of loyalties tend to be burdened with (1) *confusion,* because they do not know to which object to commit themselves, and (2) *guilt,* because no matter to which object they commit themselves, they still feel sufficiently attracted to the other objects to suffer guilt at having betrayed them; further, either (3) such persons tend to transform their guilt and confusion into *hostility,* which is projected upon themselves or the world (making other people miserable), or (4) they tend to escape into *apathy,* so as not to feel the torment of indecision, confusion, and guilt. Perhaps the extreme form of apathy is found in the person who withdraws from interaction with the world to the literal extreme of lying unresponsively in a fetal position. Such apathy can be the result of feeling no joy or meaning in life, but it can also be the result of a paralyzing inner conflict.

Hence, the wisdom of the commandment in Exodus 20:3, "You shall have no other gods before me." Why? Because having more than one god will tear you apart! As we are unified by one object of commitment, we are torn asunder by two or more. Soren Kierkegaard captured this idea in the title of one of his books: *Purity of Heart is to Will One Thing.* This doesn't mean, of course, that we cannot be committed to parents, mate, children, benevolent causes, justice, and so on, because they are multiple objects of commitment. The single, transcendent commitment of which I speak is one that enables us to unite all these other commitments in a beneficial way. I submit, then, that there is no way to become whole, to be fully released, to be drawn out into life to the full extent of our capacities except by a single object of devotion which releases, directs, and harmonizes all of our energies for its own sake. I cannot tell you what that object is for you. You must discover it yourself. But it does seem to me that to be religious is to believe that there *is* something real enough and sacred enough to release our energies and unify our lives. Whoever despairs of this possibility despairs of religious faith and must perceive religious longing as a cruel and useless passion.

INTELLECTUAL INTEGRITY

A second trait of a healthy religious faith is that it does not contradict one's sense of *intellectual integrity.* The emotional integrity that is required and created by devotion to one and only one deity must be matched by intellectual integrity. A person cannot achieve wholeness if he believes that his religion or his deity requires him to believe that which is contrary to logic or fact. More specifically, it seems to me that we sacrifice our intellectual integrity whenever we affirm as true that which we know is false, believe is false, suspect is false, or know we aren't sure about, and when we attribute to a proposition a greater degree of probability than we believe the evidence really warrants. Intellectual integrity is a precious part of personal wholeness and should not be sacrificed on the altar of church or temple membership. If it is, it will return to haunt us in the form of hostility toward ourselves for having made such a sacrifice and hostility toward our religious tradition for having required such a sacrifice. Nothing is worth the price of your sense of self-respect.

This does not mean, however, that you must choose between religious faith and intellectual integrity. To be sure, some people believe otherwise. Bertrand Russell quips that faith is "believin' what you know ain't so," and Friedrich Nietzsche says that to have faith is "to will to not know the truth." I disagree, and so does Paul Tillich, who writes in *Biblical Religion and the Search for Ultimate Reality:*

> Faith and doubt do not essentially contradict each other. Faith is the continuous tension between itself and the doubt within itself. This tension does not always reach the strength of a struggle; but, latently, it is always present. . . . Faith includes both an immediate awareness of something unconditional and the courage to take the risk of uncertainty upon itself. Faith says "Yes," in spite of the anxiety of "No." It does not remove the "No" of

doubt and the anxiety of doubt; it does not build a castle of doubt-free security—only a neurotically distorted faith does that—but it takes the "No" of doubt and the anxiety of insecurity into itself.[1]

Hence, a mature faith does not fear radical doubt. Faith confronts it. Faith grows out of it or over against it. Doubt is a *structural feature* of a healthy, mature religious faith, for we do not want to commit ourselves absolutely to that which is less than the absolute.[2] Hence, we must doubt: we must scrutinize that to which we are asked to commit ourselves, and we must scrutinize that to which we have committed ourselves. Why? In order that we may be continually assured that that to which we are committed is in our judgment at the moment the best to which we can be committed. Hence, we should affirm the best that we know while keeping ourselves open to the possibility of something better. If we don't affirm the best that we know, we can only affirm something less or affirm nothing at all. Surely we don't want to affirm anything less than the best we know, and earlier we saw the consequences of affirming nothing at all. Further, if we don't keep ourselves open to the possibility of something better, we exclude ourselves from it if it does exist, and we likely become dogmatic about the superiority of that to which we are committed.

Before we leave the trait of intellectual integrity, let's think about the so-called conflict between religion and science. Is it the case that if science is true, then religion is false? I think not. First, the statement is too broad, since by "religion" most people would mean the concrete religions of the world, and these are too diverse to be joined together by any creed which they all affirm in common and which stands opposed to science. Second, if my own definition of religion is accepted, then science and religion should not contradict one another. Rather, they should supplement one another, for they perform basically different functions. Science is intent on discovering causal relations between those kinds of things which can be sensed directly or detected by instruments, things such as gases and metals, molecules and light waves, whereas religion is intent on discovering those forces and ideas which are good in themselves or lead to good. In one sense, science can be subsumed within the enterprise of religion, for science is a means to the goods of theoretical and practical knowledge of the physical world. Insofar as one engages in scientific activity in order that people can live more fully, one's scientific activity could be considered religious.

Both enterprises are also engaged, however, in constructing a frame of orientation, and it is here that they have clashed over such issues as the creation of the universe, evolution, and the nature of humankind. Whenever science and religion do overlap and a religion makes a claim which can be investigated by scientific means, that claim should not be withheld from (and perhaps *should* be submitted to) such investigation. If the claim, such as geocentrism, is discredited by science, then it should be rejected. When the results of a scientific investigation of a religious belief are *not* conclusive, however, it should not be assumed that one has a moral or intellectual obligation to abjure the belief until it *is* proved true by science. When the need to make a decision about a matter of belief is urgent, you have the right to believe as seems best to you until the truth is made clear. That salt melts ice is clearly demonstrable. That persons determine some of their actions by means of free will is not so clearly demonstrable. Even more significantly, are there some claims that are completely outside the boundaries of scientific investigation? Are scientific methods even applicable, for example, to the proof or disproof of the existence of the biblical Lord? Further, can we by means of scientific methods prove that our senses reveal the way the world "really" is—or even that there really is a world apart from our perceptions? We won't belabor these points, for this is not an essay in metaphysics or philosophy of science. I would only urge you to be aware that not all that is claimed in the name of science is a matter of science. Perhaps the best antidote to naive optimism about the omniscience of science is a good dose of philosophy of science.

Parenthetically, an interesting question was raised in a paper by one of my students. "How," she asked, "can some invisible supernatural being create the entire universe with all its peculiarities in six days, no less?" One of the issues she was raising is this: How can something that cannot be perceived and is not physical *be* anything and *do* anything? A good question, yet I doubt that she discounts the reality of her own consciousness and the effectiveness of her own will, though the reality of neither is capable of being demonstrated by means of sensation. Further, the religious person should not be disoriented by the discovery of regularities in nature and of our ability, within limits, to control natural processes. We should be glad that the world is largely dependable and that we can control and improve it for our survival and pleasure. It would be naive, though, to conclude that because nature is dependable and we can control it to some extent, the solution to *all* our problems is just a matter of science and time. Scientific methods and discoveries can be used for weal or woe, and we, as a species, have a notorious record for working woe. Hence, we stand in need of something which will influence us so that we will use scientific methods and knowledge in intelligent and humane ways. Perhaps devotion to science itself is the means by which we can be transformed into a species of intelligent, compassionate individuals. B. F. Skinner appears to hold this point of view in his novel *Walden Two*. Yet surely it is not obvious that devotion to science will affect us this way. If it will, then perhaps it should be our deity, our object of religious devotion. But is it science, the Lord, humanity, communism, or something else to which we must devote ourselves in order to live the finest kind of human life, individually and socially? That, I think, is the question at the heart of discussions of religion.

One final word about intellectual integrity: It is compatible with a sense of mystery and even paradox. Regarding mystery, recall the statement by Einstein in the section on fear in Chapter 4. Consider also the following argument by Baron Friedrich von Hügel to the effect that a sense of mystery in religion is understandably inevitable. After commenting on the level of awareness a dog would have of its master's activities—for example, repairing a clock or composing a poem—von Hügel wrote:

> The source and object of religion, if religion be true and its object be real, *cannot*, indeed, *by any possibility, be as clear to me even as I am to my dog.* For the cases we have considered deal with realities inferior to our own reality (material objects, or animals), or with realities level to our own reality (fellow human beings), or with realities no higher above ourselves than are we, finite human beings, to our very finite dogs. Whereas, in the case of religion—if religion be right—we apprehend and affirm realities indefinitely superior in quality and amount of reality to ourselves, and which, nevertheless (or rather, just because of this), anticipate, penetrate, and sustain us with a quite unpicturable intimacy. The obscurity of my life to my dog must thus be greatly exceeded by the obscurity of the life of God to me. Indeed the obscurity of plant life—so obscure for my mind, because so indefinitely inferior and poorer than is my human life—must be greatly exceeded by the dimness, for my human life, of God—of His reality and life, so different and superior, so unspeakably more rich and alive, than is, or ever can be, my own life and reality.[3]

Hence, if a religion like Judaism or Hinduism is true, then we should *expect* that there will be much about God and God's actions that our limited minds will be incapable of understanding or evaluating.

Regarding paradox, consider the fact that contemporary physicists treat light as both a wave and a particle, because it has properties of both; yet there is no known way to make sense of the statement that light is both a wave and a particle! Perhaps the paradox will be resolved, and perhaps it won't, but in a conflict between fact and logic, it is fact that should be given the upper hand.[4] The broader significance of this point is that we should not allow the intellect to impoverish our lives when the categories of logic are too rigid or narrow to cover the facts of our experience or the richness of a reality that races beyond the categories of the mind. Logic is part of life, but life is more than logic. As John Henry Cardinal Newman put it, there is a kind of logic that does us a great disservice by dispelling our legitimate sense of mystery and paradox. How does it do this? By trivializing the profound and dismissing the difficult. "One is not at all pleased," he wrote, "when poetry, or eloquence, or devotion, is considered as if chiefly intended to feed syllogisms."[5] Newman, a nineteenth-century cardinal in the Church of Rome, also insisted that the intellectual difficulties of a doctrine do not mean necessarily that we should doubt the truth of the doctrine. Having in mind the difficult doctrines of his Christian faith—for example, the Trinity and transubstantiation, he wrote:

> Ten thousand difficulties do not make one doubt, as I understand the subject; difficulty and doubt are incommensurate. There of course may be difficulties in the evidence; but I am speaking of difficulties intrinsic to the doctrines, or

to their compatibility with each other. A man may be annoyed that he cannot work out a mathematical problem, of which the answer is or is not given to him, without doubting that it admits of an answer, or that a particular answer is the true one.[6]

Hence, the intellectual difficulties generated by the mysteries and paradoxes of a religious doctrine do not entail that we must reject the doctrine in order to preserve our intellectual integrity. Indeed, intellectual integrity may *require* that we affirm a mystery or paradox, rather than deny an aspect of our sense of reality.[7]

HUMANISTIC

A third trait of healthy religion is that it is *humanistic.* If you are used to thinking of humanism as an atheistic, antireligious movement, then you might think once again that I am trying to mix oil and water. But if we take the core of humanism to be concern for and commitment to the universal *welfare* of human beings, then I would say that humanism and a healthy religion are not only compatible but inseparable! Martin Buber put this point beautifully in the title of one of his books: *Believing Humanism.* I propose to you, then, that a healthy religion—theistic, atheistic, or otherwise—will be humanistic. It will emphasize *maximization of the quality of life on earth for all persons.* Alfred North Whitehead, in *Religion in the Making,* contends that enjoyment is the *purpose* of life, that God has brought us into being precisely in order that we might enjoy being![8] Milton Steinberg goes a step further in *Basic Judaism* and says that we have a God-given *duty* to enjoy life and that it is part of religion's function to help us do so![9] Does this purpose, this duty imply a life of crude sensualism? Not at all, for there are the joys of fellowship, of work, of creativity, and of worship, as well as of the body. Further, an intelligent religion does not limit itself to self-gratification, but involves itself also in the creation, maintenance, and improvement of a system of natural and social relations which makes *universal* enjoyment possible. The healthy and intelligent religious person is not fixated on immediate selfish pleasure, without regard for others. Such a person finds pleasure also in bringing pleasure to others, whether directly, as in the case of the chef or entertainer, or indirectly, as in the case of the community planner or ecologist who helps create and maintain an entire environment of diverse opportunities for the enjoyment of nature and society. As David Hume says in *The Natural History of Religion,* perhaps "the most genuine method of serving the divinity is by promoting the happiness of his creatures." This means, of course, that a healthy religion will oppose those things which demean or exploit people and which prevent them from enjoying existence in a manner compatible with universal enjoyment.

Karl Marx, the founder of modern communism, had a very different understanding of religion.[10] He described it as "the opium of the masses," and he made a very important point—namely, that the idea of "heaven" can be used to exploit people, to desensitize them, to manipulate them. It is a simple historical fact, for example, that wealthy slave owners favored and supported ministers who taught the slaves that *industriousness* at work and *obedience* to one's superiors will be rewarded "with pie in the sky, bye and bye." Then too, consider the teachings that the riches of this life are not to be compared to the riches of the next life (so don't worry about your poverty during this brief life), and that it will be as hard for the rich to get into heaven as for a camel to pass through the eye of a needle (so be glad you aren't rich, because being rich in this life makes it more difficult to get into heaven, and because the riches of this life last only a few decades, whereas the riches of the next life last forever!). You can see how such teachings, all adapted from the New Testament, could be used to manipulate the poor by making them reluctant to rebel or loaf, by taking their attention off their plight in this life, focusing their attention on the rewards of the next life, and by making their poverty seem an asset. I agree with Marx that such preachments are an "opium of the masses," used to maintain them in a slavish stupor, but I also believe that such preachments represent a *perversion* of religion. Religion doesn't *have* to be an opiate. It can be a stimulant. Indeed, healthy forms of religion are the *mainstay* of the hope of the masses, for these forms of religion insist on the *dignity* of every person, on the *brother/sisterhood* of all persons, on their *responsibility* for one another, and on their *right* to enjoy their existence. Finally, I do not see how Marx's theory of religion can satisfactorily explain such religious political activists as Mahatma Gandhi and Martin Luther King, Jr. Religion didn't put them to sleep; it roused them to action.[11]

REALISTIC AND HELPFUL REGARDING EVIL

A fourth trait of a healthy religion is that it is *realistic* about evil and *helpful* in the face of it. As I will argue shortly, it is a mistake to "get hung up" on evil, to fixate on it, to let it crush religious hope; yet I also believe that a religious faith will not be satisfactory to us unless we feel that it has faced up to the number and horror of natural evils, such as cancer and earthquakes, and to the depth of the human capacity for evil, such as cruelty, exploitation, and deceit. It seems that for some people, religion comes to mind only when they find themselves in a crisis situation. As a popular saying puts it, "There are no atheists in foxholes." I doubt that that's perfectly true, but I would be willing to bet that there are *fewer* atheists in foxholes! We need not restrict our discussion to the battlefront, however, for there are numerous foxhole situations in life: a student failing out of school, a student graduating from school without the least idea of what to do with the rest of her life, a marriage falling apart, a sole supporter of his family losing his job.

Clearly, a religion worth having is going to be a religion that has fathomed the frightening waters of life and found a solid foundation beneath them. A "fair-weather religion" is one of the most useless things I can think of. It's like carrying around an umbrella that has no covering: when you really need it, it is of no use to you!

Now I don't want you to think that I am promoting a foxhole type of religion. Whitehead, again, has suggested what needs to be said.[12] Namely, our religion should be capable of functioning at all temperatures and in all climates—and that includes those below-zero temperatures when the callousness of some human beings or the indifference of nature makes the human adventure seem a painful and meaningless accident. A healthy religion, then, is one that is helpful in adversity and prosperity, that augments the beauty of the good times and helps us get through the bad times. It is one in which our deity stands at the *center* of our everyday life as well as at its *periphery,* during those extraordinary moments of great fortune, misfortune, or decision.

OPTIMISTIC

A fifth trait of a healthy religion, and the final trait we shall discuss, is that it is *optimistic.* You might say, "Yes, but it is optimism based on escape from reality!" Or, as I have heard it put, "Religion is for people who can't handle reality!" Some even say, "Religion is a crutch." To be sure, religion has served as an escapist crutch in all three senses in which my students have interpreted that saying: (1) religion, like alcohol, drugs, sex, and so on, can be an escape from facing and coping with a serious problem, so that instead of acknowledging the facts and struggling with them, we hide ourselves from them with a veil of illusion or a cloak of pleasure; (2) rather than doing what is within our power to do, we can "lean" on the Lord to do it; (3) rather than accepting the responsibility for having done what we should not have done, we can blame it on the will of God. I agree that these are real and serious ways in which religion has been misused. There is yet another sense in which religion is a crutch, however, and it is a sense that calls for neither shame nor reproach. Why? Because when you're crippled, you need a crutch! And we are all crippled by the ambiguity of life: its meaning is not clear—all sorts of things *might* be the case, but none is clearly the case. Consequently, *we* have to choose *something* to stand on, something to give life unity, meaning, and direction. You may choose the crutch (the religion) that was given to you as a child, but *you* now have to choose it for yourself. Having reached the age of self-conscious deliberation, you can no longer blame your parents and educators for what you believe. You are a free agent. If you continue to believe what they taught you, you must now add that it is because *you* are convinced that they knew best!

You may decide that they were wrong, however, and where does that leave you? You can't simply divest yourself of all beliefs about reality and value, yet survive. Why? Because you'd be as helpless and dependent as a newborn infant. Hence, if you reject one set of beliefs, you are confronted with the necessity of replacing it with another set. We simply cannot get along without a crutch of some kind. It is as though we were born crippled and have to find or construct a crutch in order that we can get along in life. (The crutch that parents and teachers start us off with quickly becomes such a part of us that we don't realize it is a crutch!)

Clearly the crutch I have been talking about consists of ideas that "bake no bread." That is, religious beliefs about the nature of reality and value are of no practical value in the narrow sense of the word "practical." You can't use religious beliefs to make better cars or grow larger crops. Such ideas are, in that sense, useless. Consequently, some pragmatists and Marxists contend that such ideas ought to be barned from discourse as a waste of time. To the contrary, I would like to say a few things in behalf of nonpractical ideas.

Beliefs that "bake no bread" can make a significant difference in our lives in terms of (1) the way we feel about ourselves and others, (2) how we bear up under tragedy, (3) how we persevere under adversity and temptation. What I am claiming is that what we *believe* has a reflexive influence upon our attitudes, feelings, and actions, even when we are aware that our belief is a matter of feeling or hope and not of knowledge or probability. Consider, for example, the following contradictory alternatives: (1) that you are to some extent a free agent, able to choose what you will do and able to choose to what extent you will persevere in doing what you choose; (2) that you are in every instance the puppet of forces beyond your control—unable to choose other than as you do and unable to stop other than when you do. To adopt a metaphor from Dostoyevsky, according to the second position you are a piano upon which Nature and Society play. You have no more control over what you do than a piano has over the sounds it makes. The sounds it makes are determined by the keys that are struck; the actions we emit are determined by the natural and social forces that play upon us. Now these alternative beliefs "bake no bread," yet you must believe one way or the other, and which way you believe, it seems to me, is going to have a distinctive impact upon your feelings toward your life, its worth, its possibilities, and its meaning. It should also have an impact upon how you feel about and relate to other persons. (Reconsider in this context the sentence the student wrote before committing suicide: "I'm going to die anyway." Also, how well does a condemned man enjoy his last meal, sumptuous though it be? Clearly, the context of beliefs within which we operate makes a difference in how we feel about things.)

Having defended the value of nonpractical beliefs, I now want to claim that a *healthy religion is a mode of creativity devoted to the construction (or appropriation), maintenance, and celebration of an optimistic theory of the origin, nature, and destiny of human being.*[13] This optimism may be grounded in the Lord, humanity, science, or something else. It may be magnificent or very modest, but it is always there; for in the final analysis, religion has nothing to do with cynicism. Indeed, the opposite of healthy religion is *nihilism:* the systematic denial that there is anything truly good or that there is any reason for hope. The healthy religious impulse asks, Inasmuch as our situation is ambiguous and uncertain, why take a hopeless view of our situation when we can take an optimistic one? Why believe something that takes the wind out of your sails? that takes the fight out of you? that leaves you depressed? Within the limits set by logic, science, and your own sense of realism, why not look at the world through that set of ideas which to you is conducive to the fullest enjoyment of existence? As Tennyson bids us in his poem "The Ancient Sage," "Cleave ever to the sunnier side of doubt."

To be sure, all pessimists are not emotionally depressed. Miguel de Unamuno, Spanish author of *Tragic Sense of Life,* accuses pessimists of being arrogant snobs![14] The pessimists Unamuno has in mind are pessimists because it is stylish and because they think they know beyond question what reality is really like. Such pessimists clearly take pleasure in their pessimism. I am concerned about pessimists who do not. To them I recommend religion because I believe that religion at its best is a form of "creative insecurity."[15] A sensitive, alert person cannot escape altogether from insecurity, but it need not be crushing, and a healthy religion is committed to helping people cope with insecurity in creative, growth-enhancing ways. It is a matter of believing that which gives one the maximum of hope, of meaning, and of peak experience without compromising intellectual integrity. To put it another way, religion as a mode of creativity is the construction or adoption of an interpretation of life that (1) is compatible with one's understanding of logic and fact, and (2) causes one to have a maximum of joy in being. A healthy religion doesn't oppress us; it liberates us. It doesn't constrict us; it releases our energies and enthusiasms. It doesn't leave us drifting; it gives us direction. In order to do these things, clearly one's religion must wrestle with the problem of evil and put it into such a perspective that neither *evil* nor *indifference* is seen as the ultimate fact of existence. Why do I say this? Because I see no way to be the least bit optimistic if I become convinced that evil or indifference is the ultimate fact of reality. Again it seems to me that such a conviction must wash back over all of one's feelings toward life. Yes, people differ greatly with regard to how *much* they can hope for, but whenever the flame of hope goes out altogether, so does the heartbeat of religion.

In conclusion, without a frame of orientation that nurtures within us a deep and abiding hope, we are crippled indeed. So perhaps it is *without* a healthy religion that we need a crutch. Perhaps a healthy religious faith is our "natural" means of spiritual balance and vitality.

Reprinted by permission of UFS, Inc.

Notes

1. Paul Tillich, *Biblical Religion and the Search for Ultimate Reality* (Chicago: University of Chicago, 1955), pp. 60–61. For an explanation of the four things Tillich says faith is not, see Chap. 2, "What Faith Is Not," in Tillich's *Dynamics of Faith* (New York: Harper & Brothers, 1957).

2. Ibid., Chap. 1, Sec. 5.

3. Friedrich von Hügel, *Essays and Addresses on the Philosophy of Religion,* quoted in John H. Hick's *Philosophy of Religion,* 4th ed. (Englewood Cliffs, NJ: Prentice-Hall, 1990), p. 85.

4. For a recent analysis of paradox in both science and religion by a physicist-philosopher, see Ian Barbour's *Myths, Models, and Paradigms* (New York: Harper & Row, 1974).

5. John Henry Cardinal Newman, *Apologia Pro Vita Sua* (New York: Modern Library, 1950), p. 182.

6. Ibid., pp. 237–38. You might want to say to Cardinal Newman, "Okay, I'll accept your contention that 10,000 difficulties do not make a doubt. But what about 10,001? or 10,002? Surely at *some* point difficulties legitimately cause doubt!" For a brief and provocative statement of this kind of reaction to Newman's point, see Antony Flew's "Theology and Falsification," in Antony Flew and Alasdair MacIntyre, eds., *New Essays in Philosophical Theology,* (New York: Macmillan, 1955).

7. *The Mystery of Being,* 2 vols., Gabriel Marcel (Chicago: Henry Regnery Company, 1960). The religious existentialist philosopher gives an illuminating discussion of the difference between a "problem" and a "mystery." For a brief introduction to Marcel, see Sam Keen, *Gabriel Marcel* (Richmond, VA: John Knox Press, 1967).

8. Alfred North Whitehead, *Religion in the Making* (New York: World, 1973), p. 97.

9. Milton Steinberg, *Basic Judaism* (New York: Harcourt, Brace & World, 1947). 172 pages. Very readable.

10. For the writings of Marx himself and his colleague Friedrich Engels, see *On Religion* (New York: Schocken Books, 1964). For a brief introduction to Marx's position, see William Luijpen and Henry Koren, *Religion and Atheism* (Pittsburgh: Duquesne University Press, 1971).

11. See "Religion: Opiate or Inspiration of Civil Rights Militancy among Negroes?" by Gary T. Marx, for a sociologist's investigation of this question. Reprinted several places, including Charles Y. Glock, ed., *Religion in Sociological Perspective* (Belmont, CA: Wadsworth, 1973).

12. Whitehead, *Religion in the Making,* pp. 53–54.

13. I make this distinction between "construction" and "appropriation" of a religious faith in order to allow for both the *naturalist,* who believes that religious faith is the product of human experience and reflection, and those *theists* who believe that given the limitations and perversities of the human mind, no religion is worth our time save one that has been revealed by a supreme being—and it, having been revealed by a supreme being, should not be altered but accepted whole. Karl Barth represents the theistic position and John Dewey the naturalistic position. John Hick, contemporary philosopher of religion, believes, like Barth, that there is a God who reveals Himself to us, but Hick believes also that God reveals Himself in such a way that we are forced to *interpret* what He is saying. See Chap. V, "Revelation and Faith," of Hick's *Philosophy of Religion,* 4th ed. (Englewood Cliffs, NJ: Prentice-Hall, 1990).

14. See Miguel de Unamuno, *Tragic Sense of Life* (New York: Dover, 1954), p. 326.

15. Peter Bertocci develops this idea in his book *Religion as Creative Insecurity* (New York: Association Press, 1959).

6

Attitudes Toward Religious Propositions

QUESTIONS TO THINK ABOUT

- What are four attitudes a person may have toward religious propositions?
- How do the rationalist and the antirationalist disagree regarding the power and scope of human reason?
- Using a "hope" interpretation of faith, how can the proposition "I believe in God" be related to both the present and the future?
- In what sense do religious propositions have an aesthetic function in human life?
- What are the relations of mature religious faith to doubt and to courage?
- In what ways is the mature religious person "open" and why?
- What is the mature religious person endeavoring to discover, and what are the two passions that drive him or her?
- What is the significance of "faith as hope" for interreligious dialogue?
- What are three noetic perversions of religious faith? Explain them.

Many people believe that to have a religious faith means to be certain that what you believe is true. This attitude toward one's religious beliefs has caused a great deal of conflict in the past as groups with mutually exclusive faiths have encountered one another, each claiming to be the one true religion. Today that attitude is causing *doubt* as well as *conflict.* Why? Because an increasing number of people are asking, "Since I am not *certain* about the nature of reality and value, how can I have a religious faith at all?" Given their assumption that religious faith is a matter of being certain, these people understandably believe that they must reject religious faith. What we shall see in this chapter is that such rejection may not be necessary. Why? Because there are at least four basic attitudes one can take toward one's religious convictions; only one of them being dogmatic. I call these four attitudes *knowledge, belief, faith,* and *hope.* In ordinary language there is considerable overlap among the meanings of these four terms, and some of them are used interchangeably. As a consequence, discussions about belief and faith are often confusing because it's not clear to all parties how these terms are being used. Hence, what I propose to do is to give a narrower, more precise meaning to each term than it has in ordinary discourse. This should bring greater clarity into our thinking and talking about religious credence by providing us with four distinct forms of it, together with a different term for each form. Sometimes, however, because of your own ways of using these terms, you may feel uncomfortable with the meanings to which I restrict them. I do too, at times. Still, by restricting them as I do I am able to bring out four clear attitudes toward the truth of a proposition, and that, for our purposes, seems worth the discomfort. Further, as long as we stay with ordinary language, rather than inventing new terms (and how could we define new religious terms apart from ordinary language?), uneasiness is inevitable because—for our purposes— we will be restricting terms with many meanings to only one of their meanings. Of course, my way of restricting them may cause more dissatisfaction than is necessary. Thus, if you're sufficiently unhappy, I encourage you to improve upon my own attempt to bring clarity into our understanding of the modes of religious conviction.

FOUR BASIC ATTITUDES: KNOWLEDGE, BELIEF, FAITH, AND HOPE

As I have said, there are at least four basic attitudes you can take toward your religious beliefs. First, you can hold that your religious beliefs are *absolutely and demonstrably true.* This would mean that you are not only convinced beyond a doubt in your own mind that your religious beliefs are true, but that you are also convinced that their truth is *demonstrable* to anyone who is intelligent enough and unbiased enough to follow your presentation of the evidence. Here, then, we have rational certainty. You claim that your religion is based on knowledge, on the certainty of proof. The Roman Catholic Church, for example, holds that the existence of God can be proved in this manner (though it does not hold that all of its doctrines can be proved by reason). In 1940, Pope Pius XII asserted, in his encyclical *Humani Generis,* "Human reason can, without the help of divine revelation and grace, prove the existence of a personal God by arguments drawn from created things [that is to say, drawn from the way the world is]." Hence, Pius XII is claiming that one who can and does follow such arguments will come to *know* that there is a personal God.

There are other possible attitudes toward the doctrines of religion, however. You might hold that though you do not think that the doctrines of your religion can be proved to be true beyond a doubt, still you believe they are *the most plausible explanation of the nature of reality.* In other words, given the evidence presently at hand, you believe that your religion is more likely the true explanation of reality than any other explanation with which you are familiar. This is the kind of position taken by Richard Swinburne in *The Existence of God.* Here we have empirical confidence, of one degree or another, rather than rational certainty. Instead of saying that you *know* the claims of your religion are true, you say that you *believe* they are true, and your belief is based on *evidence* which doesn't *prove* your religion is true, but which, in your judgment, gives it a higher *probability* of being true than any other explanation enjoys. However, the fact that your commitment is based on evidence means that should old evidence be discredited, new evidence be discovered, or a more convincing analysis of the evidence be arrived at, then the strength of your belief should fluctuate appropriately; and if your present religion is in your own judgment surpassed on the probability scale by some new explanation of reality, then your allegiance should switch immediately to the new explanation—since your implicit objective is to be always committed to that explanation of reality which enjoys the highest probability of being true. This attitude is captured very nicely in a statement by James Cornman and Keith Lehrer in their *Philosophical Problems and Arguments.* They write regarding the question of the existence of God: "Although God may exist, as evidence unavailable to human beings might indeed show, the conclusion that we as rational beings should draw, based on the evidence discussed in this chapter, is that God does not exist. . . ."[1] Note Cornman and Lehrer's assumption that *as rational beings* we should always make sure that we believe only propositions which have the highest likelihood of being true, regardless of our hopes and intuitions.

Yet is the concept of probability even *applicable* to the question of the truth or falsity of a worldview? Some religious persons are unable to say that they *believe* their religion is true, much less that they *know* it is true, because they believe that it is *impossible* (either for practical or theoretical reasons) to establish the various truth probabilities of the different worldviews. John

Hick, for example, is himself a believer in the Christian God, yet he discredits probabilistic arguments to the existence of God by arguing that the concept of probability cannot be applied legitimately to the question of the existence of a unique infinite being such as God.[2]

Whether Hick is correct or not, one may be convinced that he does not *know* that his religion is true, and he may think it would be inaccurate to say that he *believes* that his religion is true, yet he may have *faith* that his religion is true. What does it mean to have faith that something is true? It means to have the *feeling* of confidence which normally accompanies knowledge, but with regard to propositions about which you are neither rationally certain nor empirically confident, since you do not think that you have either reasons which prove them true or evidence which shows that they are probably true. You do, however, have a feeling of *emotional confidence* that these propositions are true. You have the feeling of certainty without the grounds of certainty, and this, it seems to me, is yet a third type of attitude one may have toward one's religion. This kind of faith, it should be noted, is not the result of an exertion of will or of a process of reasoning; it is simply the way one's feelings are constituted at the moment. Some people, such as Karl Barth and Miguel Unamuno, would say that it is "a gift of grace." Unamuno writes in *The Agony of Christianity* that faith "issues from grace and not from arbitrary choice. He who has merely a craving for faith does not have faith."[3] Faith is received, not achieved. It is something that happens to us.

Finally, you may not be able to say in honesty about a religion that you know it is true, or that you believe it is true, or even that you have faith that it is true. Still, you might *hope* that it is true, for it may represent to you the most attractive interpretation of reality of which you are aware. Hence, in expressing your commitment to that religion, you would not be claiming it to be true on logical or empirical grounds; nor would you be claiming to feel as though it were true. You would be claiming only that you *hope* it is true and that you believe that there is a *possibility* that it is true. (It would be irrational to hope that it is true if you believe that there is no possibility that it is true, but it would not be irrational to hope that it is true if you believe that there is the least possibility that it is true, regardless of how improbable it might seem.) Miguel de Unamuno is the exemplar *par excellence* of this fourth position. See his *Tragic Sense of Life,* wherein he insists that "with reason or without reason or against reason" he will persist in his hope that there is life after death.[4]

These attitudes and their descriptions can be outlined as follows:

Knowledge: Rational certainty; based on proof
Belief: Empirical confidence; based on probability
. . . .

Faith: Emotional confidence; based on feeling
Hope: Emotional desire; based on attractiveness

The dotted line points to the question of the power and scope of human reason. Knowledge and belief assume that human reason can discern the ultimate nature of reality. Faith and hope do not. To be sure, we would like to be *convinced* by reasons or evidence that certain claims about the nature of reality are true, and we would like to *feel* that they are true. Hence, from this perspective hope is the least satisfactory of these four positions, and faith the next to least satisfactory, since hope by itself is backed by neither argument nor feeling, and faith by itself is backed by only one of these. But perhaps hope and faith are the best we can do. Perhaps it is impossible to resolve the question of the nature of reality by means of human reason. Let's take a look at two positions, pro and con.

On the one extreme, there is a tradition of thinking called *rationalism* whose proponents believe that reality is essentially transparent to the searching light of reason. It is as though reality were a large but transparent glass ball and human reason a powerful flashlight capable of illuminating every aspect of that ball. In principle, then, the rationalist believes that there is no height or depth or area of reality that cannot be fathomed by human reason. One of the most famous rationalists, G. W. F. Hegel, a nineteenth-century German philosopher, made this position quite clear in his inaugural address at the University of Heidelberg:

> Man, because he is mind, should and must deem himself worthy of the highest; he cannot think too highly of the greatness and power of his mind, and, with this belief, nothing will be so difficult and hard that it will not reveal itself to him. The being of the universe, at first hidden and concealed, has no power which can offer resistance to the search for knowledge; it has to lay itself open before the seeker—to set before his eyes and give for his enjoyment, its riches and its depths.[5]

Clearly Hegel believed that, in principle, human reason is able to answer with certainty the question of the nature of reality.

There are others, however, who believe that reality is not transparent to reason. These persons, let us call them *antirationalists,* believe that whereas reason is a very valuable tool, it is also a very limited tool. It can, for example, (1) do mathematics, (2) figure probabilities, (3) aid in the discovery of natural laws, and (4) check arguments for consistency. But it is not a metaphysical flashlight that can disclose ultimate truths about reality. Rather, as Soren Kierkegaard, a nineteenth-century Danish philosopher, put it, when it comes to questions about the nature of reality, human reason is like a judge who listens to all the evidence in a case, but then is missing from the bench when it's time for him to give a verdict! The point is that no matter how long or deeply we investigate questions about the nature of reality, we shall never find that THE answer is given to us. Rather, reality is always presented to us ambiguously—open to various interpretations, none of which is clearly true—all of which fit the data, but none of which fits it perfectly. To be sure, given your individual background (culture, family, and so on) and your present values, you will find some interpretations of reality *easier* to believe in than others. But upon philosophical analysis you will find, according to Kierkegaard, that you cannot demonstrate according to some universally accepted criteria that your interpretation is definitely true, or even more likely true than any other. Hence, your commitment must really be a matter of faith or hope.

Who is right in the debate between the rationalists and the antirationalists? I've already given myself away as some kind of a rationalist. But the debate is far too inconclusive for solemn pronouncements of "correct" and "incorrect." It is more important for you to figure out where your own sympathies lie, with the rationalists or the antirationalists, for that will help you get a perspective on how to react to a whole raft of issues, such as whether to take seriously arguments for and against the existence of God. Meanwhile, having gone over each of these four attitudes toward one's religion, now let's turn around and work our way back through them, going in the other direction and giving special attention to their epistemological relations to one another and to how they might be combined.

The simplest form of religious engagement, epistemologically, is *hope:* the hope of sheer aspiration, with no ground other than desire, or the hope of sheer desperation, with nowhere else to turn. I am speaking, for example, of the sudden hope of the unbeliever that there is a God who will vindicate justice and mercy or the hope of a distraught mother that her child will live again. Such hope, I believe, is genuinely religious and need not, in order to be considered religious, be bolstered by a feeling or by evidence that it is true. Here we have the religious attitude in its simplest, least rationalized, least assuming form. Religiousness at this level is not a matter of knowing that a particular interpretation of reality is true, or of thinking that "given the evidence it is probably true," or of feeling that it is true, but simply of hoping that it is true because it is the best that one can imagine about reality.

When one's religious adherence is self-consciously understood to be a matter of hope, the articles of one's "faith" perform a kind of aesthetic function. For the sake of enhancing the felt quality of our lives we decorate the interior of our homes with attractive physical objects: paintings, sculptures, plants, music, and so on. In like manner, we can decorate the interior of our minds with attractive propositions—not without regard for their truth or falsity, but with primary regard for the quality of their impact on our lives. This aesthetic function of religion in our lives extends to religious symbols and rituals as well as to religious propositions. Hence, a religion can make a valuable contribution to one's life apart from any determination of its truth or falsity. This is especially important to note, inasmuch as religious doctrines are usually *beyond* the pale of verification anyway. When we do not have certainty, we must act on probability, and when we do not have even probability, what better than to act on our own deepest vision of the good?

Religious allegiance becomes more complex when one's hope is accompanied by emotional experiences or feelings which give one the confidence that what one hopes is true. Such confidence *happens* to us, we know not why—though we may believe that it is "a gift of grace." To be sure, you may not think that hope is involved in your faith, and it may not have been consciously present in your religious development. But if your faith is a healthy faith, then I believe that under questioning you would conclude that even if you lost your feeling of confidence that things are as you feel they are, you would continue to hope that they are that way. Hope, I am suggesting, implicitly undergirds faith. For example, a person, who under the onslaught of criticisms loses confidence that there is a loving, omnipotent God, may nonetheless continue to hope that there is and that those criticisms can be overcome by a deeper understanding of God's wisdom, love, and power.

Regarding the relations of faith and knowledge, it is easy to confuse the two with one another because of the feeling of certainty common to both. One of my students wrote in a paper that she "knew" that she was saved and that God had forgiven her sins. I was interested in how she understood the concept of knowledge in her claim that she knew that she had been saved by God. So I asked, and she replied as follows:

> To answer that question I would like to define "faith." The best way I know of to do this is to tell you a story.
> "A minister had a son about eight years old. One day the son asked his father, 'What is faith, Daddy?' The father answered by taking the boy into his study and perching him up on the highest bookshelf in the room. He then asked his son, 'If you were to fall or jump down from there, do you think I would catch you?' The little boy was quick to answer, 'Sure, you'd catch me!' The father asked his son again, just to make certain, and the boy was just as confident in his second reply. The father then demanded that the boy jump. The boy hesitated a moment and then jumped into his father's outstretched arms."

The student continued:

> This story communicates, to me anyway, what faith is all about. My "knowledge" of God's love is similar to the little boy's implicit trust in his father. I have *extreme* confidence that God is there and that I have salvation

through Christ. There is always the possibility that the father would slip and the boy fall to the floor. But the boy had to take his father on faith that he wouldn't slip that one time. So faith involves "knowledge." The boy had *no doubt* that his father would catch him and I have no doubts that God exists, that God is loving, and that God has forgiven my sins. I *know* no other way of putting it!

This is a beautiful example, it seems to me, of that attitude toward religious propositions which we have called "faith" rather than "knowledge." Clearly, "trust without doubt" is not the same thing as "knowledge," or even "belief." We can have a feeling of absolute confidence in someone and nonetheless be let down by them. Hence, to have such a feeling about someone's trustworthiness is not to *know* that they are trustworthy, even if they have been dependable in the past. A problem with confusing knowledge with faith is that it gives us the feeling of knowing something which we do not know. Presumably, *to know* that an assertion is true involves the following: (1) It *is* true (if it were false then we could not *know* it to be true, though we could mistakenly *think* we knew it to be true); (2) we *think* it is true because of evidence or reasons; (3) our evidence or reasons *mean* that it is true (if they didn't, we might achieve the probability of belief but not the certainty of knowledge); (4) we are *aware* that our evidence or reasons mean that the proposition concerned is true (if we are not aware of this, then we don't *know* that the proposition is true).

But we have said already that faith is not based on evidence at all. Hence, it cannot be a form of knowledge, though it might be that faith can be reinforced by evidence. The confusion of faith with knowledge most likely occurs because a person takes his or her feeling of certainty about a proposition to be conclusive evidence that the proposition is true. Whereas, of course, how one *feels* about the truth of a proposition is usually irrelevant to the task of establishing its truth or falsity.[6]

Religious allegiance achieves a third level of complexity when one believes that one's hope or faith is supported by evidence which makes it seem more likely that it is true. Some people, for example, believe that religious experience itself is evidence in favor of the existence of God. Father Frederick Copleston, Jesuit priest and author of a widely used, multivolumed history of philosophy, made this point in a radio debate with Bertrand Russell, one of this century's most articulate critics of theism. "I don't regard religious experience as a strict proof of the existence of God," Copleston stated, "but I think it's true to say that the best explanation of it is the existence of God."[7] Other people emphasize order, purpose, beauty, and morality as lending credence to the idea that there is a personal God. Whether religious devotion can be confirmed legitimately by evidences of these sorts is, as we have seen, a question that is vigorously debated by philosophers and theologians. Whatever the correct answer, I believe it is fair to say that we would *prefer* that our religious allegiance be based not only on hope or faith but also on something which gives us a degree of *reasoned confidence* in what we are committed to. Without that objective basis of evidence, we feel all the more vulnerable to critics and the vacillations of our own feelings. With that support, there is a kind of security which we do not enjoy otherwise. Hence, it is understandable that many people whose commitment is of the nature of hope or faith work hard at trying to find reasons and evidence which protect their commitment from external critics and internal moods.

Still, even hope confirmed by faith and evidence is not identical with knowledge, in the sense defined earlier. Nor am I optimistic that we ever can achieve knowledge of the truth of any set of basic religious doctrines. To be sure, we *want* knowledge that x (our religion) is true, rather than having to settle for hope or faith that it is true. For that very reason we must be careful to avoid premature closure of the gap between our evidence and our convictions.[8] Or, to put it another way, we should not allow ourselves to be deceived into thinking that the nature of the closure between our evidence and our feelings is of the nature of knowledge or belief when it isn't. Neither knowledge nor belief in any legitimate sense can be achieved by allowing a feeling of certainty to replace a lack of evidence. To be sure, the believer may not be aware of what has happened. The believer is convinced that he or she *knows* that the religion is true! But upon being led through the land of philosophical distinctions, I believe he or she will see that we must make a distinction between what we *feel,* what we *believe,* and what we *know,* and having made those distinctions, I believe we can convince him or her that this devotion is based not on knowledge but on hope or faith, perhaps reinforced by belief. Let's pursue this line of thought a bit further.

Clearly, feeling that a religious belief is true is not equivalent to knowing that it is true. If that were the case, then Judaism, Christianity, Islam, Hinduism, and Buddhism would all be true, since they each have devotees who feel that their religion is true. But they cannot all be true, since if, for example, the creed of Islam is true, then Judaism and Christianity are false at crucial points. Hence, feeling that a religion is true cannot be accepted as sufficient evidence that it is true. Moreover, I am convinced presently that it is in principle impossible to prove conclusively the truth of any religious faith.[9]

I would not deny that some things relevant to religious faith can be known by means of reasons. I am, for example, convinced that there is something which is uncreated, eternal, and indestructible. The argument goes as follows: (1) Something cannot come from nothing; (2) if anything exists, then there is something which cannot become nothing; (3) something exists (at the very least, I exist while I am thinking through this argument). From these premises it can be concluded, I believe, that there is something which has always existed and will always exist. Whether that something is matter, the Lord, or something else is a question I won't go into here. The important point at the moment, if I am correct about the soundness of the argument, is the religious poverty of the conclusion. Indeed, all the conclusions of which I am convinced by metaphysical reasoning are far from religiously adequate and are compatible with a number of more inclusive theories which are mutually exclusive. Simply because something is uncreated, imperishable, and indestructible does not mean it is worthy of worship, and even if we all agree that the foundation of reality, whatever it is, is uncreated and indestructible, still we cannot by metaphysical reasoning, as far as I can see, determine whether that "ground of being" is mindless or intelligent, favorably disposed toward humans or indifferent. Further, there seems to be no conclusive means of settling the question of human destiny, for we can never *know* that our state of affairs has reached a point of eternal fixity. Even if we die and come back to consciousness in an unearthly paradise, how can we know then that we won't die again, and this time without a return of consciousness? Or, how can we know that our paradise won't turn into a nightmare? John Hick argues that "continued personal existence after death" in a paradisal kingdom such as is described in the *Bible* would provide "a religiously unambiguous" verification of the Judaic-Christian faith in life after death.[10] I have to disagree because as long as the future is before us—and that, I think, is where it shall always be—our situation is ambiguous no matter how completely we might be lulled by repetition into thinking otherwise. We could learn a lesson here from Bertrand Russell's chicken. Russell tells (with a bit of embellishment from me) of a farmer who had a chicken that he raised from an egg. Every day the farmer religiously fed the chicken at the same time and place. The chicken, never having experienced anything else, understandably expected that whenever the farmer appeared at the special time and place, it would be fed. Imagine the poor bird's surprise when one day instead of getting its stomach fed, it got its neck wrung. Such a touching tale, I fear, would haunt me even inside the pearly gates. But, if I make it, perhaps Hick will be there to reassure me.[11]

Finally, in showing some of the severe difficulties encountered in any attempt to prove a religious doctrine, I would like to say something about the practice of presuming to prove a doctrine by referring it to the authority of a sacred book or a sacred person. This, it seems to me, does not provide us with a resting place at all. It only raises the question of how we might become convinced that the book or that person speaks the truth. Here, too, I cannot conceive how we can achieve knowledge that a certain book or person *always* speaks the truth. There are, however, people such as my friends Reverend Herman Eckelmann, an electrical engineer as well as a minister, and Professor Robert C. Newman, Ph.D. in astrophysics from Cornell University, now at the Biblical School of Theology, who believe that though we cannot achieve absolute intellectual certainty in either religion *or science,* that still in religion, as well as in science, we can achieve "that level of certainty which we can attain in everyday activities and decisions and by which we would be held accountable in court, in the army, by our employer, or by our friends."[12] This strikes me as an interesting approach, worthy of serious consideration. Presumably this principle of accountability should be applied to every religion, and then one becomes "morally responsible" for following that religion which exhibits "that level of certainty" for which we are held accountable in everyday life. Clearly, there will be difficulties if one concludes that no religion exhibits that degree of certainty or that two or more religions exhibit it to an equal extent. For an application of the principle to Christianity, see *Science Speaks,* by mathematician Peter Stoner, who was assisted by Newman. Meanwhile, let's return to our analysis of the difference between knowledge and faith.

A person who is philosophically astute, I believe, will realize that the movement from his feelings, experiences, and thinking to the conclusion, let us say, that the Lord God exists, is a movement which involves "a leap of faith"—a leap which is taken because the leaper hopes that the Lord is real. A believer might object, "Look, I *know* that it was when I went to the altar and accepted Jesus that a change came into my life"—meaning: "I know Jesus is real because I felt him come into my life and I have seen the changes He has made." I agree that we must not deny the spiritual efficacy of a certain kind of context and of certain actions (such as being in a revival service, walking to the altar, and so forth), but to admit the spiritual efficacy of such a setting and such acts for some persons is not to prove that the feelings and changes which ensued were brought about by a risen Christ. To repeat, that kind of argument would also "prove" the truth of Indian religions, of Islam, of paganism, and so on. If one is philosophically rigorous, one is reduced to acknowledging what was done, what happened, and that one *hopes* or *has faith* that the changes which occurred were really brought about by the Great Spirit, or Jesus, or Allah, or whomever. But that is something we cannot *know*—any more than we can know that there are minds other than our own. We have *faith* that there are, but we can't know that there are. We never see directly another person's mind, his or her feelings or thoughts; we assume them. And when we become aware of the possibility that there *are* no other minds, but only other bodies, we hope that is not the case. We hope that we are loved in feeling as well as in behavior.

This last point raises the interesting question of the relation of hope to time. Ordinarily we think of hope in relation to the future only, but it also has important relations to the present and past. Regarding the past, one might hope, for example, that one's carelessness did not contribute causally to a friend's accidental death or that Jesus really did die for the sins of man or that the Koran really was dictated to Mohammed by Allah. With regard to the *present,* one might hope that the feeling of a divine presence is due to the real presence of a personal, supreme being and not to a chemical imbalance in the body or to a self-stimulated illusion. Also, one might hope that one's present behavior is not simply and solely a function of the past (recall our discussion of determinism in Chapter 5), and that one's suffering is serving a cause which is *genuinely worthy* and not simply a matter of personal whim. Regarding the future, one might hope that lives cut short by tragedy will be restored to growth and that loved ones will be brought together again. In spite of the unusualness of relating hope to the past and the present, all three relations appear to be present in Hebrews 11:1 (New Testament): "Faith," it is written, "is the assurance of things hoped for, the conviction of things not seen." "Assurance" refers to that feeling of confidence which is the key element of faith, as we defined it earlier. "Things hoped for" can be, as we just noted, past as well as future. A Christian, for example, might hope that his sins *were* really forgiven when he repented five years ago and that he *will* be granted eternal life in heaven after death. "The conviction of things not seen" can be read to mean *confidence* that things *in the present* are a certain way even though we do not *know* that they are. A good example here is the confidence of an Orthodox Jew that his experience of the presence of God is the result of the presence of God, rather than simply of electrochemical processes in his body. Again, our experience calls for interpretation, and even when we are not confident on grounds of reason that things are a certain way, still we may hope that they are. "For now," as St. Paul puts it, "we see through a glass darkly."[13]

To review briefly, there may be in a person's religious development a point before which he or she believes that his or her commitment is a matter of knowledge because of finding either (1) evidence or (2) personal experience to be compelling. If a person ever comes to see that this evidence is inconclusive and that there are other plausible ways to explain these personal experiences, he or she will realize that the earlier conviction was not based on knowledge. Neither is religious conviction only a matter of *belief,* for we can react to a probable proposition—including "God exists"—with enthusiasm, indifference, or aversion. If a fundamental religious proposition is greeted with enthusiasm, it is because one hopes it is true. Hence, philosophy ultimately gives religion back to us, but it gives it back in the form of hope rather than knowledge. We can *hope* that something is true and *act* as though it is true without thinking that we *know* it is true and without *believing* it is true. We can persist in our hope even when it is not accompanied by encouraging experiences and arguments, though I believe such hope will motivate us to defend and strengthen it in whatever ways we can. At the very least, I believe religious hope will employ reason to assure itself that what it hopes is a meaningful possibility. If more is possible, then blessed are those whose hopes *are* confirmed by feeling, reason, and action. Therein we have religious conviction in its richest form.

FAITH, DOUBT, AND COURAGE

If the mature religious person realizes that his commitment is based on hope and not knowledge, then Paul Tillich is correct, it seems to me, in saying that doubt will be included in a mature religious faith as a structural feature of it. Why? Because at the same time that a person seems to feel the presence of something worthy of absolute commitment, he is also capable of realizing that he is *fallible* and therefore may be wrong—no matter what or who it is, whether it be Marxism or Hinduism. It is not true, then, as one of my students claimed, that religious faith "ends having to worry about explanations." Indeed, the severe loss of self-confidence into which one can be plunged by the twists and turns of the religious venture are highlighted well in the career and reflections of Cardinal John Newman. Reared in the Church of England, Newman became a priest in the same and was convinced absolutely that the pope of the Catholic Church was the Antichrist. Gradually, however, after years of debate, discussion, correspondence, and reading, he began to lose confidence in the soundness of the Church of England and felt a growing conviction that, horror of horrors, the Catholic Church is what it claims to be—namely, the one true church. Newman was distraught by the demise of one absolute conviction, regarding the orthodoxy of the Church of England, and he was troubled by the emergence of another, regarding the Church of Rome. How, he asked himself, "was I any more to have absolute confidence in myself? how was I to have confidence in my present confidence? how was I to be sure that I should always think as I thought now?"[14] In the light of his intellectual conclusions regarding the Church of Rome, he felt it was his duty to convert, but at the same time he was fearful of becoming victimized again by illusion. "I had been deceived greatly once," he wrote:

> how could I be sure that I was not deceived a second time? I then while in the Church of England thought myself right; how was I to be certain that I was right now? How many years had I thought myself sure of what I now rejected? how could I ever again have confidence in myself? To be certain is to know that one knows; what test had I, that I should not change again, after that I had become a Catholic?[15]

Having undergone this experience even once, we rightfully become apprehensive about further changes of commitment, and even about committing ourselves at all.[16]

Because of this awareness of our fallibility, Tillich claims that a self-conscious religious faith is an act of courage, a daring affirmation of one's deepest hopes in spite of the fact that one realizes one might be wrong.[17] Hence, religious faith is a risk, and the mature believer realizes this. It does not follow, of course, that such a person, because he is aware that there might be something better than that to which he is presently committed, is continually seeking for that something. Sometimes, and perhaps most times, he doesn't feel a need for something better than he has. Moreover, he has a right to enjoy to the fullest the good that he has. But if asked about the nature of his commitment, he acknowledges that it is not a matter of knowledge and that now we "see through a glass darkly." Consequently, mature believers remain open at all times to *criticisms* of their faith and to *alternatives* to that faith, for (1) they realize that they are fallible and that therefore their critics may be correct, and (2) they want to be committed to the *best* that there is and realize that, again owing to their fallibility, what they presently believe to be the best may not in fact be so.

Mature religious people also realize that they would be foolish to reject the best they know before finding something better to replace it. To adopt Cardinal Newman's expression, 10,000 difficulties do not warrant giving something up if you have nothing better to take its place. Failure to realize this has led many a person to give up his or her religion prematurely. A person would be equally foolish to ignore the possibility of discovering something better, if it does exist. Right? Still, we can understand the anxiety of Tertullian, one of the great figures in early Christianity, who wrote:

> But if we are bound to go on seeking as long as there is any possibility of finding, simply because so much has been taught by others as well, we shall be always seeking and never believing. What end will there be to seeking? What point of rest for belief? Where the fruition of finding? There will be no end . . . and I shall wish I had never begun to seek. . . .[18]

Many of us have had that very experience of wishing we had never begun to seek. We grow weary and discouraged. But my interpretation of that state of affairs is that it is the result of either (1) the fact that we have not yet found anything worthy of our wholehearted commitment or (2) the fact that we have come across something that is worthy but we haven't understood that fact deeply enough. I sometimes share Tertullian's impatience with the person who will not, because he cannot, rest content with anything; yet that person is also a tragic figure whose life is an unresolved chord. Moreover, those persons are to be sympathized with who *are* eager and able to bring the search to an end, but who have not yet apprehended anything that enables them honestly to do so. The appropriate response to these people by those who *do* have a message is not to condemn them for not being won over, but to search for ever more effective methods of getting across the beauty of the message.

Please permit a remark about one other type of person. Given the urgent, concrete problems of the world, instead of wearing oneself out with the search for something better, one might self-consciously desist from further search, hope that one's religion is true, admit one's inability to prove it, and plunge oneself into the concrete task of feeding the hungry, housing the homeless, healing the sick, and fighting injustice. As long as abstention from the philosophical task is for such a purpose and is accompanied by epistemological humility, it has my blessing (for whatever that's worth). But we must not reason, "Hey, I'm not looking around anymore—so I must've discovered the truth!" Contentment with a position is not equivalent to knowledge of its truth. C. S. Peirce, founder of American pragmatism, once pointed out that thinking is a bit like scratching. That is, when we get an intellectual itch, we think in order to get rid of it. When the itch goes away, we stop thinking. But, of course, just because a certain way of thinking makes the itch go away does not mean that we've struck on the truth. Sometimes an error will remove an itch quicker than the truth! Hence, we should be very cautious about making inferences from our contentment with a position to its truth or superiority.[19]

Finally, let's consider whether religious devotion founded on hope is an escape from reality into the realm of imaginary wish fulfillment. Friedrich Nietzsche says of Plato, for example, that he was "a coward before reality," fleeing into a realm of utopian visions which he projected into another world.[20] Is that the nature of all religious commitment when it understands itself as hope? Not at all. In the first place, it is possible to be committed to a religion which is totally earthly; that is, one's hope can be in the possibilities of humanity and Nature. Second, those who believe that we shall live again may also believe that their faith has significance for the living of *this* life. For example, Mahatma Gandhi, a great religious spirit who helped lead India to independence from Britain, said in his autobiography that "those who say that religion has nothing to do with politics do not know what religion means."[21] Hence, rather than seeing religiousness as an escape from reality, we should see it as *an endeavor to see to what extent experience fits and confirms our most hopeful interpretation of reality and way of life.* This is consistent with the fact that though many thoughtful religious people do not claim to know that their beliefs are true, they *are* concerned to *discover* the truth about reality. Hence, they are not willing to rest content with what they feel at the moment to be true. Rather, they risk their feelings to criticisms and further experience. Why? Because they are driven by two passions, not one: (1) the desire to know the truth about reality and (2) the hope that the best that they can conceive about reality is true.

INTERRELIGIOUS DIALOGUE

To summarize, I am suggesting that religious commitment is primarily a matter of hope and faith, rather than of belief or knowledge. This understanding of religious devotion provides, I believe, a fruitful context within which members of diverse religions can enter into genuine dialogue with one another. They will not be able to do that as long as each religion is thought by its believers to be demonstrably "the one true religion." On that assumption the members of a religion must perceive all unbelievers either as persons who have not yet had their eyes opened or as people who are being intentionally obtuse. Clearly, when adherents of different religious positions take these attitudes toward one another, there can be no dialogue. They can only talk *at* one another about religious matters. None of such followers of one religion can take seriously the claims of the other, for each group is convinced already that it *knows* that its own religion is the true or the best in some objective sense. Hence, the other group's claims about the superiority of its religion must be false, and the overriding task of the speaker is to show the listener where he or she is wrong and why the speaker is right about his or her own position.

I must confess that such carryings-on with such slender evidence seem to me most inappropriate. Perhaps one reason why religious arguments so often lead to uncharacteristically rude behavior is that each participant feels that he or she has sufficient objective evidence to convince anyone who will "really listen," whereas, in fact, no one has that kind of evidence. How do we explain this blind spot on the part of each participant? Perhaps in terms of the following principle: We are more easily persuaded of the truth of that which we want to be true than of that which we do not want to be true; hence, the body of evidence which is adequate to give a person who wants a position to be true the feeling that it is true and has been proved to be such is not adequate to persuade someone who doesn't want that position to be true. When the body of evidence *is* sufficient proof that a position is true, then, of course, the second person is being obstinate; but when the body of evidence isn't sufficient, it is the first person who is being obstinate in insisting that the evidence *is* conclusive. Just what the strength of the evidence is, of course, is not something that can be determined apart from an examination of the evidence itself, and—if a *belief* claim is being made, rather than a claim of knowledge—apart from a comparison of that set of evidence to the sets of evidence set forth by other religions. My own position presently is that it is impossible to demonstrate conclusively the truth of any set of religious doctrines, and I'm not optimistic about the possibility of establishing the probabilities of religions relative to one another. Hence, I believe that the argument approach to nonbelievers is *misleading* to those who are convinced (since they too become victims of the illusion that the evidence is conclusive) and *disturbing* to those who are not (since they not only are thrown into self-doubt about whether they have in fact failed to grasp the true strength of the argument, but are also sometimes, if they persist in their doubt, accused or suspected of being dull-witted, pig-headed, sinful, or some combination thereof).

If, however, persons understood their religious commitments to be a matter of a hopeful interpretation of reality, then, it seems to me, they would be free to take one another seriously and to listen appreciatively, for they would have no vested interest in proving one another wrong. Each would understand that unless the others had been touched by something which to them was beautiful, meaningful, enriching, and empowering, they would not be religiously serious at all. All could share their hopes and feelings with one another, and also (insofar as they have them) their reasons for thinking that their hope or faith might be true. W. C. Smith suggests in this same spirit, "Might it not be that the next step in missions would necessarily be one where one religious group says to another, 'This is what we have seen of the truth, this is what God has done for us; tell us what you have seen, what God has done for you; and let us discuss it together'?"[22] In such a context, there would be no reason for anyone to become defensive, for the overriding interest of each person would be to share his or her own experience of the sacred as fully as possible and to be open to the possibility of an even greater experience—from whatever direction it might come. And surely it is primarily by means of human interchange that others learn the beauty of our religion and that we learn the beauty of theirs. Hence, such a context should enable persons to share the good which they have come to know through their religion and to continue their quest to be involved with that religion which can give their lives the greatest meaning, the finest quality, the clearest direction. That religion, of course, might not be the one held presently. Consequently, we should always perform the difficult task of *affirming* the best that we know while *holding ourselves open* to that which is better—whether the better be (1) further development in the direction we are already headed in or (2) conversion to a different direction altogether.

Such mutual openness involves the responsibility of being honest in our descriptions—not describing our religion in colors more bright or less bright than we have actually experienced. Conversely, we should be sincerely and genuinely open to the words of others, letting them wash over us in all of their brilliance and subtlety. This means, of course, that we, like Cardinal Newman, might find ourselves powerfully attracted to a new religion. No serious student of religion is immune to this risk. The only escapes I can see are to avoid other religions altogether or to never really open ourselves to the beauty others see in them. And that, I submit, is not consistent with our desire to know and have the best religion or philosophy that there is.

Before leaving the topic, I must add as a counterbalance that it would be foolish to interpret religious commitment as a mode of hope, rather than of knowledge, merely in order to put all religions on the same level for the sake of dialogue. If a religion, or its fundamental doctrines, can be proved true or false, then it should be. But until it is demonstrated objectively that positive knowledge can be achieved about the ultimate matters with which religion is concerned, I shall hold on pragmatic grounds that humanity and the individual will be better served by an interpretation of religion based on hope and faith.

NOETIC PERVERSIONS OF FAITH

As a conclusion to this section on "faith as hope," I would like to point out some of the unfortunate consequences which are likely to follow from the belief that religious conviction is a mode of knowledge. We shall call these consequences "noetic perversions" of religious conviction, because the word "noetic" refers to affairs of the intellect. First there is the attitude of *dogmatism* referred to briefly in the preceding section. Dogmatism, I am convinced, is the attitude of those who cannot live with the ambiguity of human experience—or who don't see the ambiguity (and not seeing it may be a function of not wanting to see it). The dogmatists—whether theistic or atheistic—escape from the anxiety of ambiguity into the comfortable feeling of noetic certainty, even when that feeling is not warranted. The dogmatic attitude is one in which a person has the feeling that his or her religion is true and provable but does not in fact have reasons or evidence to prove it, and so either must admit that his or her religion is not provably true (which admission would dispel his dogmatism) or, as we noted earlier, he or she must think nasty things about those listeners who object that his or her argument is not a sufficient basis for commitment. (Though—and here comes the inevitable "on the other hand" of the philosopher—we must not rule out the possibility that the listener *has* in fact failed to grasp the true strength of the argument!)

A second noetic perversion is *exclusiveness.* As we noted earlier, if you believe that you know the truth, then you don't take seriously what the person says who disagrees with you; you only try to figure out how to convert him or her. If that person proves impervious to your appeals and arguments, then you avoid him or her—which is what I mean by exclusiveness. This attitude is an obstruction to universal human fellowship, and I think I can give a good example of it. I once went to a football game and sat next to a minister I knew. The minister introduced me to a couple of seminary students who had come with him. Without further ado, one of the students looked me in the eye, asked me if I believed in the blood atonement (a doctrine some Christians hold), and added that if I didn't, he would have nothing further to do with me. Personally, I didn't feel that losing his friendship would have been any great loss, but I was disturbed by his attitude. When creedal questions of this sort destroy fraternal feeling between people (or prevent it from arising), I believe that people have gotten their priorities tragically out of line. Mutual respect and affection are more important than creedal differences—which doesn't mean that beliefs are unimportant, but that we should learn to differ in love. "We sometimes forget," writes W. C. Smith,

> that this means arriving at a point where outsiders can trust us, as well as one where we can understand, respect, and honour them. It means also arriving at a point . . . where we can appreciate other men's values without losing our allegiance to our own. The world has little profit from that broadminded relativist who accepts the diversity of men's loyalties because he feels that no loyalties are ultimately valid, nothing is inherently worthwhile. Modern relativism is sophisticated cynicism—and is a devastating, not a constructive force.[23]

A healthy religion, as we noted earlier, has no place for cynicism. Nor has it a place for dogmatic exclusiveness.

The third and final noetic perversion I would like to mention is *coercion*—that is, the willingness to use propaganda or force to make people commit themselves, or at least say that they are committing themselves, to a certain religious position, whether it be theistic, such as Christianity, or atheistic, such as communism. This, in my opinion, is one of the most pathetic and harmful perversions of religious commitment. Religious devotion should be a matter of profound personal commitment based on deep experience and reflection. In its healthy form, it is the fruit of free and unforced growth. To try to force it is to have a misunderstanding of it to start with; it is not the kind of thing that can be forced. As Blaise Pascal, a brilliant mathematician, scientist, and profoundly religious philosopher, states in his *Pensées* (#172/185):

> The way of God, who disposes all things with gentleness, is to instil religion into our minds with reasoned arguments and into our hearts with grace, but attempting to instil it into hearts and minds with force and threats is to instil not religion but terror.

Furthermore, to attempt to bring about religious commitment by means of force or propaganda is to make the poor victim conclude that that is what religion is all about. No wonder some people hate religion and see it as a threat to human freedom. I join them! But what we mutually hate is a perversion of religion and not religion itself. It has its healthy forms. Indeed, one of my reasons for writing this book is that misunderstandings of the nature of religious commitment have led some people to be unloving, arrogant, dogmatic, propagandistic, and persecuting, and have led some of their victims, understandably, to become misguided enemies of the entire religious enterprise. If I am correct, however, that religious allegiance is ultimately based on hope or faith and therefore should be humble epistemologically, then the religious person must never in the name of knowledge breach the command to love. As St. Paul put it in I Corinthians 8, we should reject knowledge that "puffs up" in favor of love that "builds up." Further, though faith and hope are precious ingredients of human life, love is even greater than these. Hence, in the event of a conflict of love with faith or hope, we should never let love be the loser.[24]

Reprinted by permission of UFS, Inc.

Notes

1. James W. Cornman and Keith Lehrer, *Philosophical Problems and Arguments*, 2nd ed. (New York: Macmillan, 1974), p. 407.

2. See Chap. 2, "Teleology and Probability," in John Hick's *Arguments for the Existence of God* (New York: Herder & Herder, 1971).

3. Miguel de Unamuno, *The Agony of Christianity* (New York: Frederick Ungar, 1960), pp. 75–76.

4. Miguel de Unamuno, *Tragic Sense of Life* (New York: Dover, 1954), p. 130.

5. J. Glen Gray, ed., *G. W. F. Hegel on Art, Religion, Philosophy* (New York: Harper Torchbook, 1970), pp. 20–21.

6. The classic introduction to the question of the nature of knowledge is Plato's dialogue *Theatetus.* For recent discussions, see Robert Audi's *Belief, Justification, and Knowledge* (Belmont, CA: Wadsworth, 1988) and Roderick Chisholm's *Theory of Knowledge* (Englewood Cliffs, NJ: Prentice Hall, 1989). Audi and Chisholm both discuss the important distinction between *knowing something* and *knowing that one knows it.* One might know something without knowing that one knows it. I have not employed this distinction here because it is very subtle and would require more attention than seemed appropriate in a text of this type; perhaps more important, it seems to me that the type of knowing that is of most interest here is the type that involves knowing that one knows. Please keep in mind that I am using "know" to refer to the knowing that involves knowing that one knows.

7. Included in John Hick, ed., *Classic and Contemporary Readings in the Philosophy of Religion,* 2nd ed. (Englewood Cliffs, NJ: Prentice-Hall, 1970), p. 291.

8. I do believe that a person with faith only would prefer that his or her faith be backed by evidence, but it should be noted that faith, because it is not built up on evidence, is superior to belief in the sense that it is not subject to disruption by the influx of new and negative evidence. Etienne Gilson, distinguished scholar in the tradition of St. Thomas Aquinas, in his book *The Elements of Christian Philosophy* (New York: Doubleday, 1960), p. 58, puts the point this way:

> Now, on the one hand, faith is a type of knowledge inferior to understanding; as a mode of knowing, merely to believe is not as good as to understand. On the other hand, if we consider these two ways of knowing from the point of view of their certitude, faith is incomparably more certain than understanding.

His use of terms is not identical with ours, but you should be able to make the proper substitutions with little trouble. Gilson claims also that what a person holds originally on the ground of faith, he or she might later come to believe or to know. Still, Gilson adds, mere intellectual belief in or knowledge of a doctrine lacks the warmth and personal depth of faith, so that faith in a doctrine remains important even once belief in it or knowledge of it has been achieved. See especially Chaps. 1, 2, and 3 of *Elements.*

9. I have been especially influenced in this regard by the writings of John Hick (see his *Arguments for the Existence of God* and *Faith and Knowledge,* 2nd ed. [Ithaca, NY: Cornell University Press, 1966], Parts I and III) and Karl Jaspers (see his *Way to Wisdom* [New Haven, CT: Yale University Press, 1954]).

10. See Hick's *Philosophy of Religion,* 2nd ed., pp. 90–95.

11. Russell's fowl philosophy can be found in Robert E. Egner and Lester E. Denonn, eds., *The Basic Writings of Bertrand Russell,* (New York: Simon & Schuster, 1967), pp. 150–51.

12. Contained in a letter from Robert Newman.

13. I Corinthians 13:12, King James Version.

14. John Henry Cardinal Newman, *Apologia Pro Vita Sua* (New York: Modern Library, 1950), p. 111.

15. Ibid., p. 230.

16. William James, American philosopher and psychologist, has a fascinating essay on this topic in which he distinguishes between (1) the person who fears being in error more than losing the truth and (2) the person who fears losing the truth more than being in error. The first person, consequently, is more conservative and the second more adventurous. The first is less frequently in error, but the second is more likely to come by the truth. The entire essay, "The Will to Believe," is worth your while. If you don't have time for the entire essay, go directly to Section VII. Reprinted in numerous places, James's essay can be found together with other interesting papers in *The Will to Believe and Other Essays on Popular Philosophy* (New York: Dover, 1956).

17. See his *Dynamics of Faith* (New York: Harper & Brothers, 1957), Chap. 6. For a much more comprehensive and difficult statement by Tillich, see his *The Courage to Be* (New Haven: Yale University Press, 1952).

18. *Early Latin Theology,* Vol. V: *The Library of Christian Classics,* trans. and ed. S. L. Greenslade (Philadelphia: The Westminster Press, 1956), p. 38.

19. Peirce's clear and interesting essay "The Fixation of Belief" can be found in *Philosophical Writings of Peirce* (New York: Dover, 1955).

20. Friedrich Nietzsche, *The Portable Nietzsche,* Walter Kaufmann, ed. (New York: Viking, 1968), p. 599.

21. Mohandas K. Gandhi, *An Autobiography: The Story of My Experiments with Truth* (Boston: Beacon Press, 1957), p. 504.

22. Wilfred Cantwell Smith, "Comparative Religion; Whither—and Why?" in Mircea Eliade and Joseph Kitagawa, eds., *The History of Religions* (Chicago: University of Chicago Press, 1959).

23. ———, *The Faith of Other Men* (New York: New American Library, 1963), p. 13.

24. For Paul's classic statement on love, see I Corinthians 13 (New Testament).

7

Commitment Without Absolutes

QUESTIONS TO THINK ABOUT

- How can the concept of the absolute retain meaning and importance for us if we are convinced that we cannot know what is absolute?
- What is agatheism? How is it related to agathism?
- What is the difference between closed commitment and open commitment?
- Why is it legitimate to say, "Buddha is unsurpassed" but not to say, "Buddha is unsurpassable"?
- What provides us with guidance for our lives in the absence of absolute knowledge of what is right and true and good?

An important problem relevant to our discussion in Chapter 6 is raised by Frederick Streng in *Understanding Religious Man.* He writes:

> The legacy of Western Enlightenment, freedom from absolute commitments, has provided the conditions for a situation often recognized today: a monotony of uncommitted lives.

The freedom attained by rejecting one value orientation does not necessarily mean freedom from the bondage of another value orientation that also turns out to be less than ultimate. To exchange one idol for another is not spiritual freedom. How one can avoid slipping into spiritual ignorance in the midst of one's highest spiritual efforts is a continuing religious problem.[1]

This statement occurs in the conclusion of Streng's book, so he pursues it no further. But it is an important problem, so I would like to pursue it—especially since in the last chapter I rejected the possibility of religious knowledge. The problem, as I shall address it, is as follows: If we do not, and cannot, have *knowledge* that our religious commitments are true, how can we justify being committed to anything at all? After all, if we have no knowledge of absolutes, then we have no way of judging with certainty whether one thing is really better than another; and if this is the case, then must not an enlightened person remain uncommitted to anything or be equally committed to all things? More specifically, how can *religious* commitment be possible for a person who shares the modern suspicion toward absolutes?

I agree that man's noetic situation is such that he can never know whether he is exchanging "one idol for another." We must reject the belief that we can know that something is religiously absolute. That does not mean that we must reject the concept of the absolute. We can still understand what it would mean for there to be absolute values and truths. Indeed, we can also understand that there might *be* absolute values and religious truths even if we cannot know for certain what they are. Our inability to *know* what is absolute means only that we must take a different attitude toward that which *impresses* us as being absolute and toward that which others *claim* to be absolute. Most obviously, we must not adopt an attitude of knowledge toward it. Yet *how,* you might ask, can the concept of the absolute retain any meaning for us after we foreswear all ability to determine what *is* absolute?

The concept of the absolute can be understood at least partially in terms of the concept of the unsurpassable. From the experience of some things being surpassable—one runner being surpassed by another in a race, one color being surpassed by another in brightness—we can construct the notion of there being something which not only *is not* surpassed but *cannot* be surpassed in some respect.[2] We have all, I suspect, had the experience of feeling one value surpass another in a specific situation—for example, while helping an acquaintance with a minor problem, we are apprised that our parents need emergency help. Hence, one value can surpass another in importance, and it is conceivable that some value is more important than all others. Similarly, we have all had the experience of replacing one proposition with another because we became convinced that whereas the replaced proposition was not completely false, neither was it as accurate or complete as its replacement. Hence, one proposition can be truer than another, and it is conceivable that there are propositions which are absolutely true—that is, to which no improvement in truth value can be made. Our problem, of course, is that even though we can understand in these terms what it means if a proposition is absolutely true or if a value is absolute, still we are never in a position to *verify* that a particular value or religious doctrine is absolute. The concept of the absolute remains meaningful and important in human thought, nonetheless, because it ever reminds us that there *may* be something better (truer or more valuable) than that to which we are presently committed.

AGATHISM & AGATHEISM

To be sure, we can and should resolve to commit ourselves to that which is absolutely good. This position that one ought to endeavor always with all of one's heart, soul, mind, and strength, with every fiber of one's being, to understand what is the highest good and to be devoted unconditionally to it, is what I call "agathism" (which is coined from the Greek word for "good"). Agathism is, however, a commitment to form, not substance. It is a resolution to commit ourselves absolutely to that which is absolutely good—whatever it is. But agathism does not tell us what in specific is supremely good.

Agatheism, does. "Agatheism" is a blend of "agathism" and "theism." It stands for the position that it is God and God alone (understood in the Near Eastern sense of a supremely perfect personal being) who is the absolute good and, therefore, that to which we ought to be devoted unconditionally. Hence, agatheism is a species of agathism; and Judaism, Christianity, Islam, and so forth are subspecies of agatheism. These subspecies constitute more specific positions on how God should be understood and how our devotion to God should be expressed. Within these subspecies there are sub-subspecies, such as the Orthodox, Conservative, and Reform versions of Judaism.

Note that agatheism implies that because we should have absolute confidence in nothing but God, therefore we should *not* have absolute confidence in our *understanding* of God. Why? Because our understanding of God is not God. It is God, and not our understanding of God, which is supremely good and therefore perfect. Consequently we should not treat our understanding of God as though it were sacred any more than a physicist should treat his or her *understanding* of what light is as though it were the same thing as *knowledge* of what light is. Scientists have been mistaken in important ways before and in one way or another probably always will be. The primary job of the physicist is to conform his or her thought to physical reality; of the religious person, to supremely perfect goodness. However, we are fallible and therefore capable of making mistakes in our understanding of the physical world and of God. Therefore we should not treat our religious convictions and interpretations as though they are infallible. To do so would be idolatry.

COMMITMENT AND OPENNESS

On the one hand, then, we are supposed to devote ourselves unconditionally to supreme goodness, whereas on the other hand, because we are fallible and are not God ourselves, we are not supposed to commit ourselves unconditionally to anything which seems to us to be supremely good. But if this is what is called for religiously, isn't it impossible? At first it seems to be, but I think there is a way to satisfy both of these seemingly contradictory obligations. We can commit ourselves unconditionally to *searching for* that which is supremely good, and we can commit ourselves wholeheartedly to whatever *at the present seems to us* to be supremely good.[3]

Our commitment to what seems to us to be supremely good should be *open* rather than *closed,* however. An open commitment involves a willingness and eagerness to consider indications and arguments either that there is something better than that to which we are devoted or that that to which we are devoted is not the supreme good. Such openness and eagerness shows the highest regard for goodness because it expresses the desire and intention to be committed wholeheartedly only to that which truly is the supremely perfect good.

You may be wondering, "But how can an open commitment be a wholehearted commitment? Mustn't it be somewhat halfhearted, as it recognizes that it might be wrong?" These are important questions. Getting the answers right is important for understanding the possibility of mature religiousness. Open religious commitment is not a wavering commitment or a partial commitment, and it is important that it be neither. There are some propositions, including religious propositions, the truth of which we will discover only if we devote ourselves to them wholeheartedly. Consider, for example, two people who marry but who, because they know the high failure rate of recent marriages, figure that their marriage probably won't last, so they maintain ties with "old flames" and avoid disagreements rather than venting them and trying to work them out constructively. When such a marriage fails, I don't think the individuals know whether it could have worked. They didn't devote themselves to one another and their marriage.

Similarly, consider someone who enters a diet-oriented program for depression. She is told at the beginning that the program has helped 80 percent of the people who have completed it. As the days go by she experiences increasing discomfort because she is required to eat foods she doesn't like and is not supposed to eat others she does like. She decides that since there is a 20 percent chance that the program will not help her, there is no sense in letting it make her miserable, so she cheats a little here and a little there—flushing some of what she's supposed to eat and sneaking some of what she isn't. When the program is over she reports no significant improvement and concludes that her depression is not responsive to diet therapy. But of course she doesn't know that. Even minor deviations from the program could have nullified a great benefit that she would have received with a bit more cooperation.

A small deviation can make a big difference. We can lower the temperature of water 100 degrees from 133 degrees to 33 degrees and it will remain liquid; just 1 more degree and it would have made a sudden, dramatic change from liquid to solid. In some cases, then, it is only by wholehearted commitment that we will discover whether the purported goodness of a thing is what it is claimed to be. Yet the point of devotion to what seems to be absolute good is not to find out whether it is; rather, the point is simply to honor it for what it seems to be. Fortunately for us, such devotion sometimes discloses that our object of devotion is not worthy of continued commitment.

By its very nature, then, an object of religious devotion calls for wholehearted commitment, so we should take every step we can to reassure ourselves that the object is worthy of such commitment on our part. To do otherwise would be irresponsible. We certainly shouldn't make such a commitment simply on the word of every missionary who reaches out to us, whether by phone, or mail, on the street, at our door, or at an airport.

Human life seems to call, then, for commitment *and* openness. It is in *refusal to admit* that there may be something better than what we have that we tend to become closed-minded, dogmatic, and socially exclusive, and run the risk of cutting ourselves off from the absolute good if it is different from what we think it is. However, it is in *refusal to commit* ourselves wholeheartedly that we fail the purpose of human life, which according to religion is to be rightly related to the supreme good.

Openness without commitment is pointless (since the point of openness is to find and become committed to the absolute good if that to which we are presently committed is not it), and commitment without openness is self-defeating (since we want to be committed to the best that there *is.* Moreover, we want to *believe* that that to which we are committed is the best but we cannot believe that in good conscience unless we are open to criticisms of it and alternatives to it. We must, then, walk a religious tightrope while aided by a balance bar weighted at one end by openness and at the other by commitment. We must be careful not to let the commitment end of the bar overwhelm the fact that there may be something better than that to which we are presently committed, and we must not let the openness end overwhelm the importance of being committed to the good as we presently understand it.

UNSURPASSED—PERHAPS NOT UNSURPASSABLE

I can imagine someone, a Buddhist let's say, responding at this point, "But I have compared Buddha to Moses and Jesus and Krishna, and he *is* the best!" This is a legitimate and important kind of response, but no matter how confident we are in our conclusion and no matter how rigorously we have made our comparisons, we cannot rule out the possibility that upon acquiring new insights into Krishna, for example, or a deeper understanding of Krishna, our convictions about Buddha and Krishna will become reversed. Such reversals have happened before and will happen again. (Recall Cardinal Newman's traumatic reversal of opinion regarding the Roman Catholic Church, discussed under Faith, Doubt, and Courage in Chapter 6.)

Another, more abstract reason for keeping our religious commitments open turns upon the difference between a finite number of things and an infinite number of things. Given a finite set of objects, x, y, and z, it is legitimate for a person to make the personal judgment "x is the best," meaning, "In my opinion, x is better than y or z." With an *infinite* set of objects, however, the best that a person can say is some form of "x is *better* than y or z." To claim to know that x is the best of an *infinite* set is always illegitimate because we can never examine all the members of an infinite set. Hence, we can compare x only to those members of the set we *have* examined. We can even endeavor to compare x to every extant religion, but given the number of existing religions, and given the fact that the smallest among them must be taken as seriously as the largest (each of the great religions began with only a few followers), this hardly seems like a task which could be completed in one lifetime. And even if by sheer dint of energy we did complete it and still judged x best, it would always be possible that a new religion would eventually appear which we would judge to be better than x.

Hence, if the set of possible objects of religious commitment is infinite, as it seems to be, then while it is perfectly legitimate for a person to say of the object of his or her religious devotion, "It is *unsurpassed* in my judgment," it would be illegitimate to say, "It is *unsurpassable*." The former can be known; the latter cannot—even if it is true. Further, the fact that a person cannot at the moment *imagine* anything eclipsing the object of his or her present religious devotion is not to be taken as evidence that this object of devotion cannot be surpassed. Rather, an inability in this respect is to be expected, for religious devotion in its purest sense is precisely devotion to that than which we neither know nor can imagine anything greater. But human knowledge and imagination can, of course, be expanded in ways and to an extent that one would have hitherto not believed possible. Indeed, that kind of radical expansion of "mind, heart, and soul" is what is involved in religious conversion.

Now let's return to the question raised in the opening paragraph of this chapter: If we do not know what is absolute, then we cannot judge varying degrees of approximation to the absolute; so how can we judge with confidence whether one thing is really better than another? To be sure, we cannot assay that x is better than y by comparing them both to the absolute and seeing which is closer, but we can assay which is better in terms of our own thought and life experience. This does not mean that our judgments about religious matters are always correct, but it does remind us that in the final analysis it is always the individual who must judge the worth of a religious doctrine or practice, and it is only by means of that individual's own reason, experience, and knowledge that he or she can make that judgment.

To be sure, we might defer to someone else's judgment on certain matters. We might trust Moses' account of how he came by the tablets of stone containing the Ten Commandments, or we might trust Jesus regarding whether there is life after death, but note that *we* must judge whether the other person's judgment is preferable to our own on such matters. Hence, there is no escaping our ultimate responsibility for the things that we believe and do, so it is important that we learn when to trust someone else's judgment and when not to. If we cannot be confident of ourselves in this regard, then we have no good reason to be confident of anyone else. Why? Because *we* must judge whether someone else is worthy of greater confidence than ourselves or others on a certain topic. Developing a sense of when to and when not to trust others then is of basic importance to religious maturation. Rational confidence in oneself must precede rational confidence in anyone or anything else.

To summarize, mature religious commitment involves (1) commitment to the best that we know now, (2) recognition that we cannot prove that there is nothing better, (3) and openness to the possible appearance of something better. Consequently, our *absolute* commitment should be not to anything specific—even though it be humanity, love, or Jesus. Rather, it should be to absolute goodness and therefore also to that kind of openness which will enable us to discover and recognize the absolute good—if it exists and when it appears to us, whether in thought, experience, or revelation. Absolute commitment of this kind is not dogmatic, for it is not a matter of absolute commitment to anything specific; hence, every specific commitment remains open to fundamental examination. Nor does this kind of absolute commitment lead necessarily to romanticism—that is, to following one's fancy of the moment, no matter how quickly it might change. Why not romanticism? Because *absolute commitment* to the supreme good should be accompanied by *disciplined defeasible commitment* to the high points of our lives. This second kind of commitment gives us a kind of depth against which superficiality cannot prevail, but without giving us the illusion that we know that the object of our commitment is unsurpassable.

We do not seem to have an absolute criterion regarding religious matters, so we have no right to claim that we know that some specific thing or person is absolutely best. However, we do have *personal* experiences of some things being *good* and of some things being *better* than others. It is by such personal experiences of good and better that we can find authority and direction for our lives. We must learn to cultivate our sensitivity and loyalty to such experiences without assuming that they must be regarded as absolute. Indeed, it seems to me that our situation is very much like that of Hesiod's "flying spiders." Miguel de Unamuno reports on this phenomenon in *The Agony of Christianity:*

> The name of "Threads of the Virgin" is applied to certain tiny threads that float in the wind and on which a certain kind of spiders—which Hesiod . . . calls flying spiders—take flight in the free breezes of the air and even in the midst of a violent storm. There are also such things as winged seeds, equipped with tufts. But these spiders spin those floating threads out of their own entrails, delicate webs by means of which they hurl themselves into space unknown. What an awesome symbol of faith![4]

And so it is, for we too must spin a web of religion from the entrails of our own experience and hurl ourselves upon it into space and time unknown, hoping that the web will sustain us through the storms and dance in the breezes, rarely aware of how precious a thing it really is.

Notes

1. Frederick Streng, *Understanding Religious Man* (Belmont, CA: Dickenson, 1969), p. 126.

2. St. Anselm, eleventh century A.D., argues in his *Monologium* and *Proslogion* that God should be understood as that being than which none greater can be conceived. This implies that by definition God is unsurpassable; *ergo* nothing can surpass or be greater than God. In the twentieth century, Charles Hartshorne has investigated and developed this conception of God most extensively. See his *Man's Vision of God* and *A Natural Theology for Our Time.* See also Alvin Plantinga's *God, Freedom, and Evil* and *The Nature of Necessity.*

3. I first encountered the idea of a "dual" commitment, that is, of two simultaneous commitments, one absolute and one tentative, in a lecture by Henry Nelson Wieman. He elaborates this idea in his *Man's Ultimate Commitment* (Carbondale, IL: Southern Illinois University Press, 1958), pp. 21, 167–69. I prefer "open" to

"tentative" because "a tentative commitment" suggests that the commitment is temporary or hesitant, whereas "open" does not. However, I prefer "absolute" to "closed" (the opposite of "open") because "a closed commitment" has negative connotations, as in "closed-minded." Perhaps "unconditional and conditional commitment" would be better than "absolute and open." A dual commitment would then involve *unconditional* commitment to searching for and being devoted to absolute goodness and *conditional* commitment to what we think is the absolute good and how we should relate to it. The latter commitment would be conditional only upon continuing to think that what we are devoted to is the absolute good and how we are related to it is fitting.

4. Miguel de Unamuno, *The Agony of Christianity* (New York: Frederick Ungar, 1960), pp. 76–77.

The Spiral
of Religious Growth

- What are four phases of the cycle of religious growth? Name and describe each.
- What are some of Rudolf Otto's main points about the nature of religious experience?
- What are some of Martin Buber's main points about the nature of religious faith?
- What are some of Carl Jung's main points about religion?
- What are some of Abraham Maslow's main points about religious experience?
- What distinction does Philip Phenix make between "the life of desire" and "the life of loyalty"?
- What does Abraham Heschel mean when he says that "*faith is faithfulness, loyalty to an event, loyalty to our response*"?
- What is the difference between the "way of Greece" and "the way of Israel"?

- What is worship? What is its function and structure in human life?
- Do people do only what they enjoy?
- Should we worship only when we feel like it?
- Should we worship together or alone?
- Why is religious growth a spiral and not just a cycle?
- What causes the cycle of religious growth to begin again?

So far, I have been doing a kind of structural analysis of religious commitment, looking from a static point of view at the way it is built and the parts that make it up. Now I would like to do a process analysis, that is, take a look at religious involvement as something that is moving, growing, developing. I see this process as cyclical in nature and passing through four fundamental phases. These phases can be described as follows: (1) the stage of pursuit, (2) the moment of revelation, (3) the moment of decision, and (4) the stage of action. Most adults have been through this cycle many times—though they may not have noticed its structure or how the successive phases contributed to their personal growth. To be human yet escape this cycle altogether seems most unlikely. Let's take a look at each of the four phases.

THE STAGE OF PURSUIT

The first stage of the religious cycle, the launching pad so to speak, is the stage of pursuit—the stage of the restless heart, of intense yearning that the void within might be filled, of profound anxiety at the prospect of ultimate meaninglessness. Something of the spirit of this moment is reflected in Psalm 42, in which the psalmist writes, "As a hart longs for flowing streams, so longs my soul for thee, O God. My soul thirsts for God, for the living God." Also, "Why are you cast down, O my soul, and why are you disquieted within me?"[1] Clearly, during this phase the present beliefs, practices, and experiences of such a person are felt as inadequate. Something *more* is desired—but what? Perhaps the most fundamental truth about religion is that it is the endeavor to provide that "something more" which brings a sense of closure to the meaning of our lives. Different religions bring about that sense in radically different ways, ranging from the very specific proposals of theistic religions (recall Augustine's statement, "Our hearts are restless 'till they find their rest in Thee") to the Zen Buddhist claim that our yearning is not an emptiness to be filled by reason or revelation, but a sickness to be cured. But all religions, as far as I can tell, major in helping us cope with our personal metaphysical uneasiness.[2]

THE MOMENT OF REVELATION

The moment of revelation is the moment at which there comes an answer to our question, a reply to our plea, a response to our groping, something that comes from we know not where and invades our consciousness. This is a necessary moment if religious concern is ever to pass over into religious faith, for the religious struggle is precisely with problems we feel unable to resolve by ourselves. As Carl Jung states, "Man is never helped in his suffering by what he thinks for himself, but only by revelations of wisdom greater than his own. It is this which lifts him out of his distress."[3] Such a revelation may be from a natural or a supernatural source; we are not concerned with that question here. But if the moment of revelation had never come at all—whatever its origin—religious faith would have never been born, for how can a person become religious if something of great value, indeed, of seemingly ultimate value, has not impressed itself upon him?

Yet, what is it that is revealed to us? What is the nature of revelation? What is the cause of religious experience? These are questions that have been answered in conflicting ways, even by persons who value religious experience highly. Consequently, what I would like to do now is to share with you some of the range of opinion of persons who all believe in the value of religious experience: Rudolf Otto, author of classic works in phenomenology of religion and mysticism; Martin Buber, Jewish existentialist philosopher, best known for his distinctions between I, Thou, and It; Carl Jung, founder of the analytic school of psychology, which emphasizes archetypes and the collective unconscious; and Abraham Maslow, who tried to make psychology more accessible and relevant to every person.

Rudolf Otto

I would like to introduce you to Rudolf Otto's analysis of religious experience. Otto was a German philosopher/theologian who lived from 1869 to 1937 and made many important contributions to the study of religious experience. He was a profound student of the world's religions and an energetic world traveler. Hence, his book *Mysticism: East and West* was not just a product of library research. His sensitivity and openness to all religions was a result of his belief that all religions are the result of different people's interactions with one divine reality. A long-standing dream came true when he succeeded in establishing in Germany an institute for the comparative study of the living faiths of the world. Otto's best known book, *The Idea of the Holy,* was published in 1923 and is still considered by many the finest analysis of religious experience ever written. It is to some of the main ideas of that book that we turn our attention now.

First, Otto claims that religious experience is a *distinctive* kind of experience which is not to be understood as some other kind of experience in disguise—such as an especially intense aesthetic experience, or a feeling of oneness with Nature, or an uplifting experience resulting from participation in a social cause.[4] Second, Otto claims that there is *no* religion in which religious experience does not live as its "real innermost core." Hence, religious experience is the lifeblood of religion, and a religion devoid of religious experience is no longer truly a religion, any more than a corpse is truly a person. Third, we can talk about religious experience, but we must do so obliquely and by means of metaphors. Why? Because our language is based on the categories of natural experience—categories such as color, shape, size, and location—but religious experience is not comparable to natural experience. The categories of natural sensory experience simply do not apply literally to the nature and content of religious experience. Thus, we should not expect our language to do a clear job of describing religious experience. Still, it's all we've got, so we must do with it the best that we can, realizing its limitations. Fourth, Otto claims that the religious experience is *of* something, or at least so it feels. It is an experience in which we feel that we are up against something, that something has encountered us. It is not as though we were daydreaming or imagining. Otto gives the name "numen" to this special something which we feel ourselves to be up against and he attributes to it the following five characteristics: (1) absolute unapproachability, (2) absolute overpoweringness, (3) energy or urgency, (4) wholly other, (5) fascinating, intoxicating. Let's take a look at each of these traits.

First, the numen has the characteristic of absolute unapproachability. It provokes within us a kind of dread, a *religious dread*. Otto insists that this kind of dread is not like natural fear, of a snake, say; nor is it like anxiety, for example, that your plane will be hijacked. It is another kind of thing altogether. "It first begins to stir," Otto writes, "in the feeling of 'something *uncanny*,' '*eerie*,' or '*weird*.'" This is an experience that tears us from our ordinary state of mind, shudders through us with an alarmingly disorienting effect, and leaves us convinced that there are dangerous powers and forces of which we are not aware in our everyday mode of consciousness. Otto goes on to say that "it is this feeling which, emerging in the mind of primeval man, forms the starting-point for the entire religious development in history."[5] This awe of the numen can cause a shudder which is well-depicted in Isaiah's experience, recorded in Chapter 6 of the book of Isaiah in the Bible. The language there is highly symbolic, but the character of Isaiah's emotion is conveyed quite effectively:

> In the year that King Uzziah died I saw the Lord sitting upon a throne, high and lifted up; and his train filled the temple. Above him stood the seraphim; each had six wings: with two he covered his face, and with two he covered his feet, and with two he flew. And one called to another and said: "Holy, holy, holy is the Lord of hosts; the whole earth is full of his glory." And the

foundations of the thresholds shook at the voice of him who called, and the house was filled with smoke. And I said: "Woe is me! For I am lost; for I am a man of unclean lips; for my eyes have seen the King, the Lord of hosts!"

The second characteristic encountered in the numen is might, power, indeed, "absolute overpoweringness." Again we can think of earthly examples of being overpowered, such as in a very uneven wrestling match, but the analogy must fail ultimately, for in our earthly experience we find that we are at least able to exert ourselves—no matter how ineffectively— against that which overpowers us. But in the religious experience we are pervaded with the feeling that we have been confronted by absolute power, to which we can offer no resistance whatsoever. "Thus," Otto writes, "in contrast to 'the overpowering' of which we are conscious as an object over against the self, there is the feeling of one's own submergence, of being but 'dust and ashes' and nothingness. And this forms the numinous raw material for the feeling of religious humility."[6] It gives rise also to a feeling of the "aweful majesty" of the divine.

Third, the object of religious experience is characterized by "urgency" or "energy." As the Bible puts it, the Lord God is a living God, an active, passionate, vital, forceful God who neither sleeps nor rests. Mystics report that their religious experiences reveal something "urgent, active, compelling, and alive."[7] Naturalists speak of nature as a pulsating, dynamic, flowing process; some naturalists attest that in mystical moments they apprehend the creative vitality and unity of nature. This picture of God as reacting, changing, and developing—whether God is thought of as transcending nature or being the same thing as nature—is taken literally by process theists, for example, A. N. Whitehead and Charles Hartshorne, and figuratively by classical theists, for example, Eleonore Stump and Norman Kretzmann, who think that because God is eternally perfect, He is also eternally unchanging. Otto's concern is not to resolve this important debate over how we should conceive of God, but, rather, to convey how God *seems* to be in the experience of mystics, so let's continue with his description.[8]

Otto writes, "We gave to the object to which the numinous consciousness is directed the name *'mysterium tremendum.'"* In his exposition of the meaning of this phrase he explains the *tremendum* aspect of the numinous object in terms of the three elements we have already explored: *awefulness, majesty,* and *energy.* The *mysterium* aspect of the numinous he explains in terms of the other two elements of the religious experience: its *"wholly otherness"* and its *aura of fascination.* Let's take a brief look at these fourth and fifth elements.

Fourth, Otto is quick to point out that the "mysteriousness" of the numinosum is not like the "ordinary" mysteries of life—the latter being things that puzzle us but that are capable of being explained. Rather, what we are up against in religious experience is something *wholly other* than anything we have ever experienced in the realms of nature and society. It is "that which is quite beyond the sphere of the usual, the intelligible, and the familiar, which therefore falls quite outside the limits of the 'canny,' and is contrasted with it, filling the mind with blank wonder and astonishment."[9]

But the profundity of the mystery of the numinosum goes even deeper than this, for the feeling we get is that it is "*beyond* our apprehension and comprehension, not only because our knowledge has certain irremovable limits, but because in it we come upon something inherently 'wholly other,' whose kind and character are incommensurable with our own, and before which we therefore recoil in a wonder that strikes us chill and numb."[10] Mystics in all ages and all cultures have been aware of this wholly other quality of the object of religious experience. Consequently, they have combined philosophy and humor to say that the numinosum is "nothing." What is God? Nothing. What are you praying to, meditating upon, seeking unity with? Nothing. There is a kind of honesty in this answer which there can be in no other because that which is being prayed to or contemplated or merged with cannot be described literally by any word or combination of words in any language. Moreover, it isn't anything we can point to—so we say with a bit of a smile, "It is nothing."

At the same time, mysticism affirms "the *positive quality* of the 'wholly other' as a very living factor in its overbrimming religious emotion."[11] The numinosum is not just an idea. Nor is it like an unsighted planet whose existence is known only through intellectual calculations. Rather, it has a direct and deeply felt personal impact. "It is through this positive feeling-content that the concepts of the 'transcendent' and 'supernatural' become forthwith designations for a unique 'wholly other' reality and quality, something of whose special character we can *feel*, without being able to give it clear conceptual expression."[12] To illustrate this, let me tell a story about a Hindu father who was asked by his child, "What is God?" The father's now famous response was, "Neti, neti," meaning, "Neither this nor that." That is, the father pointed to something, perhaps a chair, and said, "God is not that." Then he pointed to something else, perhaps a dog, and said, "That is not God." On and on he went from one thing to another, saying "neither this nor that is God," until finally the child got the point: God cannot be identified with any thing in this world or with the world itself. Hence, in terms of the things of this world, revealed to us by our senses, God is nothing; yet, the fact that God is nothing in terms of the things of this world does not mean that God is nothing at all. Indeed, the idea that God is wholly other than anything in this world and yet is something very real is precisely part of the conviction which one carries away from religious experience.[13]

The fifth and final element which Otto analyzes out of the religious experience is that of *fascination*. The mystery of the numen is not simply something to be wondered at; it is something that entrances us, that captivates and transports us "with a strange ravishment, rising often enough to the pitch of dizzy intoxication."[14] Otto acknowledges that there are similarities between this aspect of religious experience and certain aspects of ordinary experience. Love, mercy, pity, comfort, are all experienced in ordinary life and can also be present in religious experience, though in the latter they are experienced in their perfection. Likewise, experiencing the wrath or rage of God is not totally unlike the small child's experience of the wrath of a parent. Still, the content of religious experience, according to those who have undergone it, can in no way be reduced to these natural experiences taken to a higher level of intensity.

> Bliss or beatitude is more, far more, than the mere natural feeling of being comforted, of reliance, of the joy of love, however these may be heightened and enhanced. Just as "wrath," taken in a purely rational or a purely ethical sense, does not exhaust that profound element of *awefulness* which is locked in the mystery of deity, so neither does "graciousness" exhaust the profound element of *wonderfulness* and rapture which lies in the mysterious beatific experience of deity.[15]

By virtue of its fascinating quality, the numinous becomes the object of personal search, desire, and yearning. In fact, once the numen has been experienced, "possession of and by the numen becomes an end in itself; it begins to be sought for its own sake; and the wildest and most artificial methods of asceticism are put into practice to attain it." Otto continues,

> Here, too, commences the process of development by which the experience is matured and purified, till finally it reaches its consummation in the sublimest and purest states of the "life within the Spirit" and in the noblest mysticism. Widely various as these states are in themselves, yet they have this element in common, that in them the mysterium is experienced in its essential, positive, and specific character, as something that bestows upon man a beatitude beyond compare . . . one whose real nature he can neither proclaim in speech nor conceive in thought, but may know only by a direct and living experience.[16]

Otto goes on to claim that in religious experience is revealed

> an *ideal good* known only to religion and in its nature fundamentally nonrational [that is, unable to be apprehended in terms of the categories of nature], which the mind knows of in yearning and presentiment, recognizing it for what it is behind the obscure and inadequate symbols which are its only expression. And this shows that above and beyond our rational [self] lies hidden *the ultimate and highest part of our nature,* which can find no satisfaction in the mere allaying of the needs of our sensuous, psychical, or intellectual impulses and cravings.[17]

By now you may have noted that in our survey of Otto we have gone from the negative to the positive pole of religious experience. Otto started out with the element of *religious dread* and has ended up with the element of *religious fascination*. It is precisely the contrast of these two elements that provides the profound tension of religious experience—at once a feeling of dread and of rapture, of repulsion and attraction. These two contrary feelings combine in "a strange harmony of contrasts" to which mystics across the centuries have testified. Interestingly enough, if theists are correct that the *cause* of religious experience is a supreme personal being, then we *should expect* the religious experience to be "a strange harmony of contrasts"—since it would be, at one and the same time, an experience of a reality which is infinitely more powerful and frightening than any natural force and infinitely more fascinating than its most captivating creation.

Martin Buber

Martin Buber, a Jewish philosopher/theologian of the twentieth century, spent much of his life elucidating what he called "the I-Thou relationship" and distinguishing it from the "I-It" relationship. Buber was convinced that for human beings there are two basic modes of relating to something. You can relate to it as an It—that is, as a thing, a passive object—or you can relate to it in a manner of mutuality, as a Thou. Buber illustrates the difference between the two types of relationship (and also illustrates that we can relate to the same object as an It or as a Thou) by asking us to consider "the child that silently speaks to his mother through nothing other than looking into her eyes and the child that looks at something on the mother as at any other object. . . ."[18] To make the illustration a bit more pointed, consider the difference between the child looking at the mother's eyes to see what color they are and the child looking into the mother's eyes in wonder and affection. In the former act the eyes may be no more than an object of curiosity; in the latter act they are a passageway through which something is expressed and from which a response is sought.

The question with which we are primarily concerned is whether a conscious relation with God is an I-It relationship or an I-Thou relationship. Blaise Pascal, a seventeenth-century, many-sided genius, pointed out that for many philosophers God is a concept, an It, not a person, a Thou.[19] A good twentieth-century example of such a philosopher is John Dewey. In his book *A Common Faith,* Dewey states that to him the word "God" means "the unity of all ideal ends arousing us to desire and actions."[20] That is, for Dewey the word "God" refers to that idealized vision of the world which is so attractive that it causes us to act in order to actualize it. Clearly, such a God is an idea and not a person. Another impersonal conception of God was set forth in the nineteenth century by Ludwig Feuerbach. The word "God," according to Feuerbach, refers to an idealized conception of Man. This ideal conception is built up in our imagination by means of projecting onto an imaginary person whatever virtues and powers we believe would constitute human perfection. This process occurs unwittingly, of course. The believer does not realize the source of this particular idea of God. Rather, the believer operates under the illusion of relating to a divine person, only he or she isn't doing so. Once one becomes aware of the origin of the God idea, one need not reject the God idea itself, since it represents one's highest conception of man, but one can no longer presume to relate to God as to a person.

These explanations by Dewey and by Feuerbach are explanations of what is happening in religious experience. In the one case, we are being aroused by a utopian vision; in the other, we are being ennobled by an image of the powers and capacities of Man. But we must ask whether these explanations are any more adequate than theistic explanations which explain religious experience in terms of the presence of a divine person. Can all cases of religious experience be accounted for in terms of impersonalistic explanations such as those of Dewey and Feuerbach? Experiences called "religious" are quite diverse, of course, but impersonalistic explanations, Buber argues, cannot account satisfactorily for the kinds of religious experience that are paradigmatic in the biblical tradition—namely, those religious experiences in which we feel ourselves to be up against a very real though nonsensory person. We don't account for I-Thou encounters with another human being in terms of purely impersonalistic explanations—though we could. Much less, then, should we account for a *religious* I-Thou experience in impersonalistic terms, since the I-Thou experience finds its purest, most powerful expression precisely in religious experience. In Buber's own words, "I-Thou finds its highest intensity and transfiguration in religious reality, in which unlimited Being becomes, as absolute person, my partner."[21]

The Thou of religious experience is, according to Buber, the living God who approaches us and addresses us as individuals in our own concrete circumstances. Hence, religious experience in the biblical sense is an encounter in which we are convinced that we are over against someone who is real and living, and not simply a concept which is a synthesis of ideals. You might well be thinking, "But how do you know a divine person is really there and that you are not deluded?" Buber would agree that there is no way to *prove* that you are not deceived—but that is true with regard to *every* experience! How can you prove you are not dreaming now? Perhaps Pascal is right that "life is a dream a little less inconstant"?[22] When you talk to a person, how can you prove that behind that person's skin there is listening, caring, feeling, imagining? Isn't it true that when you talk to a person you do not mean to be talking to his body and nothing more? When you look lovingly into someone's eyes and tell her your appreciation for something she has done, isn't it true that you are not looking *at* her eyes and speaking *to* her ears but are communicating to what, somehow, lies "at the end" of those sense organs? And the fact that you have never "seen" that person's "mind," so as to be sure that she isn't a mindless, emotionless robot, doesn't stop you from entering into an I-Thou relationship with her. You trust your intuition that you are in the presence of a human person, and not merely of a human body; so why not trust your intuition, when it occurs, that you are in the presence of a divine person?[23]

To trust your feeling that you *have* encountered the living God does not, according to Buber, mean that you should be able to *speak* about God. Recall for a moment the limitations of ordinary language which we noted in the section on Otto. Buber claims that our lack of a language with which to describe God literally is no problem at all. "It is not necessary to know something about God," he writes, "in order really to believe in Him: many true believers know how to talk *to* God but not *about* Him. If one dares to turn toward the unknown God, to go to meet Him, to call to Him, Reality is present."[24] To be sure, there is a kind of knowledge acquired from encounter with God, but it is not the kind of knowledge which can be externalized for public investigation or set forth in the categories of ordinary language. Public knowledge is the kind we acquire from I-It relationships. God we never encounter as an It. Hence, those people are mistaken who believe that we should be able to externalize the knowledge acquired from religious experience and open it up to public inquiry. To quote Buber's difficult but exquisite language, "Philosophy errs in . . . regarding the essence of religion as the knowledge of an object which is indifferent to being known."[25] Buber has in mind here such philosophers as Aristotle and Epicurus, ancient Greeks who believed that God is real but, in His perfect state of bliss, oblivious to the affairs of the earth and the attentions of human beings. Indeed, Epicurus argued, should God choose to become involved with the human species, He would quickly lose His perfect peace of mind—and for the thanks He would get, we can be sure He won't do that! This conception of God contrasts sharply, of course, with the biblical conception that Buber affirms. The Living God, the God of Abraham, Isaac, and Jacob, is never indifferent to the attentions of human beings. And insofar as the Bible speaks of "knowledge of God," it does not portray it as the abstract, intellectual relation

> of a thinking subject to a neutral object of thought, but rather as *mutual contact,* as the *genuinely reciprocal meeting* in the fullness of life between one active existence and another. Similarly, religion understands *faith* as the entrance into this reciprocity, as binding oneself in relationship with an undemonstrable and unprovable, yet even so, in relationship, knowable Being, from whom all meaning comes.[26]

Clearly, Buber is using the word "know" in a different sense than we used it in Chapter 6. He is using it in the sense in which we say that we "know" or are "getting to know" a person. Entry into such a relationship of give and take requires faith that the other is really a person, a subject with depth, as well as an object with surfaces. God and God alone is *pure* subject, presenting no aspects that can be studied without His awareness and regard.

Because the living God is absolute subject and never mere object, the Second Commandment warns against making images of God. An image or a symbol is an "it," something impersonal, and it will likely seduce us into relating primarily to it rather than to God, the symbol thereby becoming an idol. To be sure, idols are much more comfortable to relate to than the divine person, who stands over us in judgment as well as by us in love, but idols eventually prove disillusioning or tragic. The only appropriate relationship, indeed, the only *possible* relationship to the Absolute is a direct I-Thou relationship, for the Absolute is in no way nor at any time indifferent to our approach. I may be unaware that someone is paying attention to me. God is never unaware of attention paid to Him. I may not *care* that someone is paying attention to me. God, according to Buber, always cares.

You might ask at this point, "But what about the notorious silence of God in the hearts of modern persons?" Indeed, isn't Jean-Paul Sartre's rejection of God based in part on the silence of God? The answer here is yes. Sartre, the most famous atheist existentialist of our century, reportedly once stepped from a train and announced to the waiting press corps, "Gentlemen, God is dead!" It is absurd, Sartre argues, for people to persevere in their theism in the face of divine silence. "God is dead!" That is, there never was a real God, and now even the *idea* of God is defunct! We must acknowledge this, gird ourselves with courage, and follow out the consequences of living in a Godless universe.[27]

Buber, to the contrary, sees no reason to conclude that God's silence implies God's death. The biblical tradition reports periods of divine silence at least as far back as the time of Isaiah (sixth century B.C.), and most Judeo-Christian thinkers have had something to say about God's *hiddenness* as well as His *presence.* To illustrate his point, Buber points out that an eclipse is something which takes place *between the sun and our eyes.*[28] It is not something which takes place *in* the sun; it does not mean that the sun is dead. Likewise, with regard to the silence of God, "It would be worthier," Buber writes, perhaps with Sartre in mind, "not to explain it to oneself in sensational and incompetent sayings, such as that of the 'death' of God, but to endure it as it is and at the same time to move existentially toward a new happening, toward that event in which the word between heaven and earth will again be heard."[29] Meanwhile, the perseverance of the religious need in people's lives does not reveal in these people an insecure refusal to face the truth, as Sartre claims it does. Nor does such a longing contradict the meaning of the silence of God. Rather, it reveals the confidence and trust of those who have known God and are willing to wait for the return of His felt presence. And while we are waiting in patient trust, Buber proposes, we should reflect upon God's silence and ask, "Why has it happened? What does it mean?"

A final word from Buber. He claims that genuine encounter with the Eternal Thou confirms the biblical teaching that all religious life begins with "the fear of God." It begins, he writes, "when our existence between birth and death becomes incomprehensible and uncanny, when all security is shattered through the mystery."[30] Then he issues this warning:

> He who begins with the love of God without having previously experienced the fear of God, loves an idol which he himself has made, a god whom it is easy enough to love. He does not love the real God who is, to begin with, dreadful and incomprehensible. Consequently, if he then perceives . . . that God is dreadful and incomprehensible, he is terrified. He despairs of God and the world if God does not take pity on him . . . and bring him to love Him Himself.[31]

Presumably this means something like what Alfred North Whitehead meant in *Religion in the Making* (see notes for Chapter 4) when he said that religious maturation consists of moving from "God the void" (when God is a matter of indifference to us), to "God the enemy" (when God is a source of torment to us), to "God the companion" (when God is a blessing to us). Interestingly, perhaps significantly, all three persons, Otto, Buber, and Whitehead, claim that when religious consciousness follows its full course, it begins in a negative mode but ends in a positive one.

Carl Jung

Whereas Otto and Buber are theists in a traditional sense, our next object of study, Carl Jung, is not. Yet neither is he an atheist. He falls somewhere between these two extremes in spite of the fact that he was a long-time student and associate of Sigmund Freud, one of the twentieth century's most trenchant critics of religion. Jung developed a profound sensitivity to and appreciation for religion and its importance in human life. In fact, after thirty-two years of research and practice as a psychiatrist, he made the statement we mentioned in Chapter 2:

> Among all my patients in the second half of life—that is to say over thirty-five—there has not been one whose problem in the last resort was not that of finding a religious outlook on life. It is safe to say that every one of them fell ill because he had lost that which the living religions of every age have given to their followers, and none of them has been really healed who did not regain his religious outlook.[32]

Jung is quick to add that regaining a religious outlook does not depend on adopting some particular creed or joining a particular religious organization. Nor does he mean that one must gain back the same religious outlook one had as a child. What he does mean is very complicated. It is founded on his conception of the unconscious, and we cannot take the time to examine that concept here.[33] I would like, however, to focus briefly on some of his insights into the second phase of the religious cycle—that is, religious experience. These ideas can all be found in his *Psychology and Religion.*

In that book Jung writes that by the word "religion" he means "a careful and scrupulous observation" of that which Rudolf Otto meant by the word "numinosum." More fully, religion is

> a careful consideration and observation of certain dynamic factors, under-stood to be "powers," spirits, demons, gods, laws, he had found in his world powerful, dangerous or helpful enough to be taken into careful consideration, or grand, beautiful and meaningful enough to be devoutly adored and loved.[34]

Briefly, religion in its positive mode is the zealous cultivation and enjoy-ment of that which is most precious to us. In its negative mode it consists of the fearful attention and concessions paid to that by which we are most alarmed.

In either case, negative or positive, it is important to notice that the numinosum is something which happens *to* us. It comes to us. It is not and cannot be caused by an act of will on our part. Rather,

> it seizes and controls the human subject, which is always rather its victim than its creator. The numinosum is an involuntary condition of the subject, whatever its cause may be. At all events, religious teaching as well as [the opinions of people] always and everywhere explains this condition as being due to a cause external to the individual. The numinosum is either a quality of a visible object or the influence of an invisible presence causing a peculiar alteration of consciousness.[35]

In fact, Jung adds, the word "religion" might be used to designate "the attitude peculiar to a consciousness which has been altered by the experi-ence of the numinosum."[36] Such an experience in its positive mode elicits from us loyalty, trust, confidence, and devotion to that which we believe to have brought about our new state of mind.

Jung is quick to point out a profound difference between *religious sentimentality* and the *numinosum of religious experience.* The latter is a powerful, transforming force that lifts us out of the world only to plunge us back into it, giving us a new way of seeing and feeling things and a new set of marching orders. The former, by contrast, is a melancholy state of mind; it is wistful pleasure found in childhood reminiscences; it is a mild but passive yearning for a better state of world affairs. Moreover, sentimentality is "the well-known characteristic of a religion that has lost the living mystery."[37] I would add that it is tragic when an outsider (or an insider!) mistakes sentimentality for the root of religion—since then that person will never understand the great religions which have rocked the world and of which the sentimental religions are only faded variations. It is tragic also when someone who has lost contact with the numinous rests content thenceforth with religious sentimentality, for such a religion will be a weak and lukewarm cup of tea when what is needed is hot and nourishing broth.

If we turn our attention now to the *value* of religious experience, we find Jung once again in agreement with Rudolf Otto, who, you will recall, talks about the unique value of religious experience. Jung claims that to those who have it, religious experience is not just one more valuable kind of experience. Rather, "if it means anything, it means everything to those who have it." And surely if we want to know the value of religious experience, we should ask what it means to those who know it firsthand, treasure, and believe in it. Jung goes on to say, in character with our earlier analysis, "One could even define religious experience as that kind of experience which is characterized by the highest appreciation, no matter what its contents are."[38]

Later he states that religion is one's relationship to the highest or strongest value in one's experience, whether that value be positive or negative, whether it enchants or frightens. Then he makes a point that goes right to the heart of the second phase of the religious cycle. Still speaking about religion as one's relationship to the highest or strongest value in one's experience, he points out that the relationship can be "voluntary as well as involuntary." The "as well as" indicates that the relationship is involuntary to start with, and so it is, for our deity is always that psychological factor by which we are overwhelmed. However, we can be innocently unaware of what it is, or we can try to convince ourselves and others that it isn't what it is, or we can acknowledge what it is and self-consciously affirm it. In Jung's words, "you can accept, consciously, the value by which you are possessed unconsciously." You can allow it to surface fully in your consciousness, to reveal itself, and be acknowledged.

Jung goes on to say that whenever a god "ceases to be an overwhelming factor, he becomes a mere name. His essence is dead and his power is gone."[39] Any further devotion to such a god must be a matter of self-delusion, hypocrisy, sentimentality, or mindless routine. But surely you should not accept religious sentimentality in place of numinous experience, and you should not force yourself to remain committed to a god that no longer empowers you.[40]

Jung concludes *Psychology and Religion* by defending from skeptics the legitimacy and importance of religious experience. He writes:

> Religious experience is absolute. It is indisputable. You can only say that you have never had such an experience, and your opponent will say: "Sorry, I have." And there your discussion will come to an end. No matter what the world thinks about religious experience, the one who has it possesses the great treasure of a thing that has provided him with a source of life, meaning and

beauty and that has given a new splendor to the world and to mankind. He has pistis [faith] and peace. Where is the criterion by which you could say that such a life is not legitimate, that such experience is not valid and that such pistis is mere illusion? Is there, as a matter of fact, any better truth about ultimate things than the one that helps you to live? Nobody can know what the ultimate things are. We must, therefore, take them as we experience them. And if such experience helps to make your life healthier, more beautiful, more complete and more satisfactory to yourself and to those you love, you may safely say: "This was the grace of God."[41]

These, then, are some of Carl Jung's ideas on religion, and I would like to emphasize two of them, in closing. First, religion is not man-made—at least not in the sense that chairs and maps are. A religion is not something that can be created on the drawing board, so to say. It is not the product of the conscious ego. At the very least it is the product of the unconscious ego—and it may be much more. It wells up from deep within us—we know not whence or how. Hence, Jung's position is an implicit criticism of those people who want to construct a "rational religion" founded on human reason. Such a religion would be at best like boiled water—clear but flat. The second point is that religious experience is not merely an intensely pleasurable emotion. It has a transforming impact on the individual. We will turn to a study of that impact and our reaction to it after we look at one final interpretation of religious experience.

Abraham Maslow

So far we have studied analyses of religious experience by two theists, Otto and Buber, and a third person very sympathetic to theism but not clearly a theist himself, Jung. Now we turn our attention to a man who clearly rejects theism, yet seeks at the same time to exalt the values of religious experience. I speak of Abraham Maslow, founder of the "third movement" in psychology, that is, humanistic psychology as distinguished from Freudian psychology and behaviorist psychology. The quotations that follow come from Maslow's book *Religions, Values, and Peak-Experiences.*

According to Maslow the goal of humanistic psychology is twofold. It is to help each person become as *fully human* as possible, showing regard for the values of justice and compassion; and as *fully self-realized* as possible, searching out and actualizing his or her unique, individual potential. "In a word, it should help him to become the best he is capable of becoming, to become *actually* what he deeply is *potentially.*"[42] The person who is solidly on the path to this goal is, in Maslow's terminology, a "self-actualizing individual." Unfortunately, there are many factors in our time working against self-actualization; the worst of these factors is *valuelessness.*[43] All the traditional systems of value in the West have been founded on theism and have claimed to be objectively authoritative because of the will of God. Yet history testifies, according to Maslow, that theistic value systems have failed. Unfortunately, he laments, many people who agree about the practical failures of theistic value systems and the increasing difficulty of believing in the biblical God have concluded, under the influence of Western tradition about objective values, that construction of an objective value system is now impossible. Hence, along with the existence of God, they believe they have thrown out the possibility of an objective value system. But they haven't. Indeed, by throwing out the theistic God idea they have, perhaps without realizing it, created the social climate necessary for the construction of a truly objective, *human* system of values.

Our problem is to *construct* this new system, and we will be able to do that only if we do not fall victim again to the idea that values must be grounded on a concept of God. A system of values, Maslow argues, is too precious and urgent a thing to tie to so dubious a hypothesis as that of the existence of God. Our values must be grounded in Nature, for Nature is a *fact* rather than a hypothesis; it permits observation and control rather than requiring prayer and faith. Hence, what we need to do is to construct a set of values that is *confirmed by experience* and *useful in action.* Such values "we can believe in and devote ourselves to because they are *true* rather than because we are exhorted to 'believe and have faith.'"[my italics][44]

As a result of these convictions, Maslow spends time criticizing both conservative theists and liberal religionists. The *conservative* theists he criticizes for foisting on the world the belief that values must be grounded in or by God, or otherwise lose all authority. He argues that values are a *human* phenomenon which can be investigated, clarified, and justified without reference beyond the realm of nature.

Religious liberals are criticized for thinking that in throwing out theism, they also had to throw out the emotions of religious experience such as awe, reverence, humility, and adoration. They didn't have to do that, yet they did. The result?

> A rather bleak, boring, unexciting, unemotional, cool philosophy of life which fails to do what the traditional religions have tried to do when they were at their best, to inspire, to awe, to comfort, to fulfill, to guide in the value choices, and to discriminate between higher and lower, better and worse, not to mention to produce Dionysiac experiences, wildness, rejoicing, impulsiveness.[45]

To be sure, a religion, any religion, should be "[1] intellectually credible and [2] morally worthy of respect, but it must also be [3] emotionally satisfying (and I include here," Maslow writes, "the transcendent emotions as well)."[46] Inasmuch as liberal religions neglect these emotions (which we will be examining shortly, it is no surprise that they "exert so little influence even though their members are the most intelligent and most capable section of the population. It *must* be so," Maslow emphasizes, "just as long as they base themselves upon a lopsided picture of human nature which omits most of what human beings value, enjoy, and cherish in themselves, in fact, which they live for, and which they refuse to be done out of."[47]

If liberal churches *want* to exercise a broad and profound influence on individuals and their societies, then they must reclaim the values of religious experience for contemporary people and show that these values can be had without belief in God! This is an especially urgent task today, "because of the widespread 'valuelessness' in our society, that is, people have nothing to admire, to sacrifice themselves for, to surrender to, to die for."[48] Why are they in this state? Because they have unfortunately and unnecessarily allowed themselves to be deprived of those emotions out of which our most basic values are formed—namely, the emotions of religious experience. To be sure, according to Maslow religious liberals did us a great service in leading the way from theism to atheism, but they did us a great disservice in thinking that they also had to abjure religious experience. As a consequence, we have been plunged into an era of meaninglessness, for it is in and from religious experiences that we derive our values! Without such experience we are sailors adrift on a starless night, with nothing to guide ourselves by. Fortunately, we needn't remain in this vacuum of values, for "When we are well and healthy and adequately fulfilling the concept 'human being,' then experiences of transcendence should in principle be commonplace."[49]

The experience of transcendence, Maslow contends, is the dynamic source of all the great religions. "The very beginning, the intrinsic core, the essence, the universal nucleus of every known high religion," he writes,

> . . . has been the private, lonely, personal illumination, revelation, or ecstasy of some acutely sensitive prophet or seer. The high religions call themselves revealed religions and each of them tends to rest its validity, its function, and its right to exist on the codification and the communication of this original mystic experience of revelation from the lonely prophet to the mass of human beings in general.[50]

This original revelation or mystical experience, which is transmitted from the solitary prophet to the masses, need not be interpreted in supernaturalistic terms. Rather, it "can be subsumed under the head of the 'peak-experiences' or 'ecstasies' or 'transcendent' experiences which are now eagerly investigated by many psychologists."[51] To be sure, on account of the prescientific world views of the cultures within which the classic "revelations" took place, it was natural and inevitable that they were interpreted as gifts from the supernatural. Today we can see that those experiences were perfectly natural human experiences, the causes of which can be examined scientifically. Hence, peak-experience, the core and dynamic source of religion, is an appropriate object of scientific examination and not something that lies beyond the realm of science. We shall return to this point after a fuller look at Maslow's description of peak-experience.

It might become tedious to tell you here all that Maslow has said about peak-experience (a term which he prefers to "religious experience" since it is broader and doesn't carry the theistic connotations which "religious experience" does), but it is important to mention some of the basic characteristics that will help you understand how peak-experience can be the source both of religion and of our norms and values. In the first place, Maslow claims that everything Rudolf Otto defined as characteristic of religious experience can be enjoyed by the atheist as well as the theist:

> the holy; the sacred; creature feeling; humility; gratitude and oblation; thanksgiving; awe before the *mysterium tremendum;* the sense of the divine, the ineffable; the sense of littleness before mystery; the quality of exaltedness and sublimity; the awareness of limits and even of powerlessness; the impulse to surrender and to kneel; a sense of the eternal and of fusion with the whole of the universe; even the experience of heaven and hell.[52]

Next he claims that "in the peak-experience there is a very characteristic disorientation in time and space, or even the lack of consciousness of time and space. Phrased positively," he writes, "this is like experiencing universality and eternity."[53] Clearly, this kind of experience is radically different from ordinary experience. "The person in the peak-experiences may feel a day passing as if it were minutes or also a minute so intensely lived that it might feel like a day or a year or an eternity even. He may also lose his consciousness of being located in a particular place."[54]

In addition to being filled with the traditional emotions of religious experience and being characterized by disorientation in space and time, peak-experience is, third, a type of experience in which

> the dichotomies, polarities, and conflicts of life tend to be transcended or resolved. That is to say, there tends to be a moving toward the perception of unity and integration in the world. The person himself tends to move toward fusion, integration, and unity and away from splitting, conflicts, and oppositions.[55]

Moreover, and fourth, "In the peak-experiences, there tends to be a loss, even though transient, of fear, anxiety, inhibition, of defense and control, of perplexity, confusion, conflict, of delay and restraint. The profound fear of disintegration, of insanity, of death, all tend to disappear for the moment."[56] Consequently, peak-experiences frequently have a therapeutic effect and can have a profound and enduring transforming effect which amounts to a conversion.

Regarding the formation of our values, Maslow points out that we learn in the peak-experience that "joy, ecstasy, and rapture do in fact exist and that they are in principle available for the experiencer, even if they never have been before. Thus the peaker [the person who has a peak-experience] learns surely and certainly that life *can* be worthwhile, that it *can* be beautiful and valuable." He or she learns that there are things in life "which are so precious in themselves as to prove that not everything is a means to some end other than itself."[57] Some things are ends in themselves. Hence, the peak-experience does not stand in need of justification by means of something beyond itself. Why? Because it is "felt as a self-validating, self-justifying moment which carries its own intrinsic value with it. It is felt to be a highly valuable—even uniquely valuable—experience, so great an experience sometimes that even to attempt to justify it takes away from its dignity and worth."[58] Further, peak-experiences not only enrich life; in some instances they are responsible for its continuation. How so? By showing potential suicides that there *are* things worth living for—namely, peak-experiences themselves. Hence, once experienced, they refute the proposition that life is meaningless. They give the peaker something good to remember, to look forward to, and to enjoy.

The good news, according to Maslow, is that peak-experiences are available to *everyone*—and not to just a few mystics. Moreover, by means of scientific investigation, we can determine the type of people to whom such experiences come most frequently, the circumstances under which these experiences are most likely to occur, and how they might best be blended into our lives as a whole. This knowledge can then be generalized—by means of education and counseling—from those few people who are *natural* "peakers" to anyone who is interested in increasing the peak-experiences in his or her own life or the life of someone he or she cares about. Hence, our individual ability to cause peak-experiences whenever we desire will come increasingly under our control if we investigate them scientifically and develop the requisite conditions and discipline. Eventually, then, we might, whenever we desire, have all the blessings of religious experience without any of the problems caused by questionable creeds and dogmas.

Having spent so much time on peak-experience, a brief word is in order about the *nadir-experience* and the *plateau-experience*. The nadir-experience is simply the opposite of the peak-experience. It is as intense, but it is an experience of disharmony, of fragmentation, of desolation and emptiness. The plateau-experience, by contrast, is a positive rather than negative state of mind, but it lacks the intensity of either the peak-experience or the nadir-experience. It is "serene and calm, rather than a poignantly emotional, climactic" response to the awesome or miraculous.[59] Rather than being experienced as an explosion, it is "more often experienced as pure enjoyment and happiness, as, let's say, in a mother sitting quietly looking, by the hour, at her baby playing, and marveling, wondering, philosophizing, not quite believing. She can experience this as a very pleasant, continuing, contemplative experience rather than as something akin to a climactic explosion which then ends."[60] Happily, plateau-experiences are far easier to bring about by personal volition than are peak-experiences. "One can learn to see in this Unitive way almost at will. It then becomes a witnessing, an appreciating, what one might call a serene, cognitive blissfulness which can . . . have a quality of casualness and of lounging about."[61] Moreover, by means of thought, effort, and perseverance, we can achieve and maintain ourselves indefinitely in a state of plateau-experiencing. Hence, we can reach a point where we *stay* turned on by life. I once asked a perennially happy person why she was always so happy. Her reply? "I guess I'm just stoned on life!" That kind of experience isn't like the peak-experience of suddenly ascending a mountain top and just as suddenly descending. Rather, it's like *living* on a mountain top—and that's hard to beat!

One final note: Maslow is highly critical of religious institutions—churches, temples, and the like—for the extent to which they have ignored or suppressed peak-experience rather than encouraging and cultivating it. "Most people" he writes,

> lose or forget the subjectively religious experience, and redefine Religion as a set of habits, behaviors, dogmas, forms, which at the extreme becomes entirely legalistic and bureaucratic, conventional, empty, and in the truest meaning of the word, anti-religious.[62]

When this happens, a person's purported religion becomes a pseudoreligion and his or her deepest commitments are switched elsewhere without the realization that the old religion has been superseded by a new one. A further aspect of this withering process is that "the mystic experience, the moment of illumination, the great awakening, along with the charismatic seer who started the whole thing, are forgotten, lost, or transformed into their opposites." Consequently, Maslow warns us that organized religions "finally may become the major enemies of the religious experience and the religious experiencer."[63]

What is your reaction to Maslow's warning? "Right on!"? He has pointed out a very real danger and we should heed it. Still, I believe there is a grievous omission in his treatment of peak-experience. Specifically, he does not provide for the I-Thou type of religious experience Buber speaks of. Theists would say that that kind of experience is *the* religious experience *par excellence*. They would agree that Maslow's peak-experiences are a real and valuable kind of experience, but they simply do not include religious experience in the theistic sense. This is made especially clear by Maslow's claim that by means of scientific analysis we can learn to *control* peak-experience. For surely if there is a supreme personal being, we will not be able to control that being in the least respect. Right? Further, such control is antithetical to a genuinely personal relationship, whether between God and human or human and human because an authentic friendship is not achieved by control and manipulation. And because religious experience of the I-Thou type is the result of a *personal* relationship with God, a religious experience of the biblical sort must not be a peak-experience of Maslow's kind. Again, then, Maslow's treatment of peak-experience excludes what theists would consider the most important kind of "peak" experience.[64]

Moreover, if there is a God in the biblical sense, isn't anyone who takes Maslow's attitude toward peak-experiences—considering them *all* to be natural experiences subject to scientific analysis and control—cutting him- or herself off from the possibility of developing a *personal* relationship with God? Why would that happen? Because the human person would assume that the feeling of the presence of a divine person is really only the result of natural forces—which the human will seek to manipulate as desired. Under such circumstances, it seems reasonable to assume that God would withdraw his presence. Wouldn't you?

Finally, the better part of wisdom seems to be to hold open the possibility of religious experience in the biblical sense. Why? Because if there *is* a God in the biblical sense, then considering what and who God is, and considering the testimony of theistic mystics to the beauty of his presence, it would be contrary to our own deepest desires—if my analysis in Chapter 4 is basically correct—to cut ourselves off from his presence. And if there is *not* a God in the biblical sense, then nothing significant seems to be lost by not excluding from our worldview the possibility of a theistic religious experience. Right?[65]

THE MOMENT OF DECISION

To review the cycle of religious growth, the first phase is the phase of the restless spirit, of the hungry heart, of *pursuit;* whereas the second is the phase of *revelation.* It is the moment during which something of supreme importance seems to be revealed. That it is of supreme importance is not something which someone *tells* you. It is your *own* feeling. The content and source of that revelation should, of course, be evaluated as soon as possible and appropriate. If the revelation is not discredited as false or as an illusion created by your mind, circumstances, another person, an evil demon, and so on, then you are led to the third phase of the cycle of religious growth, namely, the phase of personal *decision* about that which has been revealed. This phase consists of one's decision to live according to that revelation or to live irresponsibly toward it. I say "irresponsibly" because it was *one's own conviction* during the moment of revelation and after evaluation of it that what was revealed was something of supreme importance, something that should be honored in all the moments of one's life. Hence, if one neglects or betrays it, then—unless what was revealed has been surpassed in one's judgment by something yet greater—one is living irresponsibly toward it.

Authenticity and Inauthenticity

This moment of decision is impossible before the moment of revelation, for then we are simply another animal, seeking to survive and to enjoy ourselves in the many ways made possible by our bodies and minds. Our lives then are lived wholly within the realms of physical, social, and cultural pleasures and pains. Søren Kierkegaard calls this "the aesthetic stage" of life. Human life at a higher level than this—at the levels Kierkegaard calls "the ethical stage" and "the religious stage" of life—cannot begin until we hunger and thirst after something more than the pleasures afforded by the senses, the mind, and society. The possibility of being fully human, or at least *more* fully human, comes only when our religious needs have been aroused and spoken to. After that moment we live either *authentically* or *inauthentically*, in *guilt* or in *good conscience*—for we either lead a life of devotion to that which has been revealed or we revert to a life oriented to the satisfaction of body, mind, or ego. We should distinguish, then, between human life before the moment of revelation and human life after that moment. Life before revelation can be no more than a life of prudence in pursuit of survival and pleasure. Life after revelation is either a life of loyalty or disloyalty to that which has been revealed. It is life *unified* by revelation or *strained* by infidelity—but it can never again be life without a sense of something that is transcendently true and important. Hence, as well as being invited to "see and enjoy" in the moment of revelation, we are called to "hear and obey." I would like to expand on the nature and significance of this call by drawing on the insights of two contemporary thinkers, Philip Phenix and Abraham Heschel.[66]

Philip Phenix: The Pleasant and the Sacred

Phenix, a professor of education at Columbia University, published a book in 1961 titled *Education and the Common Good.* In this book he draws out the profound difference between a life built on *desire (pursuit of the pleasant)* and a life built on *loyalty to the excellent (good, sacred).* Without presuming to tell us what "the good" is, Phenix points out that we do each have experiences of the good. Moreover, he claims, our experience is such that we feel that the good is something objective, something that has authority over us, and not something that is merely a whim of our desires or a figment of our imagination. In our moments of religious experience, of revelation, we are convinced that what is revealed to us is not merely expedient for the moment, but is what we ought to honor at all times— whether it be to our worldly advantage or not. The sacred is not *whatever* we will, but that which *we* feel in our depths we *ought* to will. It is not our creation. It is our Creator—if we let it be. It is that which creates meaning, unity, and direction in our lives. Our experience, then, is always that the sacred possesses a validity apart from our whims and wishes. It seizes us and convicts us. It is that perfect combination of the good and the right. It cannot be equated with pleasure. Devotion to the sacred is fundamentally different from desire for pleasure. The former is other-regarding, whereas the latter is self-interested. Devotion "entails sacrifice and loyalty instead of conferring gratification and comfort. It is concerned with giving instead of getting."[67]

Now you might be thinking, *à la* Ayn Rand, author of *The Virtue of Selfishness,* "I'll be damned if I'm going to sacrifice my personal preferences to the Good, the Right, the Sacred, or anything else!" However, claims Phenix, human happiness cannot be found in self-centered satisfaction. Phenix is only inviting us to abandon an *illusory* source of happiness. After the moment of revelation, pleasure is no longer enough for us because we have become aware of a dimension of reality that transcends the pleasant, evoking worship, devotion, and adoration. It is through awareness of that dimension of reality and through loyalty to that which is revealed within it that we grow in beauty of character, unity of purpose, strength of will, and peace of mind. To live a life of loyalty does not mean to lose the will or capacity to enjoy social, intellectual, and bodily pleasures, but it does mean to discover that these sources of pleasure do not deserve top priority. It involves the discovery that when the hard choice comes between pursuit of pleasure and pursuit of excellence, our lives, paradoxically, are less impoverished and more ennobled if we choose excellence and sacrifice pleasure. Phenix makes this point in the following words: "The history of mankind and the facts of personal experience suggest that the health and fulfillment of life spring from *release from self-centeredness in loyalty to the good.*"[68] Also, "The fulfillment of personal existence comes not from grasping for it, but . . . as a by-product of self-forgetful and loving devotion to the good."[69]

Once we have become sensitive to the sacred as it is revealed in our lives, what we do on our own initiative, out of our own heads, may prove temporarily interesting, but it will never prove deeply satisfying. Its shallowness will become more and more dissatisfying until we seal ourselves off in a neurosis or begin to take the sacred seriously. It need not always be the case, of course, that what we desire and what is of worth be at variance with one another. A healthy religion affirms that these two things, the desired and the excellent, are not always the same—since sometimes we desire that which is unworthy or wrong; yet it attempts to put us in touch with that which can mold our desires so that we desire the excellent and are enabled to pursue it in spite of threats, distractions, and inertia. To be transformed in this way does not destroy our ability to enjoy the pleasurable. It only leads us to give it a lower priority, so that instead of seeking fulfillment through self-centered striving for pleasure, possessions, power, and applause, we find our fulfillment in loyalty to the sacred. Phenix should quite agree, then, with Carl Jung's statement that "man's life should be sacrificial, that is, offered up to an idea greater than man," for only in this way shall human fulfillment be found.[70] And ultimately, I add in the spirit of St. Anselm, we should give ourselves to "that than which nothing greater can be conceived."

Abraham Heschel: Faith as Faithfulness

Phenix, as far as I know, is not a theist, but a naturalist—that is, he believes that Nature is the whole of reality. Abraham Heschel, recently deceased professor of theology at the Jewish Theological Seminary in New York City, was a deeply theistic Jew. Yet in spite of their differences in philosophical orientation, Phenix and Heschel disclose basically similar understandings of the nature of the religious life. Again, as with Tillich and Fromm, my intuitions are that such a fundamental agreement between people writing from such different perspectives is probably the result of the facts imposing themselves, rather than of sheer coincidence. To be sure, there are profound differences between Phenix and Heschel, though we won't focus on these. Neither shall I discuss their similarities, for I believe these will impress themselves upon you as I simply relate some basic points from two of Heschel's books, *Man Is Not Alone* and *God in Search of Man*.

Heschel emphasizes the ephemerality of the moment of revelation and states that *"faith is faithfulness,* loyalty to an event, loyalty to our response." His approach to this definition is as follows:

> Authentic faith is more than an echo of a tradition. It is a creative situation, an event. For God is not always silent, and man is not always blind. In every man's life there are moments when there is a lifting of the veil at the horizon of the known, opening a sight of the eternal. Each of us has at least once in his life experienced the momentous reality of God. Each of us has once caught a glimpse of the beauty, peace and power that flow through the souls of those who are devoted to Him. But such experiences or inspirations are rare events. To some people they are like shooting stars, passing and unremembered. In others they kindle a light that is never quenched. The remembrance of that experience and the loyalty to the response of that moment are the forces that sustain our faith. In this sense, faith is faithfulness, loyalty to an event, loyalty to our response.[71]

I must admit that I was puzzled at first by Heschel's description of faith as "loyalty to our response"—perhaps you are too. I think what he means—and he has an important point—is that the moment of revelation is *defined* in part by the wholeheartedness of our response, by our *feeling* that *we are* apprehending that which is true and right and good and holy. Faith is loyalty to and trust of the response that we had in the moment of revelation, a response of commitment, of wholehearted allegiance. In our less exalted, more mundane, even depressed, moments, we should neither lose sight of what we felt in the moment of revelation nor betray it. Rather, we should self-consciously guide our lives by it. In brief, we should be loyal to our response during that moment, for it represents our own deepest and clearest sentiments as to what is right and good and true.

Regarding the ephemerality of the moment of revelation, Heschel writes in *God in Search of Man,* "The immediate certainty that we attain in moments of insight does not retain its intensity after the moments are gone."[72] Hence, to borrow a phrase from Archibald MacLeish's play *J.B.,* religion is a matter of blowing on the coals of the heart—that we might not lose their warmth altogether and that they might burst into flame once again. In between these moments of religious conflagration the problem of the religious person is "how to communicate those rare moments of insight to all the hours of our life? How to commit intuition to concepts, the ineffable to words, insight to rational understanding? How to convey our insights to others and to unite in a fellowship of faith?"[73] Why make the effort to do these things? Because "great events, just as great works of art, are significant in themselves. Our interest in them endures long after they are gone."[74] Hence, we should sound our lives for our personal peak-experiences and we should sound human history for its peak-experiences, in order that they might become our own. As Karl Jaspers puts it, "It is by such moments and for such moments that we live."[75]

The Way of Greece and the Way of Israel

When Heschel talks about "great events" he clearly has in mind the great events of the history of Israel, such as the exodus from Egypt and the delivery of the commandments to Moses on Mount Sinai. An atheist could also have a list of what he or she considers the most significant events in history and could use them to orient his or her life. Hence, what I shall call "the way of Israel" is not limited to theists, but it is, I think, profoundly different from what I shall call "the way of Greece." The way of Israel is to guide oneself by concrete events in human history and in one's personal life. Concepts are of secondary importance in this way and are used to unpack the meaning and richness of such events as the Exodus or Gandhi's march to the sea or Hitler's fascist regime. The way of Greece, on the other hand, the way most commonly associated with philosophers, whether correctly or not, is to guide oneself by means of timeless concepts comprehended by reason. The concrete events of human history and of one's personal life are here subordinate to concepts, in the sense that the former provide the data from which one moves by means of reason toward a *conception* of the real and the good. It is then the concept, rather than the event, by which one guides one's life. To the Israelite, by contrast, *events* are always richer than concepts, and *history* is the stage on which the good and the real are revealed. To the Greek, events are grist for the mill of *reason,* which *abstracts* from them, or sees *through* them, the truth about the real and the good. Hence, the Greek's objective is to transcend history by grasping timeless truths.

The Israelite and the Greek agree that concepts and events are both necessary to human existence. They disagree as to which should be subordinate to the other. What do you think? Should we orient our lives primarily by means of events or of concepts? Which way do you tend to go? Is there a third way? Perhaps "the way of India," that is, of mysticism which transcends concepts and events? I have made the distinction for you between the way of Israel and the way of Greece because I believe these two ways are characteristic of two large groups of people who perceive the world in fundamentally different ways and who, for that reason, have a great deal of difficulty appreciating and communicating with one another. Which group do you belong to, if either? Can you think of people who, in your opinion, clearly belong in one group or the other? Is one way superior to the other as a philosophy of life? How so? Is each way superior to the other in some respects but inferior in others? Can these two ways be combined into a third way that is superior to either taken alone?

THE STAGE OF ACTION

Whereas the third phase of the cycle of religious growth consists of the *decision* to live for that which has been revealed to us or to neglect or betray it, the fourth phase consists of our *living out a positive decision* to be loyal to that which has been revealed. Whereas the moment of decision (which is never settled once and for all but must be confronted again and again) is subjective and internal, the stage of action is objective and external, for in it what we have decided is expressed in our daily lives. Primarily, I believe, the phase of action will express itself in *worship* and in *work*. Let's look more closely at each of these.

Worship

Most of us are familiar with worship as an activity which people engage in on a certain day, at a certain time, in a certain place. What is that activity all about? Ideally, worship is that activity during which we self-consciously focus our attention on the sacred in as clear and whole-hearted a manner as possible. A full act of worship has various aspects which we will look at shortly, but first it is worth noting that worship is something which cannot be done mechanically or perfunctorily. Participation in a service of worship, when that participation is sincere, is never a mere repetition of words and acts one has learned at church, temple, or elsewhere. A person who is merely going through the motions is no more worshiping than a robot which is going through the same motions and making the same sounds. Worship requires subjective as well as outward participation.

Regarding its various aspects, worship at its fullest is that activity during which we *recall* those moments of revelation which represent the high points of our awareness. Affirmations of faith, readings of religious literature, performance of rituals, and singing of hymns are all ways of recollecting those high points, of dilating the inner eye so that the divine light might flood in again with its original intensity and clarity. "Praise," "Thanksgiving," and "Adoration" are all traditional parts of a Judeo-Christian worship service during which the high points of the tradition are remembered. Through worship we also *reappropriate* the meaning and significance of the sacred as it has been revealed to us. We reappropriate it in order to make mid-flight corrections in the directions our lives are taking, and in order that we might regain perspective on our lives as a whole, so as not to be crushed in the welter of demands, temptations, distractions, and tragedies that bombard us from time to time, and sometimes from moment to moment. Such reappropriation is assisted in some traditions by the taking of sacraments, the performance of rites, and "the hearing of the word." Many Catholics, for example, receive the sacrament of Holy Communion every Sunday. Each Sunday, Protestants hear sermons that apply some portion of the Bible to contemporary personal and social problems. Muslims around the world daily perform the perspective-inducing act of praying five times facing Mecca: upon rising, at noon, during midafternoon, at sunset, and before evening sleep. Clearly, these all are efforts not only to *recall* the sacred, but to *reappropriate* it.

Having recalled and reencountered the sacred, worship is also understandably that activity during which we face up honestly to the *gap* between our sense of the sacred and our behavior. Hence, in Judeo-Christian services of worship there are opportunities for "confession" of sins and "petition" of God's mercy and forgiveness. At that time we may also seek the strength and the transforming power to narrow the gap and eventually to close it, so that our thoughts, words, and actions come into complete harmony with our sense of the sacred. Next in worship, though not necessarily in this order, we open ourselves to *new* revelations or inspirations. Some religious groups, such as Unitarian-Universalists, open themselves to inspiration from every religious tradition, whereas others look only to the religious tradition to which they belong. Some persons expect new revelations, in the sense of new *truths* about reality. Others believe that the old revelations will not be added to but that we can expect new *inspirations,* in the sense of deeper *insights* into the meaning, truth, and relevance of the original revelations. In every case, though, there is in worship an openness to, desire for, and expectation of new and fresh contact with the sacred. Finally, worship is an activity that *issues into everyday life*—reminding us of its ideal possibilities and sending us to invest our lives in the actualization of those possibilities. This leads us quite naturally to the topic of *work*.

Work

I claimed at the beginning of this section that the fourth phase of religious growth, the phase of action, expresses itself in worship and in work. I have spoken at length about worship, but there is little I can say about work as a natural expression of religious commitment. It does seem implicit in the revelatory moment that we *act* in whatever ways we can to transform ourselves and the world in the direction of our vision of the good. The form our work should take, however, must be a highly individual matter depending upon the *content* of our personal revelations and the *circumstances* of our lives. Albert Schweitzer, who at age thirty abandoned a brilliant career in music and theology to become a medical missionary, is very careful in his autobiography, *Out of My Life and Thought,* to point out that people should not assume that his type of radical change is the path for all to follow. Some people feel that they must make a drastic career change in order to honor their sense of the sacred, but for most of us, I suspect, our religious work lies in sanctifying our everyday relationships and in solving problems close to home. In either case, there is plenty of work for each of us, work whereby we can achieve a sense of significant participation in the ongoing creation of the world.

Is Pleasure Always Our Motive?

Keeping in mind the necessary eventuation of religious action in work as well as worship, but respecting the highly personal nature of the form that one's work takes, let's turn to an examination of some further questions about worship. In Chapter 5, during our examination of the humanistic aspect of a healthy religion, I spoke sympathetically of Whitehead's claim that enjoyment is the purpose of life and of Steinberg's claim that we have a God-given duty to enjoy our existence. But can a life of worship, in the sense of *self-conscious devotion to the sacred,* be reconciled with a life of enjoyment? Ideally, worship and enjoyment shall be combined. Clearly, however, these two can come into conflict, and just as clearly, whenever they do come into conflict, we should choose worship rather than enjoyment. You may be thinking, "There's really no difference. People do only what they enjoy. Hence, if we choose to worship rather than play tennis, or whatever, it is only because we *enjoy* worshipping more than we enjoy that other thing. Pleasure is our goal all along; it just takes a different form for the saint than for the sensualist." Personally, I don't agree with this analysis. It seems to me that there is a significant difference between worship and self-gratification. Commitment to the sacred, for example, may entail sacrifice and discomfort. You might reply, "But pursuit of pleasure might also involve sacrifice and discomfort, for sometimes we must sacrifice small pleasures now for the sake of large pleasures later, and sometimes we must endure discomfort now, such as physical exercise or dieting, in order to receive accolades later." That's true. The pursuit of pleasure can entail sacrifice and discomfort. However, such sacrifice and discomfort is *for the sake of eventual pleasure.* If the anticipated pleasure is not forthcoming, we are free to abstain from further discomfort or sacrifice, for the latter were assumed solely as *means* to the former. Hence, our choice of a path to pleasure is always a matter of prudence, since if pleasure doesn't follow as anticipated, we are under no obligation to continue on that path. We are free to do whatever else gives greater promise of effectiveness.

Worship, to the contrary, is not *for* the sake of eventual pleasure. If it were, and if the anticipated pleasure were not forthcoming, we would be free to cease worshipping. But we are not. Commitment to the sacred is not a matter of expediency. Hence, it is fundamentally different from the pursuit of pleasure. Indeed, pleasure—large or small, now or later—is to be sacrificed whenever it would interfere with one's sense of harmony with the right and the good. You could say, "But that is because a feeling of harmony with the right and the good is the most pleasant of all feelings," and I don't know how to reply to that except to say that it seems strange to say that a person who dies a death by torture for the sake of convictions, and without knowing whether there is life after death, is acting for the sake of pleasure. You might concede, "Okay, such a person is not acting for the sake of pleasure in the ordinary sense. Rather, that person is seeking to avoid pain—namely, the pain of the guilt he or she would incur by betraying the sense of the sacred." This is closer to the truth, I think, yet it doesn't ring completely true either, for a martyr's intention is not necessarily the attainment of pleasure or the avoidance of pain. It may simply be unflinching testimony to that which he or she finds most precious. By suffering courageously the martyr is not attempting to achieve an ecstatic experience or avoid excruciating guilt. He or she is simply trying to witness to and preserve an appropriate relationship to the sacred—a relationship which is not always the most pleasant, but which is always the most important.

Inasmuch as our relationship to the sacred is the most important relationship in our lives, the most important thing we can do is to discern the sacred as it is revealed in our lives and then to live our lives according to it. If we are very fortunate, we will be able both to honor our sense of the sacred and to enjoy our existence. Perhaps this combination is what makes the idea of heaven so powerful—for it is difficult, and many would say impossible, to live in this world both a worshipful life and a life of enjoyment. This is not because religiousness frowns on pleasure. It doesn't. Rather, it is because it so often calls us away from innocent enjoyment to fight injustice, starvation, and other social ills. Immanuel Kant, one of the great modern philosophers, held that the supreme good for human beings is the combination of virtue and happiness. He understood virtue to be the practice of doing what is morally right *because* it is morally right. Only the virtuous, those who honor and obey their sense of what is morally right, *deserve* happiness, he reasoned. But they rarely receive it on earth. Indeed, as we noted above, their obedience to morality often deprives them of pleasure and afflicts them with suffering. Still, they, and not the immoral, deserve happiness, so Kant held to a firm *hope* that there will be a life after death in which the virtuous are rewarded with happiness. Surely the hope of heaven, for those who hold it, is an incentive for sacrificing pleasure to the sacred, since the pleasure being sacrificed now is *transient,* whereas honoring the sacred, it is believed, is rewarded with *eternal* pleasure. But what about those who believe that life after death is not even a possibility? Why should *they* sacrifice pleasure to the sacred? Simply because it is fitting and right.

When Worship?

Now let me ask another question: Do you think we should worship only when we feel like it? (Please clarify your feelings and your reasons on this point before reading on.) Most of the people to whom I have put this question believe that we should worship only when we feel like it. I disagree because it seems to me that the very logic of the moment of revelation and of our affirmative response is that we should not worship only when we feel like it. Why? Because the feeling we have *during* the moment of revelation is that we are experiencing something which is significant for *every* moment of life, something which we want always to keep freshly and clearly in the center of consciousness—and what is worship but an attempt to *recapture* the impact of earlier revelatory moments and to keep ourselves *open* to new ones—keeping aglow the coals of the heart till they burst into flame again? Hence, the nature of the revelatory moment and of our own best judgment during that moment obliges us to bring ourselves regularly back under the influence of that moment so that we do not lose its perspective and so that our lives do not fall below the new heights to which it has lifted us. It seems, then, that to worship only "when the spirit moves us" is contrary to the content of the revelatory moment and is, therefore, incompatible with living a fully religious life. Do you agree?

If I am correct about the relation of worship to the revelatory moments of our lives, then I think you can see the criteria by which the content, structure, and dynamics of services of worship should be—and probably have been—determined for the most part. Since the purpose of a service of worship, broadly speaking, is to recover and respond to the content of revelation, therefore the music, rituals, symbols, prayers, creeds, readings, sermons, dances, vestments, architecture, and other elements of worship and its supporting context—not that all people use all of these elements—should be constructed and used at such times and in such ways that they capture accurately our past response to revelation and effectively help us regain that response in a deep and moving way—and perhaps help some gain it for the first time. The next time you attend a worship service you might reflect on the ways in which its rituals, symbols, music, prayers, and so on contribute to the expression and recovery of a sense of the sacred. You might be concerned that to do such a thing would require that you take the point of view of an outsider, such as a sociologist visiting and observing the parts of the service and their coherence with one another. That is a danger you would run into if you put too much distance between yourself and what is going on in the service. But it is also possible, I think, to participate sincerely in a service and observe these things. Indeed, it can be a new and powerful experience to continue participating in a service while at the same time taking a larger point of view from which you consider yourself as one person among others participating in a certain context in a shared act of worship. Such reflections can help us to appreciate more fully and deeply what it is we are involved in as well as to become aware of ways in which what we are doing might be made more effective.

Worship Together or Alone?

Finally, I raise for your consideration the question whether we should worship together or alone. Whitehead, you recall, said that religion is what we do with our *solitariness,* not our *togetherness.* So, we might ask, *why* worship together? Indeed, if religion is so private a thing as Maslow's peaker claims (look ahead at the indented quotation in Chapter 9), how *can* we worship together? Is it really possible except in some empty formal sense?

I'm not as ready to answer these questions as I have been earlier ones. I do recall a young woman who told me that when she worships with her friends in their free-spirited Pentecostal manner, she feels that they lift one another to higher and higher heights by means of their spontaneous succession of songs, prayers, Bible readings, and personal sharing. Enhancement of one's worship experience (and enhancing the worship experience of others) certainly seems like a legitimate reason for worshiping with others. But perhaps "enhancement" is too shallow a word to convey what really goes on in group worship. From the "social construction of reality" point of view, in that social activity known as worship it may be true that for those who are already initiated into the rites of the group, the worship experience is merely *enhanced*, by being shared. However, for those who are new to the group, such as children and outsiders, it is *by means of group worship* that religious consciousness is created in the first place. The religious mode of consciousness seems to be no more natural to human beings than to cats or any other creature. It is a social phenomenon—generated, sustained, and evolved by social processes. This is not necessarily to say that the creation of religious consciousness is an entirely human affair. Judaism and Christianity both affirm the corporate nature of their respective institutions, Israel and the Church. But though they are committed to different religious institutions, Jews and Christians generally agree that anyone who voluntarily remains outside the religious community will wither like an uprooted vine. They agree that spiritual nourishment comes ultimately from a personal God, but they also agree that it is mediated to us primarily through the community of the faithful. For those people who do not believe in a divine being, the religious community becomes *all the more important* in the creation, maintenance, and advancement of religious consciousness!

To be sure, a religious community could spawn people who are then able as individuals to nourish their faith apart from the community. But if these people value their faith—and if they didn't they wouldn't nourish it—then their failure to participate in a religious community would seem to show either ignorance or ingratitude: ignorance of the source from which they derived their "great treasure," as Jung calls it, or ingratitude toward that source. Knowledge of the source would seem to occasion gratitude, and gratitude would seem to call for some kind of a constructive response to religious community (though one may, in spite of gratitude, desire to reform one's religious community or even to change to another community that is closer to one's ideal). Finally, if one values greatly a particular religious faith, then normally one would want to transmit that value to others—such as children or adult seekers. Transmission of such a value would probably be achieved more effectively within a religious community than in a strictly one-to-one relationship. Again, then, participation in a religious community seems to be called for, and especially if one believes that being part of a community is part of what it means to be religious.

Regarding the belief that community is a part of being religious, discussion seems to be in order, so let's pursue it briefly. As the revelatory moment unifies the individual and gives direction to him or her, it might also unify individuals *with one another* and give direction to them *as a social whole*. In this case, people would be united by the *best* that they know (by their sense of the sacred), rather than by the *worst* (such as fear, greed, bigotry, or chauvinism). The question we seem to come back to here is whether *human solidarity* is implicit in the revelatory moment—and that is a question you and I can answer only on the basis of our individual revelatory experiences. If we do both believe that the ideal of human solidarity was implicit in our revelatory moments, then it would seem to follow that at certain intervals we should join together with one another and with all those who share our faith, to whatever extent is feasible. Why? In order that we might express, celebrate, and deepen our solidarity with one another, and in order that we might join forces in behalf of our common ideals. If human solidarity is implicit in our revelatory moments, then perhaps Martin Buber is correct that *the best way to serve God is to build*

"And about the spiral of religious growth. There seems to be nothing systematic about the loops. They jiggle a lot and sometimes go twang. And there is a loop of faith hopefully in one's early childhood which is very large and unbending upon which the whole crazy wonderful spring rests."

Harriet Cramton

community. What do you think? Is the pursuit of human solidarity implicit in your sense of the sacred? If so, what concrete steps should (must?) be taken to honor it?

THE CYCLE BEGINS AGAIN

If we do live out our lives as best we can according to our sense of the sacred, we will almost certainly discover that we still have unanswered questions and unsatisfied needs—some of them having been generated by our very effort to be faithful! Such needs and questions bring us full circle back to the stage of pursuit, which we hope will be followed by new events of revelation. Hence, the cycle begins again. That it begins again does not mean necessarily that we have been losing ground and now must regain it. Nor does its renewal mean a monotonous repetition of earlier cycles. It involves newness, and therefore growth. It is a spiral, and not just a cycle. It is something which has been going on since infancy, which reached self-consciousness in adolescence, and which, we hope, will reach maturity—though not fixity—in adulthood. Ideally the spiral of our religious growth will never stop until we have reached a religious position which is completely and enduringly satisfying. This does not mean that we should goad ourselves to uncover every imperfection in our present religion and then to agonize over each imperfection in order to hasten our journey to a perfect religion. That seems to me only a short way to misery—for those closest to us as well as for ourselves. Rather, it means that we should *be honest* with ourselves and others about the deficiencies of our religion, or our understanding of it, and that we should *stay open* to and eager for further religious growth—whether such growth takes us farther into our present religious direction or off into a radically new direction. Why stay honest and open? Because we want to be committed to the best that there is. If what we are presently committed to *is* the best that there is, then—given an equal chance—it should come out on top in spite of criticisms leveled at it and alternatives proposed to it. If it is not the best, then it should be transcended in the direction of that which is supremely, perfectly, and absolutely good.

Notes

1. All quotations from the Bible, unless noted otherwise, are from the Revised Standard Version of the Bible. Copyright 1952 and Copyright 1946, by Division of Christian Education of the National Council of Churches of Christ in the United States of America.

2. For an introduction to Zen Buddhism and its rejection of the Western attempt to satisfy spiritual yearning by means of reason or revelation, see Chap. 1, "The Sense

of Zen," in D. T. Suzuki's *Zen Buddhism,* William Barrett, ed. (New York: Doubleday, 1956). This is an essay no Westerner should miss. Suzuki is the foremost interpreter of Zen to the West, and his essay, which appeared originally in his *Essays in Zen Buddhism, First Series* (New York: Paragon Book Reprint Corporation, 1971. Repr. of 1927 ed.), has been reprinted in many different volumes.

3. Carl G. Jung, *Modern Man in Search of a Soul,* trans. W. S. Dell and Cary F. Baynes (New York: Harcourt, Brace & World, 1933), p. 240.

4. John Dewey, in *A Common Faith* (New Haven, CT: Yale University Press, 1934), takes the opposite position from Otto and explains religious experience as a form of other kinds of experience, such as were just mentioned in the text.

5. Rudolf Otto, *The Idea of the Holy,* trans. John W. Harvey (New York: Oxford University Press, 1958), p. 14. Perhaps Otto had in mind here the following passage from *Faust* (Pt. II, Act I, Scene V), by his compatriot J. W. von Goethe: "The chill of dread is man's best quality. Though from the feeling oft the world may fend us, Deeply we feel, once smitten, the Tremendous" (trans. Victor Lange; New York: Modern Library).

6. Ibid., p. 20.

7. Ibid., p. 24.

8. See Alfred North Whitehead's *Process and Reality,* Charles Hartshorne's *Omnipotence and Other Theological Mistakes,* and Eleanore Stump and Norman Kretzmann's "Eternity," *The Journal of Philosophy,* 78/8 (August 1981), 429–58.

9. Otto, *Idea of the Holy,* p. 26. Recall Gabriel Marcel's distinction in *The Mystery of Being* between a problem (which is solvable by humans and which therefore we grasp) and a mystery (by which *we* are grasped and which is not solvable by us).

10. Ibid., p. 28.

11. Ibid., p. 29.

12. Ibid., p. 30.

13. My story is freely adapted from the *Brihadaranyaka Upanishad.* There the dialogue is between a sage and his king, rather than father and son, and the things pointed to are the physical, mental, and vital aspects of reality, rather than a chair and a dog. None of these things is Brahman, either individually or taken together, but each of them points to Brahman, who transcends and includes them all.

14. Otto, *The Idea of the Holy,* p. 31.

15. Ibid., pp. 31–32.

16. Ibid., p. 33.

17. Ibid., p. 36.

18. Martin Buber, *Eclipse of God* (New York: Harper & Row, 1952), p. 44.

19. For a brief introduction to Blaise Pascal, see Alban Krailsheimer's *Pascal* (1980). For a provocative intellectual and emotional experience, read some of Pascal's *Pensées* (Krailsheimer trans.; Penguin, 1966).

20. Dewey, *A Common Faith,* p. 42.

21. Buber, *Eclipse of God,* pp. 44–45.

22. Pascal, *Pensées* (New York: Modern Library, 1941) p. 386.

23. To go more deeply into these issues would require a preliminary study of two metaphysical positions, materialism and idealism, and two epistemological positions, realism and phenomenalism. Many "Introduction to Philosophy" books treat all four topics; or see the appropriate selections in *The Encyclopedia of Philosophy,* Paul Edwards ed. (New York: Macmillan, 1967), 8 vols.

24. Buber, *Eclipse of God,* p. 28.

25. Ibid., p. 32.

26. Ibid., pp. 32–33. Italics mine.

27. A good introduction to Sartre is his own *Existentialism and Human Emotions* (New York: Philosophical Library, 1957). Sartre's major philosophical treatise is *Being and Nothingness* (New York: Washington Square Press, 1946), in addition to which he has written numerous plays, such as *No Exit* and *The Devil and the Good Lord.* Parenthetically, there are many modern people who testify that God is *not* silent in their lives. The extent to which people in the last quarter of the twentieth century feel that there is or is not a living God is a matter for sociologists to determine by sound research, not for philosophers to infer from a very narrow, highly personal range of evidence.

28. Buber, *Eclipse of God,* p. 23.

29. Ibid., p. 68.

30. Ibid., p. 36.

31. Ibid., pp. 36–37.

32. Jung, *Modern Man in Search of a Soul,* p. 229.

33. For an introduction to the work of Jung and many other leading psychologists, see *Theories of Personality,* 3rd ed., Calvin S. Hall and Gardner Lindzey (New York: Wiley, 1978).

34. Jung, *Psychology and Religion* (New Haven, CT: Yale University Press, 1938), p. 5.

35. Ibid., p. 4.

36. Ibid., p. 6.

37. Ibid., p. 37.

38. Ibid., p. 75.

39. Ibid., p. 98.

40. Professor Michael Meilach, O.F.M., has pointed out to me that the failure of a god to any longer empower a person may be the result of the person allowing or causing his relationship to that god to deteriorate. Hence, before abandoning a god, one should question seriously whether it is the god or oneself who is failing. A person who is going deaf may think that church bells are tolling ever more softly.

41. Jung, *Psychology and Religion,* pp. 113–114.

42. Abraham H. Maslow, *Religions, Values, and Peak-Experiences* (New York: Viking, 1964), p. 49. This and other quotations from *Religions, Values, and Peak-Experiences* are used by generous permission of Kappa Delta Pi, an Honor Society in Education, owners of the copyright, P.O. Box A, West Lafayette, Indiana 47906.

43. See also Maslow's preface to *New Knowledge in Human Values,* edited by Maslow himself (New York: Harper & Row, 1959).

44. Maslow, *Religions,* p. 83.

45. Ibid., p. 42. Maslow's analysis was prophetic of the decline of the popularity and influence of liberal, rationalistic denominations, such as, the Methodist and Presbyterian churches, in the 1970s and 1980s, and, by contrast, the startling surge of conservative, evangelical denominations, such as, Assemblies of God and Southern Baptists, during that period. The strong need for religion which is "emotionally satisfying," to use Maslow's words, also helps account for the success during that era of more exotic religions like the Hindu Hare Krishna movement and

the Unification Church of Korean minister Rev. Sun Myung Moon. The resurgence of Muslim fundamentalism in the Middle East is also often explained as a reaction against the shallowness and insipidness that many Muslims perceive in Western rationalistic liberalism.

46. Ibid., p. 43.

47. Ibid. Rev. Jack Taylor, himself a liberal religionist who is sympathetic to Maslow's emphasis on religious experience, remarked to me that Maslow has failed to appreciate the profoundly emotional experiences liberal religion has afforded its adherents by virtue of its emphasis on social action. Consider, for example, the emotional experiences religious liberals must have undergone when they marched on Washington in the sixties and heard Martin Luther King, Jr.'s, oration, "I Have a Dream," or when they joined hands in Selma, Alabama, and waded into a sea of hostility and violence that took the lives of two people, one a young liberal minister. It does appear that Maslow has neglected something important here.

48. Prominent secular substitutes for religious experience have been mind-altering drugs, sexual pleasure, and Dionysian music. Unfortunately, such drugs are often addictive and damaging, and sex without respect leads people to treat one another as mere objects by which to achieve selfish ends. The music that celebrates and intensifies these values often shares their frustrating character of being intensely sensual, even orgasmic, yet profoundly unsatisfying. Note, however, the religious role of drugs (for example, peyote and wine), emotional affection (for example, hugs and other expressions of caring), and "Dionysian" music (found in some worship services normally, such as, African-American Baptist worship, and in other services occasionally, examples being Handel's "Messiah" and Schiller's "Ode to Joy," set to music in the finale of Beethoven's Ninth Symphony). Regarding drugs and religion, see Huston Smith's "Do Drugs Have Religious Import?" *The Journal of Philosophy,* 61/18 (October 1, 1964), pp. 517–30; he argues that drugs *can* be a legitimate means to authentic religious experience.

49. Ibid., p. 32. The practical problem, of course, is how to restore ourselves to a state of health. For a full statement of Maslow's prescription, see his *Motivation and Personality,* 2nd ed. (New York: Harper & Row, 1970), or more recently, *Toward a Psychology of Being,* 2nd ed. (New York: Van Nostrand Reinhold Company, 1968).

50. Maslow, *Religions,* p. 19.

51. Ibid., pp. 19–20.

52. Ibid., p. 54.

53. Ibid., p. 63.

54. Ibid.

55. Ibid., pp. 65–66.

56. Ibid., p. 66.

57. Ibid., p. 75.

58. Ibid., p. 62.

59. Ibid., p. xiv.

60. Ibid., p. xv.

61. Ibid., p. xiv–xv.

62. Ibid., p. viii. A caveat: the external features of a worshiper can be misunderstood. Some people are most affected by the majesty of God the Creator or the peace of God the Comforter rather than by the ecstasy of God the Spirit. They may be deeply moved emotionally without appearing to be so.

63. Ibid.

64. Paul Tillich has an important and pertinent passage on the nature of personal relationships in his *Biblical Religion and the Search for Ultimate Reality* (Chicago: University of Chicago Press, 1955), pt. IV, sec. 1. See also Martin Buber's *I and Thou,* trans. Walter Kaufmann (New York: Scribners, 1970).

65. The classic version of this "wager" type argument is by Blaise Pascal. See his *Pensées,* sec. 3, esp. no. 233, in the Modern Library edition, or no. 418 in the Krailsheimer translation (Penguin). Whereas Pascal emphasizes the negative reason for wagering one way rather than the other, I have emphasized the positive.

66. For valuable reflections on the nature and significance of fidelity, see Gabriel Marcel's *Creative Fidelity,* trans. Robert Rosthal (New York: Farrar, Straus, and Giroux, 1964), Chap. 8, and his *Homo Viator: Introduction to a Metaphysic of Hope,* trans. Emma Craufurd (New York: Harper & Row, 1962), Chap. V. Also, Sam Keen's *Gabriel Marcel* (Richmond, VA: John Knox Press, 1967), pp. 34–40.

67. Philip H. Phenix, *Education and the Common Good* (New York: Harper & Brothers, 1961), p. 25.

68. Ibid., p. 26. Italics mine.

69. Ibid., p. 8.

70. Jung, *Psychology and Religion,* p. 94.

71. Abraham Heschel, *Man Is Not Alone* (New York: Harper & Row, 1966), p. 65.

72. Heschel, *God in Search of Man* (New York: Harper & Row, 1966), p. 132.

73. Ibid., p. 163.

74. Ibid., p. 211.

75. Karl Jaspers, *The Perennial Scope of Philosophy* (Hamden, CT: Archon Books, 1968), p. 73.

9

Conclusion

QUESTIONS TO THINK ABOUT

- What is the difference between the experimental attitude toward a commitment and the religious attitude?
- What is W. C. Smith's distinction between personal faith and cumulative tradition?
- How does Smith's distinction help show that religious faith is inevitably personalized?
- What is a sad irony of religious education? How can it be overcome?
- What is Richard Rubenstein's recommendation regarding religious education?
- What are the three most radically different religious positions you can think of? What makes them so different?
- Where do you go from here?

THE EXPERIMENTAL ATTITUDE AND THE RELIGIOUS ATTITUDE

Throughout this book I have emphasized that the individual should determine a particular religious commitment out of the depths of his or her own experience and reflection. Now I would like to make a distinction lest you think I believe that a mature religious faith is a calculating, selfish thing constructed for the sake of achieving peace of mind, mystical ecstasy, heaven, or something else. The experimental attitude is appropriate when we are trying to figure out the best means to an end: We try this and that, use the best means available, but stand ready to discard it at any time. After all, it's just a means. The end is what is important.

A mature religious faith, by contrast, is not an experimental affair in the sense that we pick and choose our religious beliefs and objects of devotion according to how well they suit us. Rather, an object of religious devotion chooses us, compels us, convicts us. Religious faith is *not* a matter of experiment, but of *submission*—an idea captured nicely in the name of the religion established through Mohammed: "Islam" means "submission," and a Muslim is "one who submits to God." To be religious, I am suggesting, is not to choose, but to submit. I would not recommend blind submission, as you know; but neither would I recommend submission with an ulterior purpose. That would not be sincere submission. What I do recommend and I believe is at the heart of all sincere religious faith is *personal submission to the best that one knows.* The word "submission" has unfortunate connotations of servility which I do not mean to imply. Mature submission in a religious sense would consist of acknowledging through thought, word, and deed the sacred as it has been revealed to oneself. This kind of submission, it seems to me, ennobles the individual and deserves admiration. It is what I have most frequently called "devotion."

It is true that by *living* according to our sense of the sacred, we discover the riches and the deficiencies of that which has been revealed to us; in view of these deficiencies we may seek a more adequate sense of the sacred. But if we live according to our sense of the sacred *in order* to discover its riches and deficiencies, then we have abandoned the attitude of religious commitment and are acting out of a self-gratifying motive. We are "using" our religion. Religious action is "practical" in the sense that it has concrete consequences which may lead us to reevaluate our commitments, and in the sense that we can experiment in order to discover those means which are most effective in helping us worship, work toward our ideals, and communicate our faith. But at the fundamental level of commitment, the experimental attitude is not compatible with the religious attitude. A mature religious faith consists in wholehearted (though not closed-minded) commitment to that which affects us as right and true and good. It does not consist in choosing something *because* it gives us peace of mind or leads us into religious ecstasy. To be sure, commitment to what affects us as right and good may give us peace of mind and bring about religious highs, but the commitment is not for the sake of these things and is maintained in spite of their absence.

TOWARD A FAITH OF YOUR OWN

The upshot of all that I have been saying is that you and I need a fully self-conscious, evaluated faith of our own in order to live at the highest level of human existence. Such a faith cannot be taken over from others in a mechanical way. An authentic faith is inevitably constructed or appropriated in a highly personal manner, so that even when the *content* of two persons' faiths is basically the same—for example, two Roman Catholics—the *accents* may differ greatly. Wilfred Cantwell Smith does an excellent job in *The Meaning and End of Religion* of arguing for the inevitable uniqueness of religious faith.[1] He begins by arguing that there is no such thing as religion, in the sense of "a certain kind of thing." The word "religion" has meant many, many different things at different times in history and during any given period of history. Ultimately, then, there is no singular thing that can be designated correctly by the word "religion." There is only your faith and her faith and his faith and my faith. Smith becomes more specific and argues that there is no such thing as Hinduism or Judaism, either! What justifies our calling two persons Hindus, and what justifies their calling themselves Hindus, is not that their faiths are identical or that they perform the same religious acts or that they belong to the same "thing." Two Hindus may not be identical or even clearly similar in any of these ways. Rather, we identify them and they identify themselves as Hindus because of their common participation in that tradition of literature, ideas, practices, and rituals to which we refer by the term "Hinduism." But Hinduism, according to this usage, is not a clear-cut thing with well-defined boundaries by means of which we can determine whether someone is a member of it or not. Just where Hinduism begins and where it ends, just what are the necessary and sufficient conditions of being a Hindu, are highly disputable questions. The same dispute applies to perhaps every other religion.

To be sure, in nearly every religious tradition, there are groups which claim to be the only legitimate representative of that tradition. Such groups should be listened to earnestly; one of them may be right. But until a person is satisfied that one group is the only legitimate representative of that tradition, he or she must—if desiring to identify with that tradition—draw deeply and broadly from its resources and create his or her own personalized commitment and participation. The person who does this may meet a group that says, "If you don't believe as we do, then not only do you not have the truth, but you shouldn't identify yourself (or think of yourself) as an *X* (whatever the religion might be)." The practical thrust of such a group is to force the individual to choose their brand of *X* or to reject *X* altogether. But even if such a group is correct that its position is true and all others false, it does not follow that an individual who is not able to agree in good conscience with that contention should abjure perceiving him- or herself as an *X-ist* of some sort. The person knows from where his or her greatest sense of inspiration comes—riddled though it may be with questions and gaps—and should not allow anyone or anything but personal growth to displace their sense of being an *X-ist* rather than a *Y-ist!*

We do not, then, possess Buddhism, Christianity, Islam, and so on in clear-cut, well-defined forms. All we have for certain are the faiths of the individuals who participate in these various traditions. Such faiths, when they are living, dynamic faiths, are inescapably personalized, and should be. In order to make this point clear, Smith distinguishes between *personal faith* and *cumulative tradition*. Cumulative tradition refers to all things of a religious nature that are public and transmissible from one individual and generation to another, for example, cathedrals, symbols, art, creeds, music, rituals, literature, and dances. These are things we have in common because of their external, physical nature. Moreover, they can be passed on relatively unchanged from generation to generation. Faith, by contrast, is not external but internal. Nor is it the same thing from person to person, as the Nicene Creed is from church to church. Consider identical twins raised by the same parents in the same church or temple. Smith's point would be that they share the same cumulative tradition—they hear the same chants, sing the same hymns, read the same readings, perform the same symbolic acts, and so on. Yet, their faiths will be different because faith is not something that is impressed upon us from the outside. It is the result of our *personal appropriation* of the impact upon us of our cumulative religious tradition, our own thoughts, and of other traditions, including secularism, as we are exposed to them. John Dewey explains in his *Individualism Old and New* that individuality is a *distinctive* way of *feeling* the impacts of the world upon us and of *reacting* to them. As individuals, each of us feels differently the impacts of religious influences, and consequently each of us reacts differently, be it ever so slightly—rejecting or being indifferent to that which others treasure, treasuring that which others are indifferent to or reject, cherishing more intensely or less intensely than others that which all cherish in common.

It is only natural that the materials for our faith are drawn first from the religious tradition in which we have been reared—if, indeed, we have been reared in any religious tradition at all. It would be foolish, however, to turn away from the lure of other traditions once we are exposed to them. It would be foolish also to reject the religious tradition of our childhood simply because it *is* the religious tradition of our childhood! Our response to the religious tradition that is passed on to us should not be unreflective acceptance or unreflective rejection, but appreciative evaluation and critical appropriation or rejection.

An aside about religious education seems appropriate here. One of the saddest ironies of religion is the extent to which adults intent on passing their religious heritage to children actually create in the children an intense dislike for the heritage. In my religion courses I frequently invite students to write a personal statement of their religious beliefs, and the students often begin with an autobiographical account of their religious background. Frequently they share with me the extent to which they were bored to intense dislike of their religious heritage by their religious education. What a tragedy, especially given the good intentions and many volunteer hours invested by the teachers. Perhaps no religious education would be better than one that is counterproductive? Some people object to religious education not because it is counterproductive, but because they believe it unfairly biases a child in favor of one religion and against the others. It would be better, they say, for parents to give their children no religious education at all, so that when the children reach maturity they can make an unbiased choice among the established religions or construct a religion of their own. That, of course, assumes a narrower definition of religion than the one with which we are operating—as though religious education were merely a matter of being exposed to various religions, like so many cellophane-wrapped sandwiches in a fast-food delicatessen. Further, there is a sense in which people must be *sensitized* to religious matters in order that they can make mature choices, even as people must be sensitized to classical music before they can appreciate it fully or make sophisticated decisions about it.

Personally, I can think of no adequate way to come to understand what religion is all about other than by being *a part* of a religious tradition. The person who has participated in the Jewish heritage from childhood is, it seems to me, in an infinitely better position to evaluate *other* religious traditions than is a person who has never participated in any religious tradition but has only read about them. Some of my students have been reared in isolation from self-conscious religion and with the idea that religion is something "out there" about which they will make a decision when they become adults. Some of these students have expressed their regret to me that their parents had reared them this way, for they felt that a void had been left in their lives. First, they had been misled into thinking that religion is something "out there" and has, therefore, a tenuous relationship to human life. Second, they had *not* been introduced to the various religions and therefore had not been prepared to make an educated choice when the time for choosing did come. Third, because religious education, like aesthetic education, must involve the body and emotions as well as the intellect, such people sometimes cannot appreciate or even perceive the multifaceted richness of religious life. Hence, it is difficult to see how religious education can be carried out effectively apart from actual immersion in some religious setting—whether it is an ancient and elaborate one, such as Orthodox Christianity, or a new and simple one, such as the deism that an antiinstitutional parent might favor.

Further, not only should each individual be raised in a self-conscious religious tradition (even if it is a tradition that begins with the individual's parents), but the *entire* tradition should be passed on to the individual so that he or she can experience the full range of its richness. The older generation *owes* this opportunity to the younger generation. Professor Richard Rubenstein, the Jewish theologian to whom I am indebted for this insight, makes his point in the following words: "Jews are free to accept or reject all or part of the Torah as individuals. Freedom carries with it the responsibility that each generation make its own commitments in the light of its insights, while leaving the inherited corpus of tradition intact for subsequent generations."[2] By contrast, liberalism and conservatism in religious education tend to impoverish students by transmitting only the convictions of the teacher or the specific religious group and those portions of the heritage which back up those convictions. This tends to lead to a decrease in what is transmitted. To be sure, it is appropriate for teachers and groups to share their own insights and convictions with students, but students should be provided with the entire body of material from which and against which those convictions were arrived at so that they, the students, can discover whether *they* find the same things or other things more important and convincing. Rubenstein is himself a Jewish atheist. Nonetheless, he writes with regard to the 613 commandments in the Torah, "I hope it will be possible for subsequent generations to confront all 613 commandments in the light of the insights of their time in order to decide what sector is meaningful for them. I seriously doubt that they will respond as we have."[3] Rubenstein recommends, then, that each generation should be confronted with the whole heritage, but that each member of that generation should be left free to determine his personal response to that heritage. This seems to me a wise recommendation for every religion, for though it places a burden on the adults who must carry it out, it provides maximal advantages to the young as they enter into their heritage and begin to decide their place in it.

Religious faith, then, is inevitably personalized to some extent, large or small. Abraham Maslow describes well the person whose faith is almost completely individualized. "From the point of view of the peak-experiencer," he writes, each person has his own private religion, which he develops out of his own private revelations in which are revealed to him his own private myths and symbols, rituals and ceremonials, which may be of the profoundest meaning to him personally and yet completely idiosyncratic, that is, of no meaning to anyone else.[4]

At the other extreme of the spectrum is the person whose faith consists of personal appropriation of his or her parents' faith in its entirety. Most of us fall somewhere between these two extremes, our faith being the result of a more even balance between our own insights and what we have acquired from our religious nurture. While I do not agree with Maslow that the private religion of the peaker is what we should all strive for (I'm much more of a community person like Buber), I do agree with him that any faith worth having must be personal. It must be something which *happens within us* and is *nurtured by us.* As Carl Jung puts it, religious faith is *loyalty to one's own experience.*[5] It is concern for, confidence in, and commitment to your own deepest experiences—which may or may not be reinforced by the religious institution or tradition in which you were reared or, indeed, by any existing institution. The person who is "looking for a religion" is sometimes, I think, looking not for a religion, already having that in a private sense. He or she is looking for a group of people who embody to a significant extent that which is already the seeker's religion, whether it be naturalistic humanism, transcendentalism, or theism (each of which will be discussed in the next section). In order to cultivate your own faith, you are going to have to spend time in solitary reflection *identifying* your deepest experiences, *clarifying* them, *taking direction* from them, and *moving toward* yet further such experiences. Again, it is important to remember that such experiences can come from reflection upon events in which you have not participated and from ideas you did not originate, as well as from those in which you did participate and which you did originate. You can benefit from, for example, the experiences and reflections recorded in the *Bhagavad-Gita* or the *Dhammapada* or the Bible, as well as from your own experiences and insights. Both types of experience are worthy of thoughtful consideration.

NATURALISM, TRANSCENDENTALISM, AND THEISM

William James wrote a book titled *Varieties of Religious Experience;* another book could well be written titled *Varieties of Religious Hope and Faith.* Yet in spite of the endless variations of religious hope and faith, I would like to suggest in closing that there are three fundamental modes of religious faith which have dominated the history of humankind, East and West: the *naturalistic* mode, the *transcendentalist* mode, and the *theistic* mode. Religious naturalism is characteristic of atheistic humanists both East and West. For the religious naturalist, Nature—that which is presented to us by our senses, science, and ordinary introspection—is the whole of reality (though extraordinary experiences sometimes mislead us into thinking otherwise). The ultimate good is earthly happiness—often conceived of as some combination of physical health, material comfort, meaningful work, invigorating challenges, refreshing leisure, and intimate friends. The means to such happiness is human activity based on scientific knowledge of nature, self, and society.

For the *transcendentalist,* Nature is not the whole of reality. Indeed, it is only a veil we must penetrate in order to reach the One of which all things are a part. All things are part of the One as waves are part of the ocean. The appearance of individuality, uniqueness, and separateness is an illusion. The truth is that you and I and all things are homogeneous with the One, even as the waves are one with the ocean. Hence, the ultimate good, according to the transcendentalist, consists in the blissful immersion and dissolution of our spirits in the One, which is Absolute Spirit. The consequent loss of individuality is not to be feared, for it is precisely the ego (our sense of separate individuality) that is responsible for our mental and spiritual confusion and suffering. By shedding the ego, we emerge from the chrysalis that has been preventing us from seeing reality as it is and feeling our oneness with it. The way out of the chrysalis is disciplined meditation.

For the *theist* there is a creator and sustainer of the universe who is personal in nature but eternally distinct from ourselves. Hence, there is no merger of the individual self with the Absolute Self. Rather, there is an eternal I-Thou relationship between God and the individual as there is between person and person. The ultimate good lies in the interaction of persons, including the Divine Person, with one another, and in the responsibility of persons, including the Divine Person, for one another. The means to this end are dialogue (including prayer), mutuality, and action.

With which of these three types of person do you feel most closely identified? What do you think of the other types? Is there any objective way of evaluating the relative merits of these three positions? Indeed, is there any *subjective* way of evaluating them? Can you think of another fundamental mode of faith which should be added here? I'm sure my trinity of modes, plus their opposite, secularism, is not exhaustive, but if it has served to heighten your awareness of who you are and who you can become, then I am satisfied.

Finally, wherever you find yourself coming down now—as naturalist, transcendentalist, theist, secularist, or something else—I hope you will never again think of religious faith as blind, cowardly assent to a set of propositions, but as intelligent, courageous consent to the best that you know. And lest you be lulled by all my talk of religion into thinking that I believe that religion is the most important thing there is, I say "for the record" that the focus of a healthy religion is not on religion but on God. "Those who make religion their god," warns Thomas Erskine of Linlathen, "will not have God for their religion." Far better it is, if we must choose, to have God than religion. But the choice hardly seems necessary or even possible, for it is through the forms of religion that we touch and are touched by God.

"Now look what you've done!"

Drawing by Lorenz; © 1971 The New Yorker Magazine, Inc.

Notes

1. Wilfred Cantwell Smith, *The Meaning and End of Religion* (New York: New American Library, 1963), esp. Chaps. 6 and 7.

2. Richard Rubenstein, *After Auschwitz* (Indianapolis, IN: Bobbs-Merrill, 1966), p. 122.

3. Ibid., p. 146.

4. Abraham Maslow, *Religions, Values, and Peak-Experiences* (New York: Viking, 1964), p. 28.

5. Carl Jung, *Psychology and Religion* (New Haven, CT: Yale University Press, 1938), p. 52.

For Further Reading

This bibliography is for readers who are just starting out in their study of religion. Hence, it is short, and most of the books are written on a level that the general reader can comprehend. Readers who become keenly interested in a topic will find in nearly every category a book that contains an extensive bibliography on that topic. The notes at the end of each chapter of the book also provide valuable leads for further reading. Because my book and nearly all of the books below embody a positive attitude toward religion, I have provided as a next-to-last category a section titled "Antireligious Literature." As to the last category, "Women and Religion," please see the preface, if you have not done so already. I hope you will become motivated to achieve "lay expertise" on at least one of the following topics. Peace.

Reference Books

ELIADE, MIRCEA, EDITOR-IN-CHIEF, *The Encyclopedia of Religion.* 16 volumes. New York: Macmillan, 1986. Brand new. This encyclopedia by dozens of authorities will be "the" place to turn for expert knowledge and opinion on nearly every topic in religious studies for many years to come.

MEAD, FRANK, AND SAMUEL HILL, *Handbook of Denominations in the United States,* 8th ed. Nashville, TN: Abingdon Press, 1985. States briefly the beliefs, practices, and organization of nearly every religious group in the United States.

Introductions to Religion and Religions

ELIADE, MIRCEA, *The Sacred and the Profane: The Nature of Religion.* New York: Harcourt, Brace & World, 1959. Good introduction by a leading force in the field.

NOSS, JOHN B., AND DAVIS NOSS, *Man's Religions,* 7th ed. New York: Macmillan, 1984. Comprehensive, excellent textbook on the religions of the world, from ancient to contemporary, Eastern to Western.

SLATER, PETER, *The Dynamics of Religion.* New York: Harper & Row, 1978. An excellent companion to *Religion and Doubt.* Slater provides a rich, illuminating analysis of the role of symbols and stories in religion.

SMART, NINIAN, *Worldviews: Crosscultural Explorations of Human Beliefs.* New York: Scribners, 1983. Another excellent companion to *Religion and Doubt.* Separate chapters on the experiential, mythic, doctrinal, ethical, ritual, and social dimensions of religion.

SMITH, HUSTON, *Religions of Man.* New York: Harper & Row, 1965. Brief, sensitive, inexpensive, readable. Chapters on seven major religions.

History of Religions

ELIADE, MIRCEA, *The Quest: History and Meaning in Religion.* Chicago: University of Chicago Press, 1969. Papers by a pioneering phenomenological historian.

MARTY, MARTIN E., *Pilgrims in Their Own Land: 500 Years of Religion in America.* New York: Penguin, 1984. Excellent example of religious history in the traditional empirical style.

SMITH, WILFRED CANTWELL, *The Meaning and End of Religion.* New York: New American Library, 1963. An important alternative to Eliade's approach.

Comparative Religion

COBB, JOHN B., JR., *Christ in a Pluralistic Age.* Louisville, KY: Westminster John Knox Press, 1984. Also *Beyond Dialogue: Toward a Mutual Transformation of Christianity and Buddhism.*

ELIADE, MIRCEA, *Patterns in Comparative Religion.* New York: New American Library, 1958. Helpful chapter on the sacred and the profane, followed by studies of ways in which the sacred has been manifested in different cultures through the sky, water, woman, and other natural phenomena.

HICK, JOHN, *An Interpretation of Religion: Human Responses to the Transcendent.* New Haven, CT: Yale, 1989. A cutting edge contribution by a sensitive, global thinker.

SMITH, WILFRED CANTWELL, *Towards a World Theology: Faith and the Comparative History of Religion.* Louisville, KY: Westminster John Knox Press, 1981.

SWIDLER, LEONARD, ED., *Toward a Universal Theology of Religion.* Maryknoll, NY: Orbis Books, 1987. Papers by Hans Kung, Wilfred Smith, John Cobb, and Raimundo Panikkar, with numerous responses.

Anthropology of Religion

LESSA, W. A., AND E. Z. VOGT, EDS., *Reader in Comparative Religion: An Anthropological Approach,* 4th ed. New York: Harper & Row, 1979. Comprehensive, widely used.

NORBECK, EDWARD, *Religion in Human Life: Anthropological Views.* Prospect Heights, IL: Waveland Press, 1988. A very brief introduction. Good bibliography.

Sociology of Religion

BELLAH, ROBERT N., ET AL., *Habits of the Heart: Individualism and Commitment in American Life.* New York: Harper & Row, 1986. One of the decade's most exciting books. Based on a massive five-year study of various communities. Shows how insistence on individualism is preventing Americans from building and enjoying the communal values that they also need.

BERGER, PETER L., *The Sacred Canopy: Elements of a Sociological Theory of Religion.* Garden City, NY: Doubleday, 1967. Important approach. Seeks to understand how systems of religious belief and practice are generated from, maintained, and modified by social interaction. Rewarding, but not easy. The theoretical foundation for *The Sacred Canopy* is *The Social Construction of Reality—A Treatise in the Sociology of Knowledge* (1966) by Peter L. Berger and Thomas Luckmann. More difficult still. For an easy introduction to Berger's approach try his *Invitation to Sociology: A Human Perspective,* Garden City, NY: Doubleday, 1963. Luckmann's major statement on religion is *The Invisible Religion: The Problem of Religion in Modern Society.* New York: Macmillan, 1967.

GLOCK, CHARLES, AND ROBERT BELLAH, *The New Religious Consciousness.* Berkeley: University of California Press, 1976. A broad look at the new religions and religious movements which proliferated in the United States, especially on the West Coast, during the 1960s and 1970s. Some examples: the Hare Krishna movement, the Divine Light Mission of Guru Maharaj Ji, Synanon, and the Catholic Charismatic Movement.

Psychology of Religion

ALLPORT, GORDON W., *The Individual and His Religion.* New York: Macmillan, 1950. Excellent essay on the role of religion in personal maturation.

For writings by Erich Fromm, Carl Jung, and Abraham Maslow, see the index of *Religion and Doubt* and notes to Chapter 8. For writings by Sigmund Freud, see bibliography under Antireligious Literature. See also *Castillejo* under Women and Religion.

Philosophy of Religion

HICK, JOHN, *Philosophy of Religion,* 4th ed. Englewood Cliffs, NJ: Prentice Hall, 1990. Excellent short introduction by leading thinker.

PLANTINGA, ALVIN, *God, Freedom, and Evil.* New York: Harper & Row, 1974. One of this century's most exciting and influential philosophers of religion provides a brief introduction to the "possible worlds" way of understanding God and the "free-will defense" of God's permission of evil.

WAINWRIGHT, WILLIAM, *Philosophy of Religion.* Belmont, CA: Wadsworth, 1988. Excellent introduction to the "possible worlds" understanding of God and to recent discussion of the rationality of religious belief.

Science and Religion

BARBOUR, IAN C., *Issues in Science and Religion.* New York: Harper & Row, 1966. Comprehensive survey by a physicist who is also a philosopher/theologian. See also his *Myths, Models, and Paradigms* (1974).

NEWMAN, ROBERT AND HERMAN ECKELMANN, JR., *Genesis One and the Origin of the Earth.* Downers Grove, IL: Intervarsity Press, 1977. Newman has a Ph.D. in astrophysics from Cornell University; Eckelmann a B.S.E.E. They argue that science is finally coming around to the Biblical story of creation, which has been misunderstood and maligned but true all along.

ROLSTON, HOLMES, III, *Science and Religion: An Introduction.* New York: Random House, 1987. A highly respected, up-to-date survey and analysis.

Religious Existentialism

BUBER, MARTIN, *Eclipse of God.* New York: Harper & Row, 1952. Demanding but rewarding. An easier introduction to Buber's thought than *I and Thou* (cited under 'Theism').

HERBERG, WILL, *Judaism and Modern Man.* New York: Atheneum Press, 1951. A clear, sensitive, and comprehensive statement by a Jew who was a Communist. For an explanation of his conversion see "From Marxism to Judaism" in *Commentary* (January 1947).

JAMES, WILLIAM, *The Will to Believe and Other Essays in Popular Philosophy.* New York: Dover, c. 1900. Very readable, provocative.

JASPERS, KARL, *Way to Wisdom.* New Haven, CT: Yale University Press, 1951. The best introduction to a profound thinker.

KIERKEGAARD, SØREN, *The Sickness Unto Death,* trans. Hong & Hong. Princeton, NJ: Princeton University Press, 1980. Difficult, but profound and revolutionary in its time, 1849. For an introduction see C. Stephen Evans's *Kierkegaard's Fragments and Postscripts: The Religious Philosophy of Johannes Climacus* (Atlantic Highlands, NJ: Humanities Press, 1989).

MARCEL, GABRIEL, *Creative Fidelity.* New York: Noonday Press, 1964. Difficult but rewarding.

PASCAL, BLAISE, *Pensées,* trans. A. J. Krailsheimer. New York: Penguin, 1966. Some of these brief jottings are too obscure to struggle with, but many are clear, brilliant, and provocative.

TILLICH, PAUL, *Dynamics of Faith.* New York: Harper & Row, 1957. Excellent introduction to Tillich on faith.

UNAMUNO, MIGUEL DE, *Tragic Sense of Life.* New York: Dover, 1921. Classic example of hope that refuses to yield as long as there is a possibility.

Immortality and Resurrection

BADHAM, PAUL AND LINDA BADHAM, EDS., *Death and Immortality in the Religions of the World.* New York: Paragon House, 1987. Includes statements by Buddhists, Christians, Hindus, Jews, Muslims, naturalists, and more.

HICK, JOHN, *Death and Eternal Life.* New York: Harper & Row, 1980. Hick surveys the field, then makes a creative contribution which is influenced by Oriental as well as Western thought.

MOODY, RAYMOND, *Life After Life.* New York: Bantam, 1984. Moody's intriguing account of near-death experiences and their similarities has stirred much discussion of whether these experiences are good evidence of life after death.

Religious Experience

JAMES, WILLIAM, *The Varieties of Religious Experience.* New York: Modern Library, 1902. Very readable, classic study with many examples.

OTTO, RUDOLF, *Mysticism: East and West.* New York: Meridian Books, 1932. Compares religious experiences from different religious traditions. Also *The Idea of the Holy.*

SMITH, HUSTON, "Do Drugs Have Religious Import?" *Journal of Philosophy,* LXI, No. 18 (October 1, 1964). Examines similarities between religious experience and drug-induced experience. Discusses whether a genuine religious experience can be induced by drugs. See also *Varieties of Psychedelic Experience,* R. E. Masters and Jean Houston.

UNDERHILL, EVELYN, *Mysticism.* New York: E. P. Dutton, 1911. Considered by many to be the best single study of mysticism.

Religious Naturalism

DEWEY, JOHN, *A Common Faith.* New Haven, CT: Yale University Press, 1934. Excellent statement of the naturalist vision of human unity by "the dean of American philosophers."

FEUERBACH, LUDWIG, *The Essence of Christianity,* Waring and Strothmann, eds. New York: Frederick Ungar, 1957. A very short abridgment of a classic. Feuerbach's thesis is that religion is the institution by means of which humankind strives toward perfection of itself; the concept of God is humankind's attempt to conceptualize its *own* perfection.

LAO TZU, *Tao-te ching.* A brilliant Chinese expression of religious naturalism. Many translations. I prefer Wing-Tsit Chan's scholarly edition *The Way of Lao Tzu* (Library of Liberal Arts), and Lin Yutang's philosophical translation *The Way of Wisdom* (Modern Library), which includes the brilliant stories of Lao Tzu's greatest follower, Chuang Tzu.

MENDELSOHN, JACK, *Being Liberal in an Illiberal Age: Why I Am a Unitarian-Universalist,* revised ed. Boston: Beacon Press, 1985.

WIEMAN, HENRY NELSON, *Man's Ultimate Commitment.* Carbondale, IL: Southern Illinois University, 1958. Fascinating attempt to modernize our concept of God. See also his *The Source of Human Good.* Carbondale, IL: Southern Illinois University Press, 1946.

Transcendentalism

BURTT, E. A., ed., *The Teachings of the Compassionate Buddha.* New York: The New American Library, 1955. Sensitive selection of Buddhist literature with glossary of Buddhist terms.

CHANG, GARMA C. C., *The Practice of Zen.* New York: Harper & Row, 1959. Excellent introduction by a Chinese master.

DASS, RAM, *Be Here Now.* San Cristobal, New Mexico: Lama Foundation, 1971. Designed to hold reader's interest. Dass was formerly Dr. Richard Alpert, teacher of psychology at Harvard University.

JASPERS, KARL, *Way to Wisdom.* Cited earlier. Excellent example of the intellectualist's way to transcendental consciousness.

RADHAKRISHNAN, SARVEPALLI, *Hindu View of Life.* New York: Macmillan, 1939. Excellent introduction by an outstanding Hindu thinker and person of action. See also his *Recovery of Faith.* Thompson, CT: InterCulture Associates, 1962.

The Song of God: Bhagavad-Gita. New York: New American Library, 1951. Perhaps the most important single piece of Hindu literature. Short, engrossing.

SUZUKI, D. T., *An Introduction to Zen Buddhism.* New York: Grove Press, 1964. Very readable introduction. Forthright discussion of ways in which the Western mentality interferes with an appreciation of Zen. Foreword by Carl Jung.

WATTS, ALAN, *Joyous Cosmology.* New York: Random House, 1962. One of many books by a Westerner absorbed by eastern religion.

Theism

BARTH, KARL, *Dogmatics in Outline.* New York: Harper & Row, 1959. Perhaps the most influential Protestant theologian of this century.

The Bible. The holy book of Jews and Christians, but Christians add a "New Testament" to the Jewish Bible.

BUBER, MARTIN, *I and Thou.* New York: Scribners, 1970. A classic work by a Jewish philosopher. Explores the I-Thou relation between God and humans.

HARTSHORNE, CHARLES, *Omnipotence and Other Theological Mistakes.* Albany: State University of New York, 1984. A brief, readable statement of process theology by its most penetrating, influential proponent.

HESCHEL, ABRAHAM, *God in Search of Man: A Philosophy of Judaism.* New York: Harper & Row, 1955. Rich and comprehensive statement by an orthodox Jew. See also his *Man Is Not Alone.* New York: Harper & Row, 1966.

KUSHNER, HAROLD, *When Bad Things Happen to Good People.* New York: Avon Books, 1981. A very popular, sensitive application of the process conception of God to the problem of evil.

McINERNY, RALPH, *St. Thomas Aquinas.* South Bend, IN: University of Notre Dame, 1982. Includes a statement of the Roman Catholic conception of God as developed by Thomas Aquinas, the official philosopher of Catholicism and one of the great philosophers of Western history.

MUHAMMED, The Holy Qur'an. The sacred book of Muslims, who believe it to have been revealed to Muhammed by God. The translation by A. Yusef Ali is majestic and includes valuable verse-by-verse commentary. For a complimentary copy write the Amana Corporation, 4411 41st St., Brentwood, MD 20722.

ROUSSEAU, JEAN-JACQUES, *The Creed of a Priest of Savoy,* A. H. Beattie trans. New York: Frederick Ungar, 1957. A wonderful statement of deism, selected from Rousseau's novel *Emil.*

Autobiographies with a Religious Dimension

BONHOEFFER, DIETRICH, *Letters and Papers from Prison,* rev. ed. New York: Macmillan, 1967. Gentle but outspoken German Protestant theologian who joined an abortive effort to assassinate Hitler. Imprisoned and executed by Nazis.

DASS, RAM, *Be Here Now.* Cited earlier. See opening section for story of an American Jewish psychologist's journey into India and Hinduism.

GANDHI, MOHANDAS K., *An Autobiography: The Story of My Experiments with Truth.* Boston: Beacon Press, 1957. Hindu lawyer, civil leader, and saint. Practitioner of "love-force." Frequently jailed, finally assassinated.

KELLER, HELEN, *The Story of My Life.* New York: Dell, 1902. Totally deprived of sight and hearing at the age of nineteen months, yet developed a profound appreciation for religion. See also her later statement, *My Religion.* New York: The Swedenborg Foundation, 1960.

KING, MARTIN LUTHER, JR., *Stride Toward Freedom.* New York: Harper & Row, 1958. Black civil rights leader in the United States. Followed Gandhi in advocating loving but aggressive nonviolence. Assaulted, jailed, assassinated. See also *Why We Can't Wait* and *Strength to Love.*

MALCOLM X, *The Autobiography of Malcolm X.* New York: Grove Press, 1965. From criminal to Black Muslim to orthodox Muslim. A fascinating story.

MERTON, THOMAS, *The Seven Storey Mountain.* San Diego: Harcourt Brace Jovanovich, 1948. Reared Protestant, Merton became one of Catholicism's most eloquent converts.

SAINT AUGUSTINE, *The Confessions.* Perhaps the greatest religious autobiography. Augustine (+A.D. 430) speaks candidly of his anguished journey from Roman paganism, Manichaeism, and Skepticism into Christianity. Good editions by Image Books & by Penguin.

SCHWEITZER, ALBERT, *Out of My Life and Thought.* New York: New American Library, 1933. A profound philosophy of life emerges from Schweitzer's account of his own many-sided development as musician, biblical scholar, philosopher, and missionary physician.

WATTS, ALAN, *In My Own Way: An Autobiography.* New York: Random House, 1972. Another testimony by a Westerner to the beauty of Hindu religion.

Antireligious Literature

AYER, A. J., *Language, Truth, and Logic.* New York: Dover, 1946. Argues that the concept of God is meaningless.

CLIFFORD, W. K., "The Ethics of Belief," in *Philosophy of Religion: An Anthology,* ed. Louis Pojman. Belmont, CA: Wadsworth, 1987. Clifford's essay is *the* classic attack on the rationality of religious belief. Pojman's volume also contains William James's "The Will to Belief," which is *the* classic response to Clifford. Pojman's volume is the most up-to-date anthology of philosophy of religion of which I know.

FREUD, SIGMUND, *The Future of An Illusion.* New York: Doubleday, 1927. A forceful critique by means of psychological explanation. See also Freud's *Civilization and Its Discontents; Moses and Monotheism; Totem and Taboo.*

HUME, DAVID, *Dialogues Concerning Natural Religion.* This brilliant eighteenth-century dialogue played a powerful part in putting theists on the defensive and atheists on the offensive regarding arguments about the existence of God. Hackett edition well-edited, inexpensive.

KENNY, ANTHONY, *The Path from Rome.* Oxford: Oxford University Press, 1986. Kenny, an important analytic philosopher, explains why he gradually abandoned his deep involvement with the Roman Catholic Church.

MARX, KARL, AND FRIEDRICH ENGELS, *On Religion.* New York: Schocken Books, 1964. By the founders of modern communism. Explains religion as a form of alienation. Selections compiled in Moscow.

NIETZSCHE, FRIEDRICH W., *Thus Spake Zarathustra; Gay Science;* and *The Anti-Christ.* Most of these three works can be found in *The Portable Nietzsche,* ed. Walter Kaufmann. New York: The Viking Press, 1954. One of theism's harshest critics. Originated the statement: "God is dead."

RUSSELL, BERTRAND, *Why I Am Not a Christian.* New York: Simon & Schuster, 1957. Popular writings against religion, and especially Christianity. Points made forceful by author's stinging wit and authoritative tone. See also *Religion and Science.*

SARTRE, JEAN-PAUL, *Existentialism and Human Emotions.* New York: Philosophical Library, 1957. Another withering blast at theism.

Women & Religion

ALLIONE, TSULTRIM, *Women of Wisdom.* London: Routledge & Kegan Paul, 1984. On the feminine in Tibetan Buddhism.

CASTILLEJO, IRENE DE, *Knowing Woman: A Feminine Psychology.* New York: Putnam, 1973. A Jungian perspective.

CHRIST, CAROL, *The Laughter of Aphrodite.* New York: Harper & Row, 1987. About the goddess in religion. Christ is a pioneering author.

CHRIST, CAROL, AND JUDITH PLASKOW, EDS., *Womanspirit Rising.* New York: Harper & Row, 1979. A feminist reader in religion.

FIORENZA, ELIZABETH, *Bread Not Stone: The Challenge of Feminist Biblical Interpretation.* Boston: Beacon Press, 1984. Important biblical scholar. See other works, such as *In Memory of Her.*

KOLTUN, ELIZABETH, ED., *The Jewish Woman: New Perspectives.* New York: Schocken Books, 1976. A spectrum of voices.

RUETHER, ROSEMARY, *Religion and Sexism; Liberation Theology; New Woman/New Earth.* A major feminist theologian.

SPRETNAK, CHARLENE, ED., *The Politics of Woman's Spirituality.* Garden City, NJ: Doubleday, 1982.

Index

*Some of the entries in this index refer to the notes at the end of each chapter. The endnote number is indicated within parentheses.